A CHILD GOES FORTH

New, Revised, Enlarged Edition

A CHILD GOES FORTH

New, Revised, Enlarged Edition

A CURRICULUM GUIDE
FOR TEACHERS
OF PRESCHOOL CHILDREN

BARBARA J. TAYLOR

Brigham Young University Press, Provo, Utah

Library of Congress Catalog Card Number: 74-23255
International Standard Book Number: 0-8425-0247-5
© 1975 Brigham Young University Press. All rights reserved
Brigham Young University Press, Provo, Utah 84602
New, revised, enlarged edition
First edition © 1964 by Barbara J. Taylor
Second printing 1965
Revised and enlarged, 1966
Revised, 1970
Third printing 1972
75 15M 4738

Library of Congress Cataloging in Publication Data

Taylor Barbara J
    A child goes forth.

    Bibliography: Within each chapter
    1. Education, Preschool—Curricula. I. Title.
LB1140.2.T28   1975   372.1'9   74-23255
ISBN 0-8425-0247-5

CONTENTS

WHY THIS BOOK

"Ideas, ideas; my fortune for some ideas!" plead teachers and parents, imprisoned in a room with even <u>one</u> energetic preschooler. A three- or four-year-old demands an adult's combined creativity and patience. Unless a child's interest is aroused, his educator (teacher or parent, male or female) often despairs of teaching him anything.

But young children <u>can</u> learn if they are exposed to many experiences and activities so that they can discover where their interests lie. Of course, a generation or two ago when parents said, "We want our son John to become a doctor" or "We're preparing our daughter Jane to become a school teacher" and educators prescribed the steps for them to achieve that goal, no one worried about children's interests; John and Jane did pretty much as they were told and thought what they were taught to think. Nor did anyone (with perhaps a rare exception) express concern with trying to "educate" a three- or four-year-old; it simply couldn't be done. How many would-be doctors and school teachers failed, how many preschool children blasted their energies into unproductive, even character-destroying, activities are dead statistics. Let John or Jane discover their own interests, however, and they tacitly show their parents and teachers what their future might be. Given access to materials and allowed to be independent in using them, they begin to formulate ideas on their own.

The problem of parents and teachers, therefore, is providing young children with motivating, educational experiences. That is why, when a book like <u>A Child Goes Forth</u> appears, it is snatched up by preschool teachers and parents alike. "Oh, thank heaven for all these ideas!" they exult. And what they find so stimulating is that the ideas in the book become sparks that set aflame their own creativity. They can take Barbara Taylor's suggestions and modify them to fit their own values, their backgrounds and experiences. The result, of course, is a greater confidence in their own abilities as teachers of the very young.

Imagine, for example, finding under one cover numerous suggested curriculum topics; ways of planning the curriculum; sample lesson plans; ideas for teaching groups or individuals; techniques for teaching creative expression, language, music and rhythm, the sciences, mathematics, and a host of everyday, indoor and outdoor activities for young children.

And children, bombarded with elemental information about many disciplines, participating in unstructured, spontaneous experiences, develop interests in one or more subjects or activities that motivate them to learn more. A grateful parent or teacher, observing a child's interest in a subject, comments, "Maybe <u>that's</u> what she'll become."

This book, then, not only provides parents and teachers with ideas and techniques for becoming creative teachers; it offers a fascinating world for young minds to explore, increasing the likelihood of a future generation of motivated—and motivating—adults. We highly recommend for your use and your liberation Barbara J. Taylor's <u>A Child Goes Forth</u>.

—The Editors

CHAPTER 1

PLANNING THE PRESCHOOL CURRICULUM

Creative planning for preschool children is essential. Opposing the belief that children younger than five or six waste time until they are old enough to enter school formally, research in the field indicates the importance of the early formative years. (Elkind, 1971; Highberger and Teets, 1974.) Early educators (such as Froebel and Montessori) felt that development was a process of "unfolding" related to maturation, and that the rate of unfolding was determined genetically. (Spodek, 1973.) More recent educators and researchers have learned that a stimulating and planned environment can influence the learning capabilities of young children, especially those from deprived homes.

Young children have a great thirst for knowledge, but it must be given on each individual's level of understanding. How thrilling it is to be with them as they have firsthand experiences. So many things we see and take for granted every day are marvelous discoveries to these youngsters. They need understanding and patient adults to help them build upon these experiences.

David, four, asked his mother, "Why is it raining?" Her reply was, "So the grass and flowers can get a drink." She thought that was a good answer, but his quick reply was, "But they don't have mouths!" What an observant youngster and what a teachable moment! This is but one indication of the mental capacity and keen observation of a preschool child.

Many people in the field of child development agree that a child is ready for preschool around the age of three years. But great differences in development exist among children of the same age; some are ready for preschool training earlier than others. Factors other than chronological age must be considered in evaluating the total growth of the child (social, emotional, spiritual, physical, and intellectual). Some questions that help in that evaluation follow: How secure or insecure does the child feel in the home? Is his physical development within the expected range for his age? Does he have opportunities to be with other children his age? How does he respond to strangers (peers, adults)? What is the relationship between the child and his parent or parents? Are there some significant happenings in the home that might be disturbing to him (new baby, recent move)? What could the child gain from a group experience that he couldn't get at home? Would the cost or arrangements cause a hardship on the family?

A group experience for three-, four-, and five-year-old children is usually a child's first experience outside the home and must be entered into with caution. It may take a period of time, or he may adjust rather rapidly. At any rate, he should be given the time necessary to make the adjustment.

As a child enters a group experience, he comes with a background unique only to him. Each experience is related to his own background. Teachers, learn about him and then move forward together.

Parents, the selection of a preschool should be made only after careful and thorough investigation. Are the goals and philosophy of the school compatible with yours? Will your child grow and develop successfully under a particular program? Are the teachers well trained? What are their personal characteristics? Are they patient and understanding? Are they stable mentally, physically, socially, and emotionally? Are the needs of the children of prime interest? Is there provision for active as well as quiet play? Is language an important factor? These are but a few of the questions you should ask before enrolling your child in a preschool.

GOALS

Teachers, in formulating goals for yourself and the children, remember that some goals are short term, while others have a long-range effect. Whatever the duration, good planning is necessary. Good teaching does not just happen; it is the result of careful planning and foresight.

To determine realistic and appropriate goals, consider the children individually, then the philosophy or model used at the school. Setting up goals without considering the children first is ineffective. It's like saying, "We'll mold the children to fit the program" when we should be saying, "Children are more important than programs, and we'll plan to meet their needs." It is very possible that goals for one group or year would not be effective for another group or year.

Here are some possible goals for children in a preschool group:

- To help them develop a good self-image, a wholesome attitude toward their bodies, and a good start toward reaching their potentials.
- To provide opportunities for them to develop their whole personalities through (a) firsthand experiences in social relationships, (b) physical development of large and small muscles, (c) finding acceptable outlets for their emotions, and (d) stimulating experiences which encourage them to think, analyze problems, and arrive at different possible solutions.
- To encourage them to express themselves through materials, movement, and language by providing ample time and adequate opportunities.
- To stimulate language development through hearing and using language.
- To develop an awareness of their five senses.
- To encourage independence.
- To give them a thirst for and to increase their knowledge by asking questions and exploring their environment, and to help them develop a sense of curiosity through providing ample firsthand experiences.
- To give them some basic experiences for future learning.
- To provide experiences with other children of the same age.
- To meet their needs as individuals and as a group.
- To encourage them to develop a positive attitude toward teachers, school, and learning.
- To provide some experiences which they do not have at home.
- To build a tie between the home and the school.

ROLE OF THE TEACHER

For convenience only, throughout this text the teacher is often referred to as "you" or "she." Male teachers, however, are essential to preschool programs.

Interested and qualified male teachers should enter the field. From them children often learn appropriate male behavior that is otherwise unclear or neglected. Note that the child is often referred to as "he." Again, this is merely a convenience.

Being a teacher is a great responsibility. Like a steward on a ship, she plans for and is held accountable for everyone under her supervision. Teachers, take your stewardship seriously. Build good relationships with and among staff, parents, and children.

Sometimes it is said that a teacher "merely furnishes a body" when she is in the preschool group, a comment implying that she is unaware of her surroundings or obligations and does not take an active part; instead, she uses this period to reflect upon matters which do not pertain to her immediate setting. Here are some suggestions for more successful teaching.

It is important that a teacher get adequate rest and proper nutrition, since much of her energy is consumed as she participates in the group. She should also leave her problems outside the door as she enters. A student teacher who was upset over an argument with her roommate was to spend the afternoon in the preschool group. Realizing that this was not the place to take her troubles, she said to herself as she entered the door, "I'm not going to let this bother me while I am with the children." But it did bother her. Finally, near the end of the day, a four-year-old said to her, "Why aren't you happy today, teacher?" She thought she had hidden her feelings, but they were obvious to this verbal youngster. Another teacher, tired and distressed, was interacting with some four-year-olds when a boy asked, "Teacher, is it your nap time?" She replied in the affirmative. Then they moved to a table which contained clay. A second child said to her, "You don't like clay, do you?" Before she could answer, the first child said, "Sure she likes clay, but it's her nap time."

A teacher, moreover, must be professional at all times. Incidents which happen at the school should be kept confidential. It is easy to make snap judgments when you do not fully understand what is behind certain actions. Frequent contact with parents therefore helps to unify the home and school.

The number of teachers required to operate a preschool group efficiently varies with the age of the children, the physical facilities, and the experience of the teachers. One teacher for five children is ideal. The type of program (whether for small, structured groups or a more informal setting) must be considered in determining the number of teachers needed. Regardless of the smallness of the group, there should always be at least two teachers present in case of injury or any other kind of emergency which might arise.

The teacher should provide for various kinds of activities and "zones" within the room. Materials are readily available but rotated to create new interests. Through supervision the teacher remains warm and supportive, allowing legitimate choices while providing for interaction, individuality, discovery, and exploration of ideas, materials, and relationships.

Some of the responsibilities of a teacher are:

- To oneself
  - To grow professionally
  - To remain in good physical and emotional health
  - To be progressive and creative
  - To be enthusiastic

- To the children in the group
  - To build good relationships with them
  - To determine and meet their needs
  - To enjoy planning for and being with them
  - To respect them as individuals
  - To help them build a good self-image and realize their self-worth
  - To help them toward reaching their potentials

- To the parents of these children
  - To build a good relationship with them
  - To provide good counseling
  - To value them and their ideas
  - To plan with them for the well-being of the child
  - To bridge the gap between home and school
  - To keep them informed about school practices and activities
- To other staff members
  - To build a good relationship with and among them
  - To support them
  - To share ideas and knowledge
  - To value them and their ideas
  - To encourage them to grow professionally
- To the community
  - To be aware of its problems and try to solve them
  - To participate in local professional organizations connected with early childhood education
  - To inform them of the importance of a child's years before public school entrance.

Regardless of what curriculum or what method of instruction is used, the basic inner qualities of the teacher are more influential on the learning of the child. (Elkind, 1970; Katz, 1969 and 1970; Levin, 1964; Siefert, 1969.)

SUGGESTIONS FOR TEACHERS

- Dress for the job. Clothing should be comfortable and easily cared for and should permit freedom of movement. Proper clothing for out-of-doors is a must.
- Be prompt. The teacher who is on the job and ready for the children will find that the day will run much more smoothly. Once the children "get ahead of the teacher," it is difficult for the teacher to gain control.
- Keep current. Monthly professional periodicals, recent books, and pamphlets contain timely information and will aid you in being a more effective teacher.
- Make sure the setting is child-centered. Give the necessary support needed, but give the children an opportunity to explore and solve problems.
- Allow time for children to help themselves.
- Be aware of every child. Consciously build a good relationship with each one. Put the child's needs before your own.
- Know how many children are in the group each day; know where they are and what they are doing, and know the location of the teachers. Occasionally count the children to make sure they are all being supervised.
- Have the next activity ready before warning children that it is time to move from the present activity. Give them time to finish their play or to put things away.
- Plan ahead. Make sure that all materials needed are readily available before beginning an activity (sponges for fingerpaint table, books for story time, aprons for water play).
- When another teacher is handling a situation, do not interfere unless your help is requested.
- Be a good "housekeeper" both indoors and outdoors so that the school will be clean and attractive. At the same time, avoid being so involved in cleaning that children are unsupervised.
- When limits are necessary, see that they are set, understood, and maintained. Be consistent in what is expected of the children without being inflexible.

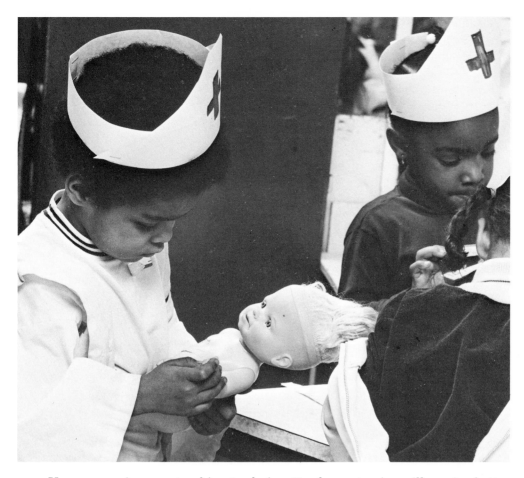

- Use your voice as a teaching tool. A soft, pleasant voice will receive better response than a loud, gruff one. Get on the child's level—by kneeling or sitting.
- Make sure your words and actions indicate the same thing. When it is time to go inside, for instance, tell the children and then go inside yourself.
- Share your ideas and experiences with other staff members.
- In all ways support the person who is planning the activities.
- Use verbalization as a technique in gaining cooperation from the children. Help them to understand what is expected of them.
- Be enthusiastic and enjoy being with the children. Relax and smile!

FOR WHAT DO WE PLAN?

First, you must consider each individual child in the group. What are his needs and interests? What have been his past experiences and how has he met them? Then consider the group's needs and interests. In order to plan effectively, the teacher should have a good relationship with each child.

Second, the ages of the children will have a marked effect upon the planning. Three-year-olds are still becoming acquainted with surroundings, materials, and possibilities, while four-year-olds are improvising and exploring with materials, ideas, and personal relationships. Their abilities and maturation may be very different, and plans should be made accordingly. Some teachers prefer that the children be within one year of the same age. They feel there are enough differences among children of similar chronological age at best, and it is easier to plan when the age span is narrow. Others prefer that the children be grouped vertically (wide age span) because the older children can be models for the younger ones; more variation in planning is possible, and experiences are more challenging to both children and teachers. Vertical grouping also makes available enough children to form an adequately sized group.

Third, the plans should include a variety of experiences: interpersonal relationships, sensory experiences, exploration of natural and physical surroundings, intellectual stimulation, development of large and small muscles, and many opportunities to hear and use language.

Fourth, provision should be made for periods of active and quiet play, solitary and group play, indoor and outdoor play.

HOW TO PLAN

A teacher should ask the following questions:

- What do I want to teach?
- What do the children already know about the subject? Are they correctly informed? (If not, clarify misconceptions before teaching new ideas.)
- Why do I want to teach it?
- How will I teach it?
- Is this the most effective way to teach it?
- What will I need in order to teach it?
- Are these materials the best for this purpose?
- Am I teaching true concepts?
- Are the concepts on the developmental level of the children?
- Are there some new terms to introduce and define?

The curriculum for preschool children provides for teaching interrelated things at the same time. For example, a particular experience may include teaching new words, the process of order and sequence of events, new concepts, new techniques, and/or social skills. It is difficult to teach things that are not related to another experience and that teach isolated ideas.

When a teacher plans for a new group of children, or for the beginning of a year, the plans need to be simple. Time must be afforded the children in order for them to assimilate the experiences. As the children become more familiar with the setting and the program, new things can be added. This is a gradual process. Occasionally go back over previously taught concepts so that the child will have another exposure to the material.

While adults often tire of repetition, young children thrive on it. They learn a routine; they know the sequence of events and depend upon it. The first time they are exposed to an experience, they explore its many possibilities. They may not use it in the way it was intended, and the adult may feel mistakenly that the experience was unsuccessful or even chaotic. As the children become more familiar with something, they find specific uses for it or different ways it can be used. For example, the first time a child is exposed to a new creative material such as clay, he may taste it, smell it, feel it, pound it, or even sit on it. After several exposures, he may use it only as dough for cookies. With musical instruments, he may simply try to find out how much noise he can make. Later he will combine rhythm, sound, and skill into a satisfying experience.

While it is desirable to follow a similar routine each day, the schedule should be flexible. When a child discovers something of interest to him, that is the time to explore with him. Putting him off until another day will destroy rather than build a sense of awareness. Spontaneous events can provide such teachable moments. However, if you are totally unprepared to discuss the topic at the moment, make some good plans and use them soon.

Provide broad guidelines and then allow freedom within them. This does not mean that only a skeleton of a plan is made. Much thinking must go into each activity, but leave leeway for freedom of exploration. Behavioral objectives could be assigned to each activity provided.

Have an open mind and absorb the many things which are available. Regardless of how many years of experience a teacher has, she can still learn from others—from children as well as adults. This is a sharing of ideas that can be most profitable to all concerned. Teachers learn from each other; they share their successes and their failures.

It is important to skillful planning to know the growth norms of children at specific ages. What is appropriate for one stage of development may be inappropriate for another. Planning above the developmental level of a child will frustrate him; planning below his level will bore him.

Determine the readiness of the children and build upon it. Teachers who capitalize upon the readiness of children are rewarded with great response. Take your cues from the children as you observe and listen to them.

Large blocks of time should be provided in order that the children may have sufficient time in which to play out the things which are important to them. To begin play only to be told it is time to do something else tends to discourage children; they need time for sustained play. Two children spent about twenty minutes building a block structure only to find that as soon as they started to play in it they were told to get ready for another activity. Their comment, "But we didn't have time to play yet" was of no consequence to the teacher, though most meaningful to the children.

The plans for each day should include group experiences, free play (both inside and outside), creative time for children to explore materials and express their feelings, music, story, and food experience—either snack or lunch. Intellectual stimulation, social relationships, muscle development, and opportunities for language development are interwoven into these activities.

Some teachers find planning much easier if they use a theme for the day or week. Other teachers have unrelated materials they want to try. Whether or not a theme is used often depends upon the philosophy of the head teacher. Either way can be successful if it is well planned.

Daily outside play is a must. For some children who are "house plants" and do not get outside to participate in the activities and enjoy the fresh air, equipment can be rotated or relocated so as to stimulate new interests. In inclement weather a covered shelter makes it possible for children to be out of doors. Set up some stimulating "pacers" to draw them outside. Eliminate the idea that outside play is only for warm, sunny days. A child delights to play in the snow or rain or wind if he is properly dressed.

Sufficient time should be allowed at the end of each daily session (after the children have departed) for the teachers to evaluate the day. Sharing experiences, problems, and ideas is a valuable learning experience. Suppose that a teacher had had an experience she had felt inadequate to handle. By discussing this experience with other members of the staff she can gain constructive suggestions that may help her in dealing with this problem and with other problems in the future. Suppose that a teacher noticed something new or different in a child's behavior. She can share this with the staff so that they will be more aware either of the child's progression or of his regression. Suppose that a teacher found a new way to do something or became upset because she did not understand the planning or reasoning or lacked techniques for working with certain children. These experiences should all be shared and discussed. The evaluation period is very important.

Be specific in planning. The objectives and concepts which are to be achieved should be clearly defined for all staff members. As a result, reinforcements can be made by all. Rather than saying, "Today we are teaching about turtles," say, "Today we are teaching that turtles live in shells, walk very slowly, and eat flies." Then there is no question about the information which they are to impart to the children. Or you might say, "Today we are going to help Robin in her relationships with other children, and this is how we are going to go about it." Or even, "Today we are going to talk about a community helper (such as the mailman, the policeman, or the doctor). These are the concepts we want to convey to the children. . . ."

At least once during each day, plan an activity which brings the children together as a group. This can be for a snack, a story, a special experience, for concept teaching, or for any combination of these. While children need to have

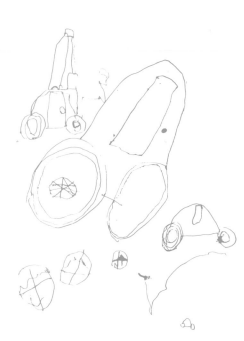

freedom for self-development, their being members of a group is also valuable. Through interacting with other children, a child learns about himself, about property rights, about sharing and taking turns, and about the interests and ideas of others. He also gains a more realistic self-concept, tries new techniques, and expresses himself verbally.

Planning should be made so that smooth transitions occur from one activity to another. A teacher could be assigned to finish up an activity with some children while another teacher moves on. It is important that the teacher be "one step" ahead of the children.

Involve the children in "cleanup." As a child begins to lose interest in a certain activity, he should be encouraged to put away or clean up the things he has been using (hand him a sponge as he finishes fingerpainting; encourage him to shelve his blocks or return his trike to the shed, etc.). Materials and equipment should be placed so that children can have access to them and can also return them. This is another way of encouraging independence and creativity.

Make a conscious effort to bring real objects to the attention of the children. If they are not available or if it is impossible to bring them to school, choose the next best way to teach about them. Pictures and other aids are good but should not be used if the real object is available. Children need firsthand experiences rather than vicarious ones.

WRITTEN PLANS

It is wise to write down the plans for the day. To the question, "Does the use of written plans cause rigidity?" the answer is "No." Allowance can be made for changes and additions, but by writing down what is to take place, a person is forced to plan thoroughly. Flexibility comes in the implementation.

Posting a copy of plans so that the other teachers and parents have access to it means that all staff members can be aware of the activities of the day. When a teacher has her plans "in her head," it is difficult for other teachers to interpret them.

Sometimes an experienced teacher does not post her plans; that does not necessarily mean that little or no thought has gone into her preparation for the day. However, it is meaningful to new teachers to see plans made by an experienced teacher so they are more aware of the many facets which must be considered.

The more thorough a teacher is in her planning, the less chance exists of her leaving some important details uncovered. If for some unforeseen reason the teacher who has made the plans is absent, the other teachers can easily carry on if the plans are in sufficient detail and if they are posted.

As a guide, see the Daily Lesson Plan Outline on page 9. (See Chapter 1 of *When I Do, I Learn* by Barbara J. Taylor for more information.) Briefly, the outline includes these items:

Theme

Decide on something of interest or value to the children and support that concept occasionally in the lesson plan. If all activities are geared to the theme, the activities become dull and boring. The theme itself suggests the best ways to put over the concepts. Supporting a theme using creative materials may not work, but it might be accomplished at story time, or vice versa. Integrate learning into the schedule of activities. Each day plan some diversions from the theme to add interest and variety.

Preassessment

In order to do adequate teaching, you need to determine what the children already know about the theme. If there is great variation, provide ideas that will help the child move beyond his present knowledge—whether it is great or small. Periodically integrate previously taught material with new so the child can see how his world fits together.

Daily Lesson Plan Outline

_____   _____
(School or teacher's name)   (Date)

Theme: The subject matter of the day.

Preassessment: Finding out what the children know about the theme.

Concepts: Specific truths to be taught.

Behavioral Objectives: What you expect the children to do or say as a result of this particular experience.

Learning Activities: The activities you provide to help the children accomplish the behavioral objectives.

Schedule of Activities:

Review plans for the day
Check-in
Setting the learning stage
Free play
    Housekeeping area
    Food experience
    Blocks—large and small
    Creative expression
    Manipulative area
    Cognitive, sensory, and/or science area
    Book corner and books
Prestory activities
Story time
Music
Snack or lunch
Outside activities
Check-out

Learning Card: Providing information and follow-through for parents.

Evaluation: Summarizing strengths and weaknesses of the plan and the day.

Plan For Tomorrow: Focusing on the goals you hope to accomplish in short- and long-range planning for individual children as well as for the group.

Books Available Throughout the Day: A list of books which support the daily theme or provide appropriate diversion.

Preassessment can be done casually or formally. Here's an example of a type of preassessment on shapes. A casual way to teach shapes is to approach individual children or a small group and ask them if they know any shapes. If so, which ones? Place articles with the different shapes you will teach on a table and see what the children say about them or do with them. A more formal approach would be to prepare some of the desired shapes, then individually ask each child to hand you a specific shape. Also ask him to look around the room and tell you if he can find things in the room that are of the same shape. The casual approach yields general information through observation, while the formal approach yields specific information through interaction.

Accurate preassessment should lead to adequate planning.

Concepts

Make several true statements related to the theme that the children can understand. The number of concepts depends on the amount and depth of information to be taught.

Behavioral Objectives

Because of your teaching this theme, you will expect the children to have a change in their behavior, through either verbal or physical means.

When you first begin using behavioral objectives, you may make them either too difficult or too simple for the children. Try writing a few. Be specific in what you expect; then if your expectations are not met, revise them until they are more realistic for the children with whom you are working.

Another term for behavioral objectives could be *desired outcome.* How do you expect the children to be different (in behavior or knowledge) because you provided this experience for them? Will their actions be different—will they have more skills? Will their verbalizations be increased?

Behavioral objectives should include some cognitive (intellectual), affective (attitudinal), and psychomotor (applicational and experiential) elements. However, it may not be possible to use all three of these in every objective you write. Some objectives will apply more to one of these areas than to the others. Actually, you want the child to have the attitude and knowledge which will affect his behavior (in a positive way, of course).

It may be easier for some teachers to establish the behavioral objectives (or desired outcomes) first, and then write the concepts and learning activities. For others, it may be easier to write the concepts and learning activities and then, based on them, write realistic objectives. Use whichever procedure is easiest and most productive for you.

In writing behavioral objectives, use terms which are appropriate for a preschool child, who has a rather limited behavior repertoire. For example, he doesn't write, outline, sketch, or perform other more advanced actions; he can tell, select, or describe, but he is more adept in "doing." ("Show me how. . . .") To say that a child will "know" or "understand" or any other vague term does not define the goal specifically enough. Mager (1962) states, "One characteristic of a usefully stated objective is that it is stated in behavioral, or performance, terms that describe what the learner will be *doing* when demonstrating his achievement of the objective."

Learning Activities

Plan as many or as few activities as you need to help the child toward the behavioral objectives. Give him opportunities to be a participator rather than a spectator.

Schedule of Activities

The sequence of activities can be arranged so that it best meets the needs of the children and the facility. Make provisions for the following activities, but be flexible in their use:

Review plans for the day. Each day before the preschool group begins, the teachers should sit down together for a few minutes and go over the plans for the day. In this way all the teachers are aware of the planned activities and concepts and can make the day more meaningful to the children.

Check-in: If children arrive over a period of time, have some simple objects or books (something that doesn't require excessive cleaning-up) until all children arrive.

Setting the learning stage: This is where teachers and children meet together, with the teachers setting the tone of the day and introducing some new concepts. It is well planned but rather informal, the children being the center of the activity. This is a good place for the children to express themselves verbally and be introduced to the concepts and activities for the day.

Free play:

- Housekeeping or domestic area (see pages 49-52).
- Food experience (see Chapter 10).
- Blocks—large and small (see pages 38-41).
- Creative expression (see Chapter 2).
- Manipulative area (see page 66).
- Cognitive, sensory, and/or science area (see page 65 and Chapters 5 and 11).
- Book corner and books (see Chapter 3).

Prestory activities (see Chapter 6).

Story time (see Chapter 3).

Music (see Chapter 4).

Snack or lunch (see Chapter 10).

Outside activities (see Chapter 9).

Check-out: The children put away their toys and get a Learning Card.

Learning Card

This is some type of written information to inform the parents of the activities and ideas that have been presented to the child during the day or week. For an example and more information, see pages 15 and 18.

Evaluation

After the children have departed, the staff will again sit down together to evaluate the activities of the day. Specific questions are used to begin the evaluation period. (Some examples are listed following the lesson plan on page 15.) Ask questions about what the teacher says and does (e.g., does she ask questions, interact with the children, give praise or attention to each child for appropriate behavior, include first-hand experiences for the children, plan for the "whole" child, vary her methods of presentation, plan for individual children as well as for the group?). Ask questions about what the children say and do (e.g., do they ask and answer questions, make related comments, look interested and alert, participate as suggested, express emotions?). Through these means, the teachers should be able to determine whether the concepts were understood, whether the activities supported the concepts, and whether the children were able to do the things which were designated as behavioral objectives. If there is some doubt, go back and teach the concepts over, making them either more basic or more advanced, geared more to the individual child.

Plan for Tomorrow

Based on today's activities and responses, what would be effective for tomorrow or some later date? Do you need to include or exclude something that you had previously planned? Looking at the long-range goals for each child, what progress is being made?

If you were to teach today's theme to another group or at another time, what changes would you make?

Books Available Throughout the Day

All books do not have to support the daily theme but some of them could. Have six to ten books available for individual browsing.

Now let's check to see if you are on target:

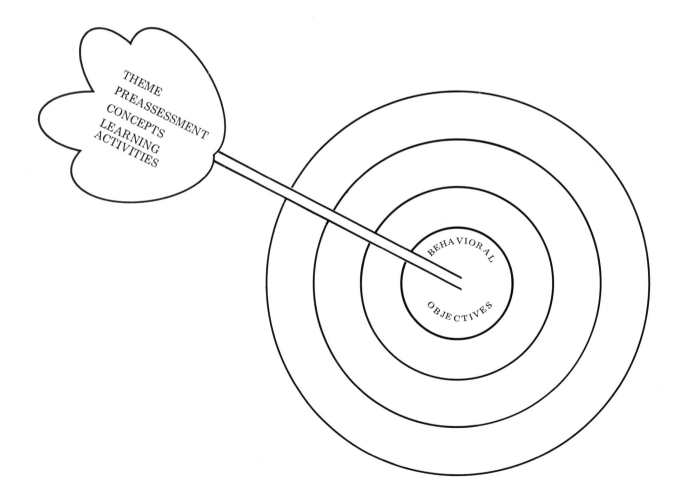

Did you hit the bull's eye? If so, keep it up. If not, make some adjustments in the size of the bull's eye (behavioral objectives), the feathers on the arrow (preassessment, concepts, and learning activities), or your aim (theme). Keep trying; it really is worth the struggle.

The following sample lesson plan is geared more to a type of preschool group where the emphasis is on the whole child, and the curriculum is less structured than in some types of small-group teaching. No time schedule is suggested; it should be flexible. Children determine how long they spend in each activity or area. Also, no specific time is scheduled for toileting. The children are free to use the toilets as necessary. Some need reminding while others do not.

SAMPLE LESSON PLAN (DAY)

Theme

Shoes.

Preassessment

Several days before this theme is to be taught, use one or more of the following ways to preassess the children's knowledge of shoes:

1. Ask the children what they are wearing on their feet. See how many of them are wearing shoes with similar characteristics (type of shoe: tie, buckle; type of fabric: canvas, leather; color). Ask them why they wear shoes (protection, warmth, comfort).

2. Show the children pictures of different kinds of shoes and ask them what person would wear those shoes (father, mother, child, hunter, athlete).

3. On a table have shoes with which most children should be familiar (tennis, sandals, booties, boots) and some with which they are probably not as familiar (ballet, wooden, clogs [Oriental], football). Let children investigate and explore.

4. Using different types of shoes, ask the children if they can identify the different functions (buckle, strap) and/or parts (tongue, sole, heel, eyelets).

5. Ask the children if they know why shoes are made out of different types of material (warmth or coolness, waterproof, inexpensive, colorful).

6. Show the children a variety of kinds of shoes and see if they can identify when (or for what activity) they are worn.

Concepts

1. Different people wear different kinds of shoes.
2. The parts of shoes have specific names.
3. Shoes are made from different kinds of materials.
4. Different kinds of shoes are worn for different activities.
5. When wearing different kinds of shoes, people move differently.

Behavioral Objectives

After this experience, the children will be able to:

1. Match shoes to the appropriate person when given a number of pictures of shoes and people.

2. Name the parts of at least three different kinds of shoes.

3. Tell at least three materials used for making shoes (leather, fabric, plastic, rubber, straw, wood).

4. Demonstrate how a person would move when wearing different kinds of shoes (cowboy boots, ski boots, ballet slippers, high-heels, sandals).

Learning Activities

Pictures of shoes are on the bulletin board. Visual aids with poem and story are used. Different kinds of shoes will be shown to the children, and the

13

discussion will include type of shoe, what it is made of, when it is worn, the names of different parts, and who wears that particular kind of shoe. Some pictures of people will be used. (Shoes for babies: booties, soft-soled shoes; shoes for girls and boys: slip-ons, buckle, tie, athletic; shoes for women: high-heels, dress, sport, athletic; shoes for men: boots, dress, sport, athletic; shoes for specific people: wooden shoes, Indian moccasins, Eskimo boots). At music time, the children will pretend they are wearing the different kinds of shoes and demonstrate how they would move while wearing them.

Schedule of Activities

Review plans. Teachers make necessary preparations for the day. Prepare bulletin board.*

Check-in. Children arrive and are checked in by nurse or teacher. Free play: manipulative toys and table activities (puzzles, peg boards).

*Setting the learning stage.** All children and teachers assemble together. One teacher brings out the box of shoes and the discussion outlined above takes place.

Free play.
- Housekeeping: available but not emphasized today.
- Food experience: not used today.
- Blocks: small unit blocks and small cars.
- Creative expression: cutting pictures of shoes from magazines and pasting them on shoe boxes*; paper weaving, easel, and paints.
- Manipulative area: lacing, buckling, and other frames; peg boards.
- Cognitive, sensory, and/or science area: magnifying glass and various objects.
- Book corner and books: (see list at end of plan).

Transition: Children are encouraged to help clean up the various areas.

Prestory activities: Wolfe, Ffrida. "Choosing Shoes"* [poem]. In *I See a Poem*, edited by Jane Ellen. Racine, Wisconsin: Whitman Publishers Div., Western Publishing Co., 1968; miscellaneous fingerplays: "Ten Little Indians," "Eency-Weency Spider."

Story time: "New Shoes"* by Sam Vaughan. (Doubleday, 1961); "Looking for Susie" by Bernadine Cook. (New York: Young Scott Books, 1956). To be used if needed.

Music and movement: Children are encouraged to move as if they were wearing some of the different shoes presented earlier.

Snack or lunch: Let children's conversation be spontaneous.

Outside activities: The children play with trikes, wagons, and climbing equipment.

Check-out: The children put away their toys and get a Learning Card before departing.

*Supports theme.

Learning Card Example

(School or teacher's name)   (Date)

Theme: Shoes.
Today we talked about shoes. There were pictures, a poem, and a story about shoes. A variety of shoes were shown to the children, including those for babies, children, and adults. Discussion included the type of shoes, what they are made of, when they are worn, what the different parts are, and who wears the particular shoes.

Perhaps it would be meaningful for you and your child to continue this topic casually as the opportunity arises.

Evaluation

 1. Which children were responsive to the materials and ideas presented? Which ones asked and answered questions?
 2. Which of the learning activities interested the children the most? the least?
 3. Which of the children knew the most about the theme? the least?
 4. How many of the children participated in the music and movement activity?
 5. What are some follow-up ideas for this theme?
 6. Were there some children who needed special attention today? If so, give names and situations.
 7. As a whole, how did the day go? Give examples.
 8. Discuss some of the interactions of children and teachers.
 9. Discuss some of the teaching techniques as to appropriateness, variety, reinforcement, etc.

Plan for Tomorrow

Books Available Throughout the Day

Brenner, Barbara. *Somebody's Slippers, Somebody's Shoes?* * New York: Wm. R. Scott, 1957.

Buckley, Helen. *Grandfather and I.* New York: Lothrop, Lee and Shepard, 1959.

de Regniers, Beatrice. *What Can You Do with a Shoe?* * New York: Harper, 1955.

Ets, Marie H. *Play With Me.* New York: Viking, 1955.

Friskey, Margaret. *A Shoe For My Pony.* * Chicago: Children's Press, 1950.

Zion, Gene. *Harry, the Dirty Dog.* New York: Harper & Bros., 1956.

Zolotow, Charlotte. *Someday.* New York: Harper & Row, 1951.

*Supports theme.

TEACHING IN SMALL GROUPS

In small group teaching, the most common parts of the curriculum are music, mathematics, reading, language, and creative expression with art materials. Each small group includes one or two teachers and a limited number of children. The children participate in one group for a period of time, then rotate groups until they have had an experience in each group. Many things that have been stated about daily lesson plans apply here. One thing that is different in this type of teaching is that each teacher is responsible for only one aspect of the curriculum each day. She may plan music one day and a creative experience the next. She plans just as thoroughly as if she were planning the entire day. Behavioral objectives are written, and the experience is planned so that the objective is reached. A theme for the entire day may be decided upon, or the teachers may plan various group activities that they feel would be meaningful to the children.

Small-group teaching is more structured than the traditional type and is often geared toward intellectual development. An example of this type of teaching follows:

SAMPLE LESSON PLAN (SEGMENT OF DAY)

Theme

Noses.
Specific aspect of curriculum: language stimulation.

Preassessment

Several days prior to teaching this theme, use one or more of the following ideas (or make up your own) to preassess the children's knowledge about noses:
1. Ask the children to describe and name the parts of a face as you draw them or paste a picture on an outline. Ask them to tell the uses of each part.
2. Ask them if they know how we can taste things. Do they know the part the nose plays?
3. Ask them if they know any other words for nose (snout, beak).
4. Make some different shaped noses out of paper or clay. Place them on a table with several large mirrors. Let the children experiment.
5. Ask them if they can explain the following ideas: "Somebody got his nose bent out of shape," "She's just nosey," "He's got his nose where it doesn't belong," "Don't stick your nose into my business."

Concepts

1. People and animals have noses.
2. The nose has special functions.
3. We learn through our nose. It is one of the five senses.
4. Our nose helps us taste things.

Behavioral Objectives

At the end of the experience, the child will be able to:
1. Describe three shapes of noses.
2. Tell two uses of the nose.

Learning Activities

The teacher will begin the discussion by showing pictures of people who don't have a nose. She will ask: "What is wrong with these pictures?" The children will undoubtedly respond quickly if they have not already commented on the absence of the nose. Then pictures of people who do have a nose will be

presented. The teacher will encourage the children to describe the different shapes of the noses, then will hand the children mirrors so that they can examine and describe their own noses. The children will point out differences. Next the teacher will ask: "What can you do with your nose?" or "Why do you have a nose?" Spontaneous responses such as "To smell with," "To hold my glasses up," "To breathe air," or "To be on top of a moustache" are expected, but many unexpected ideas will also appear. Ask a child to hold his nostrils closed with his fingers and then taste something. Ask someone to demonstrate how glasses could be kept on without the use of the nose. Ask someone else how he could breathe if his nostrils were closed. Teach the song "Ker-Choo!" (Dalton, Arlene, et al. *My Picture Book of Songs.* Chicago: M. A. Donohue & Co., 1947, p. 47.).

The same ideas and questions for evaluating a whole day can be used with each small group. (See "Evaluation" at the end of full-day lesson plan, page 15.)

Mini-Plans

In the chapters on Music, Movement, Sound and Rhythm, and also on Science are some "mini-plans" (see pages 96, 98, 99, 100, 111, 112, 114, 115, 116, and 117). You will note that only the theme, the behavioral objectives, and the learning activities are included for each plan. This was deliberate. With these objectives and activities as suggestions, write appropriate preassessment methods, concepts, and evaluations which would be of interest and value to the children in your group. Or, using these objectives and activities as a springboard as to what could be done, formulate preassessment methods, concepts, behavioral objectives, learning activities, and evaluations for these themes.

A mini-plan is a partial, or skeletal, plan, requiring more elements before it can be used with the children. It could apply to a full-day lesson plan or to a segment of the day.

ABOUT PARENTS

In order to make children's experiences at school something that can be shared with parents and other family members, plan some type of communication with the home. One example is to send a small card (3" x 5") home with the child each time there is a change of theme at school. This would include the teacher's name, the date, the theme, and some of the learning activities written in a less formal way than in the actual lesson plan. An example of a card that could accompany the day on "Shoes" can be found on page 15. The advantages of always using the same size card is that parents are more likely to keep and use them and that their preparation is simplified.

The main reason for sending the cards home is to inform the parents of the experiences the child is having at school. Parents can discuss the information with their children in a sharing vein but never in one demanding performance. Parents often give valuable feedback to teachers as to misconceptions, comments, or interests of the children.

Another way to inform parents is to have a copy of the daily lesson plan for them to see as they bring their children to school each day. Encourage them to read it and make comments.

Parents *are* interested in what their children are learning and doing at school. Make sure you help them feel a part of the education of their children by encouraging them to visit the school and to participate when it is possible. They can help with excursions and special activities, and many would be willing to share their talents if they were asked.

Parental involvement is essential to the success of any preschool program. Home visits, individual parent conferences, group parent meetings, observation by and with parents, and parent participation are some of the elements that bring school, home, and child together. When you do have contact with the parents, make sure that a quality relationship exists. Make them feel valued, useful, wanted, and appreciated. An occasional phone call or communication by mail is important if personal contacts are infrequent. Most parents want and appreciate help in raising happy, successful children.

Graphically the success of a child's education looks like this:

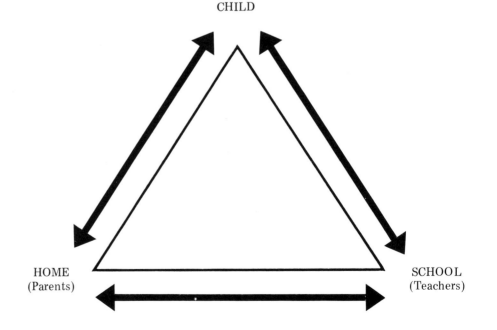

ESPECIALLY FOR PARENTS

Suppose there isn't a preschool group available in your community or that the one in your community doesn't support your philosophy; or suppose you simply choose to have your child remain at home until public school entrance. How could the information in this chapter be of use or value to you?

First of all, you know your child better than anyone else does. You are with him day and night, through health and sickness, through fun and frustration. If you are objective—and flexible—you will be the greatest teacher he will ever have. You will be his guide and model.

Second, you will have many opportunities to observe your child—his needs, his interests, his growth, his interactions with people and materials, his fears, and all other things that contribute to his total development.

Third, you will be able to respond to him on a one-to-one basis, which is often difficult in a school setting. As spontaneous questions or experiences occur, you can satisfy his individual questions and create learning situations just for him. Even if it is short, you can spend some quality time with him each day.

Fourth, you can help him understand about his community by taking him with you, first briefly, but casually, talking about where you are going and what you will do there. He isn't excess baggage, he is an eager learner.

Fifth, you can preassess the child's knowledge in various areas (similar to what a teacher does), but because you are planning for your own child, you can increase his knowledge and help him integrate that knowledge into his world.

Sixth, some parents feel there are special experiences they want to have with their children (going to the zoo, visiting the train station or airport, riding a horse) and they should have this privilege. Some experiences are automatically eliminated from a school setting because of cost, distance, or danger.

Seventh, if you see that your child is avoiding certain situations (art, books, social contacts), you can plan some enjoyable, stimulating experiences to encourage him in these activities.

Eighth, you can help your child become independent and dependable by sharing in family responsibilities.

Ninth, you can demonstrate through your daily living your religion and philosophy of life.

SOME SUGGESTED CURRICULUM TOPICS FOR PRESCHOOL CHILDREN

(Additional topics are listed at the end of chapters 4 and 5 and throughout the book):

- Animals (see pages 113-114 and 119)
  Learning the care of various animals
  Learning the names of young and adult of each animal
  Learning the names of the male and female animals
  Learning where the animals live
  Learning how they live
  Learning how they help man
  Learning about the different coverings of various animals (shell, fur, feathers)
  Learning the products obtained from different animals
  Learning which animals make good pets
  Learning about wild animals
  Learning about circus animals
  Learning how animals protect themselves (claws, camouflage, hibernation)
  Taking care of an animal at school or home
  Learning characteristics of animals in same category (dogs) and in different categories (dogs, birds, insects, reptiles)

- Birds
  Learning the names of various birds
  Learning ways to distinguish various birds
  Learning the sounds made by various birds
  Learning where birds live
  Learning how birds feed their young
  Learning how birds help man (beauty, sound, eat insects)
  Learning about the different kinds of nests
  Learning about the different kinds of eggs birds lay (color, size)
  Learning characteristics of different birds
  Learning habits of different birds (nesting, migration)

- Categories
  Learning to categorize (vehicles, food, animals, birds, clothing, furniture, persons, buildings, toys, plants, tools—building, garden or household—containers, appliances, things to write with)
  Learning about multiple classification (things can be classed in more than one category)
  Learning about ways to help us discriminate between categories (use senses, experiences)
  Learning why categories are useful and helpful

- The Children
  Learning one's own name and worth
  Learning where to hang clothing
  Learning names of other children, teachers, nurse, others
  Gaining self-confidence
  Building a good self-image
  Learning parts of the body
  Following actions—stand-up
  Learning self-mastery and control

- Clothing
  Learning the names of different garments
  Learning the different seasons for wearing different types of clothing
  Learning the sequence for putting on clothing
  Learning types of fabrics (cotton, wool, leather, plastic)
  Learning about clothing for different occasions (play, party, sleeping)
  Learning about and manipulating different types of fasteners on clothing (zippers, buttons, snaps)
  Learning the variety of uses of certain pieces of clothing (shoes, hats)
  Learning about color or patterning in clothing (printed, woven)
  Learning to dress and undress dolls.

- Color
  Learning the names of the primary colors
  Learning the names of the secondary colors
  Discovering how various colors are made
  Discussing how various colors make you feel
  Discussing the uses of different colors (red for danger)
  Discussing the color of specific objects (fruits, vehicles, animals)
  Discussing how colors are made and actually making some (berries, leaves)
  Participating in "tie-dying" experience
  Discussing shades of same color

- Communication
  Learning ways of communication with others (physical, verbal)
  Learning that some people speak a different language than we do
  Learning about different forms of communication (radio, TV, newspaper, books, telephone)

Learning proper names of people, places, and things so that we understand
   meanings
Learning that some animals help carry messages (dogs, pigeons)

- The Community
  Learning locations within the community
  Learning about kinds of buildings, industries, parks, highways
  Learning to recognize certain community landmarks
  Learning about different communities

- Community Helpers
  Learning about various community helpers—places of work, activities,
     services (suggested people: fireman, policeman, postman, doctor, nurse,
     dentist, baker, milkman, grocer, merchant)
  Learning how community helpers work together
  Learning to recognize different community helpers by uniform or clothing
     they wear

- Comparatives
  Learning the names and relationships in comparisons of two things (biggest-
     smallest, hottest-coldest, heaviest-lightest; bigger-smaller, fatter-skinnier,
     taller-shorter; too loud-too soft, too long-too short, too fat-too skinny)
  Learning the names and relationships in comparisons of more than two
     things (big, bigger, biggest; short, shorter, shortest; long, longer, longest)
  Learning that one object can be big when compared to some things and small
     when compared to others
  Learning the concept of "middle"
  Learning ordinal numbers (first, second, third)
  Learning opposites through comparisons (soft, rough)

- Days of the Week
  Learning the names of the days of the week
  Learning the sequence of the days
  Learning about activities for certain days (e.g., Saturday or Sunday)
  Learning why the days of the week have special names
  Learning about the calendar (days, weeks, months)

- Environment
  Learning about the characteristics of the community (lake, mountains)
  Learning what "pollution" is and how we can help prevent it
  Learning about natural resources (coal, gas, oil)
  Learning about conservation of natural resources (forests, water)
  Learning about recycling (water, paper, metal)
  Learning how to act in public places

- Families
  Learning who lives in immediate family (mother, father, sister, brother,
     baby)
  Learning who lives in extended family (aunt, uncle, cousin, grandparents)
  Learning what families do together
  Learning what a family is
  Learning about different jobs and responsibilities of various members
  Learning about friends and their names
  Learning about people (different physical characteristics, different abilities,
     likes)
  Learning how we can entertain guests
  Learning how to get along with family members
  Learning good social techniques

- Food (see pages 116-117, 120 and Chapter 10)
  Learning the names of various kinds of food
  Tasting various kinds of food

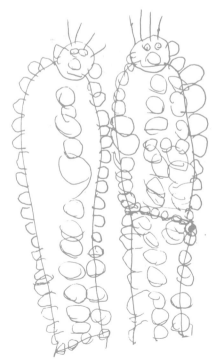

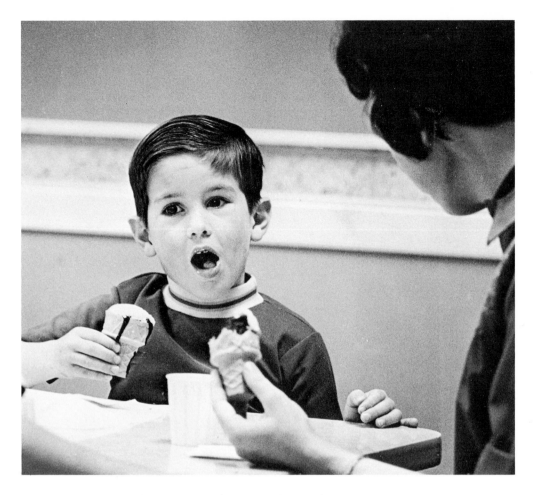

Learning about the taste buds (sweet, sour, salty, bitter)
Preparing food in a variety of ways
Learning about the different parts of the plant that we use as food (roots, stalk, flower)
Discussing things that look alike but taste different (salt, sugar, soda)
Learning about food consumed by different animals
Preparing for and participating in lunch or snack
Learning about a good diet (basic four)
Learning where different food products come from (animals, grown, manufactured)
Learning different ways of preparing food (raw, boiled, baked)

- Growing Things (see pages 115-116, and 120)
Learning the names of common flowers and plants
Learning how to care for plants
Learning different things that plants grow from (bulb, seed, start)
Learning the different parts of the plant (root, stalk, vine, leaf, flower)
Learning about the different parts of the plant which are edible (root: carrot, turnip; head: lettuce, cabbage; stalk: celery)
Learning about the different sizes and kinds of seeds
Learning about the length of growing time (grass and beans grow rapidly; corn and squash require longer time)
Learning about various fruits grown on trees
Learning about the things needed for growth (sunlight, water, warmth)
Learning about food that grows above and below the ground
Learning about growing things that are not edible
Learning how we store fruit and vegetables
Learning why we wash or clean food before eating it

22

- Health and Cleanliness
  Learning how we clean various parts of the body (hair, nails, skin, teeth)
  Learning about professional people who help us
  Learning reasons for keeping clean and healthy
  Learning how we keep clean and healthy (exercise, rest, clothing)
  Learning about a proper diet
  Learning about things which are edible and nonedible

- Holidays (see Chapter 8)
  Learning the names of various holidays
  Learning about activities unique to holidays
  Learning about the importance of holidays to children (birthdays, Christmas, Valentine's Day)
  Learning which holidays come during which seasons
  Learning about family customs for different holidays
  Learning about national, religious, cultural, and personal holidays of self and others
  Preparing for and participation in child-centered holiday activities

- Homes
  Learning where each child lives
  Learning what a house looks like (inside and out)
  Learning the rooms in a house
  Learning about the different types of homes in the community
  Learning to care for homes (inside and outside)
  Learning about homes in other countries or areas
  Learning about furnishing various rooms
  Learning about different building materials
  Visiting a home or apartment

- Identification
  Matching animals (mother and young)
  Categorizing what is sold in a specific type of store (What things would one find in this store?)
  Selecting type of store for certain item (Where would you go to find _____ ?)
  Selecting things that belong together (fork and spoon, hat and coat, shoe and sock)
  Learning how to recognize something by one or more of the senses
  Learning how to group objects with similar characteristics (color, material, shape)
  Learning how to discriminate between objects

- Machines
  Learning about machines for the home or for industry; how they work and what their function is
  Learning the names and values of various machines
  Learning to operate machines (mixer, egg beater, gears)
  Learning how machines make work easier for man

- Materials
  Learning the names of different building materials (brick, wood, fiberglass, cement, steel, cinder blocks)
  Learning the names of various materials (metal, glass, plaster, paper, cardboard, cloth fabrics, leather, rubber, foil)
  Learning why certain materials are used for certain purposes (glass, waterproof)
  Learning about various fabrics

- Mathematics (see Chapter 11)
  Learning to count, using familiar things (children, blocks, crackers, clapping)

Learning to count similar and dissimilar objects
Learning to recognize written symbols
Learning about parts of the whole (fractions)
Exploring with unit blocks (different shapes and numbers to make other shapes)
Learning to make things equal
Learning that we tell different things by their number (phone, sport participant, house, time)
Learning that we buy some things by weight, size, amount
Learning some mathematical terms (more—less, how many)

- Music (see Chapter 4)
Learning to sing different songs
Learning to play and listen to different records
Learning the names and uses of various musical instruments
Learning different ways of making sounds
Learning classes of instruments (wind, percussion, string)
Discussing different ways different music makes us feel
Learning to participate with music
Discovering rhythm in everyday life (clocks, water dripping, walking)
Observing different instruments being played
Initiating music or movement in nature (trees, animals, water)

- Objects
Learning the names of parts of an object (e.g., a pencil has a point, lead, shaft, eraser)
Learning about the different materials used to make same or different objects
Learning the specific uses of different objects (spoon, screw driver, belt)
Learning to identify objects through one or more of the senses
Naming several objects which could be used for the same purpose (hold water, improve surroundings)

- Opposites
Learning opposites (big-little, fat-skinny, loud-soft, hot-cold, long-short, fast-slow, wet-dry, smooth-rough, tall-short, dark-light, etc.)
Learning to combine opposites (big, rough and dark)
Learning to discriminate (an object may be big compared to some things and small compared to others)

- Pattern
Learning about different patterns (striped, flowered, polka dot, plaid, plain, checked)
Learning if the pattern is woven into fabric or printed
Learning to create own patterns using art materials
Learning how patterns (shapes) are combined in environment

- Piaget concepts
Learning about conservation of volume or substance
Learning about reversibility (water to ice to water)
Learning to determine differences in weight of objects (in hand or scale)
Learning how objects can be grouped in a variety of ways (color, shape, size, material)
Discovering that learning is enhanced through the senses and through movement (sensorimotor)

- Plurals
Learning that most plurals are regular (in the way they are formed)
Learning about irregular plurals (foot-feet, child-children, man-men, tooth-teeth, mouse-mice, sheep-sheep)

Learning that some terms are used when you have more than one of an object (many, few, group, some)

Learning that you may have one of an object but it is still called a "pair" (scissors, glasses, pants)

- Prepositions

  Learning the names of relationship of various prepositions (in, on, over, under, next to, in front of, in back of, inside, outside, between)

  Learning how to carry out simple commands

  Using one's body in space to learn prepositions (obstacle course)

- The Preschool

  Learning labels for materials and objects in the room

  Learning storage place for toys

  Learning place for certain activities

  Learning about the adults

  Learning limits, responsibilities, and privileges

  Learning routine

- Safety

  Learning about times and places where we must be careful (roads, around water)

  Learning to prevent accidents

  Learning about the care of injuries

  Learning about professional people who help us

  Learning about safety at school and home

  Learning reasons for limits under different circumstances

  Learning about using tools and materials

- Science

  Learning about magnets

  Learning about magnifying glasses

  Learning how to make measurements

  Learning about heat and how it changes various things

  Learning about light and prisms

  Learning to distinguish heavy and light objects

  Learning about liquids, solids, and gases

  Exploring physical science (see chapter on science)

  Exploring social science (see chapter on science)

  Producing and preparing food

  Working with levers

  Exploring biological science (see chapter on science)

  Discovering things about community, nation, and universe

  Learning how to get along with others

- Seasons

  Naming the seasons

  Learning characteristics of each season

  Learning what people do during different seasons

  Learning what people wear during different seasons

  Learning why we dress differently for different seasons

  Learning how seasons affect family, animals, and plants

  Learning to identify different seasons from pictures

- Shapes

  Learning the names of shapes (square, circle, triangle, rectangle, oval, diamond, trapezoid)

  Discovering the uses of different shapes

  Looking for various shapes of objects in the room

  Discussing the shapes of various objects in our daily life

  Learning about why certain things are the shapes they are (e.g., wheel)

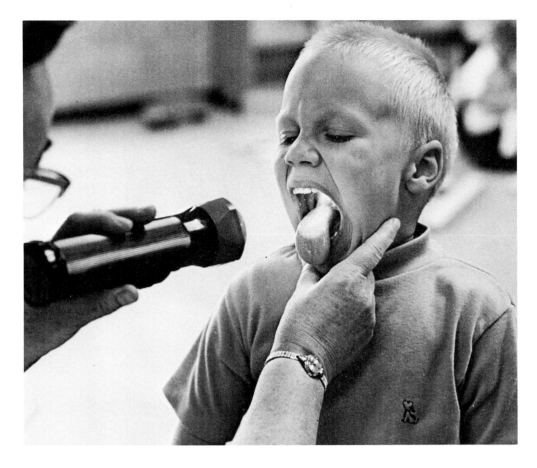

Discovering how various shapes can be formed (two semicircles make a
    circle, two triangles make a trapezoid)
Discussing how similar objects (leaves, flowers) are different shapes
Using a variety of shapes, make an original design (could be art project or
    with plastic disks, for example)
Discussing characteristics of (or explaining) various shapes (a triangle has 3
    corners, and the lines may vary in length.)

■ Sound (see also pages 65, 98-99, and 101-2.)
Listening for sounds in everyday life
Distinguishing things by sound only
Distinguishing differences in sound (high or low, loud or soft)
Learning different ways of making sounds
Making sounds of the different animals
Making sounds of different transportation vehicles
Making sounds that express different emotions
Saying rhyming words
Learning to recognize objects from verbal descriptions only
Telling something interesting about child's self or activity
Learning to follow simple directions

■ Temperature
Learning the terms used with heat (hot-warm, cool-cold, hot-cold)
Learning about temperature as it relates to the different seasons
Learning about temperature and heat as related to cooking
Learning how a thermometer registers heat or cold

■ Time
Learning about the present, past, and future
Learning about the sequence of things (before and after)
Learning about ways to tell time (clock, sun, sundial)

Learning about things that we do when it is light outside, and things we do when it's dark

- Transportation
  Learning the names of various kinds of transportation (boat, airplane, bus, train, automobile)
  Learning various ways they work
  Learning what they carry and how it feels to ride in each
  Learning about vehicles
  Learning about wheels and how they work
  Learning about transportation in air (airplanes, balloons, helicopters), on or in water (boats, submarines, ferries), on land (cars, trucks, busses), and underground (subways)
  Learning about animals used for transportation (horse, camel, elephant)

- Weather
  Learning about precipitation (rain, snow, sleet, hail)
  Learning about lightning and thunder
  Learning about visibility (cloudy, foggy, sunny)
  Learning labels for different kinds of weather
  Learning what happens to plants, animals, and people in different weather
  Learning about water (solids, liquids, gases)
  Learning about air (evaporation, movement)
  Learning about wind (windy, breezy, calm)
  Learning about different occupations related to weather (hunting, fishing)
  Learning how a thermometer indicates temperature
  Learning how weather is predicted
  Learning how weather affects the way we feel

BIBLIOGRAPHY FOR CHAPTER ONE: PLANNING THE PRESCHOOL CURRICULUM

BOOKS

Hess, Robert D., and Doreen J. Croft. *Teachers of Young Children.* Boston: Houghton Mifflin Company, 1972, pp. 2-59.

Hildebrand, Verna. *Introduction to Early Childhood Education.* New York: The Macmillan Company, 1971, pp. 3-20, 49-65, and 293-317.

Leeper, Sarah H., Ruth J. Dales, Dora Sikes Skipper, Ralph L. Witherspoon. *Good Schools for Young Children.* New York: The Macmillan Company, 1974, pp. 131-71.

Mager, Robert F. *Preparing Instructional Objectives.* Palo Alto, California: Fearon Publishers, 1962.

Read, Katherine. *The Nursery School.* Philadelphia: W. B. Saunders, 1971, Parts 1, 3, 4.

Spodek, Bernard. *Teaching in the Early Years.* Englewood Cliffs, New Jersey: Prentice-Hall, 1972, pp. 1-11.

Spodek, Bernard. *Early Childhood Education.* Englewood Cliffs, N.J.: Prentice-Hall, 1973.

Taylor, Barbara J. *When I Do, I Learn.* Provo, Utah: Brigham Young University Press, 1974, Chapter 1.

Todd, Vivian E. *The Aide in Early Childhood Education.* New York: The Macmillan Company, 1973.

Todd, Vivian E., and Helen Heffernan. *The Years before School: Guiding Preschool Children.* Toronto: The Macmillan Company, 1970, pp. 160-90.

Vance, Barbara. *Teaching the Prekindergarten Child.* Monterey, California: Brooks Cole Division, Wadsworth Publishing Company, 1973, Part 1.

ARTICLES

Berman, Louise M. "Not Reacting but Transacting: One Approach to Early Childhood Education." *Young Children*, June 1973.

Caldwell, Bettye M. "What Is the Optimal Learning Environment for the Young Child?" *American Journal of Orthopsychiatry*, January 1967.

Casey, Vera M. "High School Parent-Child Education Center." *Young Children*, January 1974.

Chittenden, Edward A. "What Is Learned and What Is Taught?" *Young Children*, October 1969.

Crase, Dixie Ruth, and Nancy S. Jones. "Children Learn from Recycling." *Young Children*, January 1974.

Elkind, David. "The Case for the Academic Preschool: Fact or Fiction?" *Young Children*, January 1970.

Elkind, David. "Sense and Nonsense about Preschools." *Parent's Magazine*, March 1971.

Gross, Dorothy W. "Teachers of Young Children Need Basic Inner Qualities." *Young Children*, November 1967.

Harms, Thelma, "Evaluating Settings for Learning." *Young Children*, May 1970.

Highberger, Ruth, and Sharon Teets. "Early Schooling: Why Not?" *Young Children*, January 1974.

Katz, Lillian G. "Children and Teachers in Two Types of Head Start Classes." *Young Children*, September 1969.

Katz, Lillian G. "Teaching in Preschools." *Children*, April 1970.

Lee, Patrick C., and Annie Lucas Wolinsky. "Male Teachers of Young Children: A Preliminary Empirical Study." *Young Children*, August 1973.

Levin, Carolyn W. "The Teacher Is the Nursery School." *Young Children*, November 1964.

MacDonald, James B. "A Proper Curriculum for Young Children." *Phi Delta Kappan* 50 (March 1969):406.

Marion, Marian C. "Create a Parent-Space—a Place to Stop, Look and Read." *Young Children*, April 1973.

Mendelson, Anna. "A Young Man around the Class." *Young Children*, June 1972.

Seifert, Kelvin. "Comparison of Verbal Interaction in Two Preschool Programs." *Young Children*, September 1969.

Spodek, Bernard. "Early Learning for What?" *Phi Delta Kappan*, March 1970.

PAMPHLETS

Baker, Katherine Read, Editor. *Ideas That Work with Young Children.* # 304. Washington, D.C.: National Association for the Education of Young Children, 1834 Connecticut Avenue N.W., 20009. 1972. 144 pp. $3.00.

Beyer, Evelyn. *The Teacher Sets the Stage.* Washington, D.C.: National Association for the Education of Young Children, 1834 Connecticut Avenue N.W., 20009.

Dittmann, Laura L., Editor. *Curriculum Is What Happens: Planning Is the Key.* # 119. Washington, D.C.: National Association for the Education of Young Children, 1834 Connecticut Avenue N.W., 20009. 1970. 72 pp. $1.75.

Tarnay, Elizabeth Doak. *What Does the Nursery School Teacher Teach?* # 106. Washington, D.C.: National Association for the Education of Young Children, 1834 Connecticut Avenue N.W., 20009.

Weikart, David P., et al. *The Cognitively Oriented Curriculum: A Framework for Preschool Teachers.* # 127. Washington, D.C.: National Association for the Education of Young Children, 1834 Connecticut Avenue N.W., 20009. 1971. 196 pp. $3.50.

CHAPTER 2

CREATIVE EXPRESSION

Nothing is quite so delightful as seeing a young child wholly absorbed in expressing himself creatively. Some people believe that creativity in children is linked strictly with the actual use of materials, such as paint or clay. This assumption, of course, is erroneous. A child may express his innermost thoughts in other ways as well. For example, children may be creative when they move to music, engage in dramatic play, or exercise large muscles. This section will be devoted to areas where such expression might take place, whether it be at the "creative table" or at other areas in the nursery school. Music will be covered in a later section, but it should be kept in mind that this section could apply also to music.

Not all children find it easy to participate in things which are "messy," but the need for expression is still within each child. It is the teacher's responsibility to see that he has many opportunities for expression.

VALUES FOR CHILDREN

Sensory experiences are very important to the young child; it is through these experiences that he learns about his world. The steady flow of dry sand through a child's fingers is very different from the maneuverability of wet sand. The free movement encouraged by the use of finger paint contrasts markedly with the more controlled use of woodworking tools and materials.

INDEPENDENCE

Keeping materials and supplies where children have access to them helps to stimulate independence in children. The old saying, "Strike while the iron is hot," applies equally to children and adults. When interest is high in a certain area is the time to explore it. If a child feels inclined to make a picture, play a record, or enter into dramatic play, and if "props" are at his disposal, he can make the transition smoothly rather than having to wait for adult help.

Through the use of creative materials we can encourage and stimulate children to be individuals and to share their ideas with others.

Ronald, three years old, had been given several different opportunities at nursery school to finger-paint. He thoroughly enjoyed each exposure. The

request came from his mother to "quit finger painting at school because Ronald finger paints with everything at home—especially his food at mealtime." Here was a child who needed a greater number, not fewer, of sensory experiences.

AESTHETIC APPRECIATION

By setting a good example, having a wholesome attitude and atmosphere, encouraging the children, and giving them honest praise, adults can help them gain an appreciation for the beauty surrounding them. If a child develops appreciation for aesthetics at a young age, his environment will become more meaningful. By taking an interest in what a child does, an adult can, by helping him see the unusual in the usual and hear that which he has not heard before, make him more aware of his environment.

SATISFACTION AND ENJOYMENT

It is enlightening to listen to the conversation of young children while they are engaged in creative or dramatic play. They should be encouraged to give verbal expression. "It's gushy!" "It holds onto my fingers."

Two essentials for gaining the most value from the use of creative materials are time and space. Much thought and planning need to be done here. Time is so important in the life of a preschooler. He needs time to live through each experience of importance to him—in his own way. He needs time in which he can investigate materials. When children have ample space in which to function, their activities are more enjoyable. To have an activity in a traffic lane, in cramped quarters, or in competition with other experiences discourages the child from the outset.

When a child knows that he can complete an activity without being interrupted, he is more likely to develop a sustained interest in it. Analyze this episode: Several children were finger painting; some entered eagerly into the activity while others watched. Ann sat debating whether or not to get involved. Some of the children finished and left the table. Ann gingerly put one finger into the mixture. It seemed acceptable; so she put her finger in again and sat quietly pondering the situation. She was about to involve herself again when the teacher came with a sponge and told her they were through for the day. She helped Ann away from the table and finished cleaning it. Would it have been better for Ann if she had been allowed to stay a while longer—or if she had been encouraged to help in cleaning the table? This is a case where a child did not have sufficient time for exploration and development of interest.

Creative expression can help a child realize that he is a worthwhile person, that he has good ideas, and that more than one way exists to do things. Adults stifle creativity in young children through remarks such as, "What is that?" "Nobody draws like that!" "You must do it this way!" Adults encourage creativity when they take pride in what the child does.

Betty carefully guarded a finger painting she had made so she could take it home after nursery school. She tenderly carried it to the car. A few moments later an angry young uncle stormed into the classroom with the painting and shouted, "If you think you're going to put that junk in my car and mess up the upholstery, you're sadly mistaken." Betty ran after him with tears in her eyes but made no comment; she was heartbroken. One wonders how long it was before she tried finger painting again.

David sat quietly on a chair waiting for his father. As his father appeared, David proudly displayed a picture he had made. The father studied the picture appreciatively, nodded his head, and smiled. After a short pause, the child looked at his father and asked, "Well, what is it, Dad?" as if the father saw much more in the painting than the child did. Think how much more David was encouraged to pursue creative activities than was Betty.

EMOTIONAL RELEASE

Creative expression can be an avenue for emotional release. Beating a drum, squeezing clay through the fingers, playing a domestic role in the domestic area, or moving to music are excellent ways through which a child can relieve his pressures.

John was aggressive one day because he had experienced a number of distressing incidents. He got on a stick horse and galloped around and around the play yard. When he returned, he said, "I feel better now. Let's go read a story." Russ had been frightened by a dog on his way to school. At the finger painting table, he made a resemblance of the dog and then quickly rubbed it out with the remark, "He can't bark at me now." Susan picked up a doll and rocked it, saying, "You'll feel better if I sing to you and hold you close." She had experienced these same feelings when an understanding adult had come to her rescue.

GOOD WORK HABITS

Even work habits can involve creative expression. Wiping up finger paint made from soap flakes gives the experience a new and exciting light. Lisa felt it was important to stay clean. She would stand near the creative tables and watch the other children as they enjoyed the materials. She would often wipe her hands on her clothes as though trying to remove some of their mess from her already clean hands. Whenever cleanup was initiated, she was the first one to get a sponge. She had the feeling that it was unacceptable to get dirty but that it was very acceptable to clean up a mess. This was the way she began her acquaintance with creative materials.

Children enjoy participating, and valuable learning experiences can be gained from it. They need to be involved in the whole cycle of an activity. Encourage them to mix the paints, for example, to use them, to clean them up, and to prepare them for storage. It may take longer, but the satisfaction experienced by the children is priceless.

MUSCLE DEVELOPMENT

Through self-expression, children can develop their muscles. The use of large muscles can be encouraged by providing such activities as woodworking, movement to music, block building, or use of outdoor equipment. Small muscle activities include cutting and pasting, working with collage, coloring with large crayons or chalk, figuring out puzzles, or having fun with peg boards. Activities involving large muscles should predominate over small muscle activities for a preschool child. Too much close or fussy work should be eliminated. Some children delight in the use of materials which involve small muscles, and these activities should be introduced, giving the child time to develop dexterity and eye-hand coordination.

EXPLORATION

Through the use of raw materials, children often learn to do individual thinking. Some children wait for other children or adults to tell them what to do and when to do it. They could profit from experience with raw materials. It is important to remember, however, that the use of the material is more important than the finished product.

Children enjoy repetition of materials and activities—not to the point of limiting experiences but to the end that they can explore, manipulate, and exercise their imaginations and initiative. The actual doing is important to them. When new ideas or materials are introduced to children, plans for repeated use of them should be included. One exposure is not enough.

It should be recognized that children may want to watch an activity before entering into it. Watching is the child's way of learning. Adults must feel comfortable in recognizing that some children enter in readily while others need to survey the activity before attempting it. Allow them time to discover and explore.

Most children have a tendency toward creativeness. Some, however, have been encouraged in it while others have been stifled. A recent study indicated that preschool children increase in creativity until about the age of five, when a sharp decrease begins. What could be the cause of this decrease—parental influence, conformity, patterning, adherence to unrealistic standards, peer pressure, commercial materials? All of these things, and more, contribute.

If a child feels free to explore, he can use materials such as cardboard, candy papers, containers, egg shells, and other usually discarded items in many different and creative ways. Be the supplier; let the child be the architect and builder.

Involvement with materials and ideas which allow children freedom to have firsthand experiences on their level of development starts them on a path of self-expression that will likely continue throughout life. All children have some creative ability, but some need more encouragement and experience than others. Moreover, some children need help in discarding erroneous concepts about their abilities.

ROLE OF THE TEACHER

ATTITUDE

It is unnecessary for a teacher always to express herself verbally in order for a child to learn of the teacher's feelings. It is important for a teacher to have a wholesome, accepting attitude toward the use of creative materials. She may not have this characteristic as she begins her preschool experience, but it can come with time, understanding, and the desire to help children live their lives to the fullest.

In one school, when the head teacher was absent, a substitute teacher, unknown to the children but known to the other teachers, went to assist. As creative materials were being prepared for the day, the substitute asked: "Why not use this bucket of earth clay which is already prepared?" Several teachers agreed with one who replied, "Our children don't like clay." The substitute teacher persisted, volunteering to supervise, and the teachers agreed. As the children entered the school, they drifted to the clay table. There the substitute teacher was rolling and pounding the clay and remarking that it was cool, soft, and so forth. Many of the children sat down to the clay table and remained for a long period of time. The conversation was delightful. Some of the children remained a short time, but during the period, all of the children had been to the clay table. At the end of the day, the teachers remarked, "We don't understand why the children went to the clay table. They haven't liked it before." What was the magical thing that drew the children? It was the attitude of the substitute teacher. She was enjoying the material and the children! The children felt her enjoyment and enthusiasm and sat down to share it with her. In talking with the teachers, the substitute teacher learned that none of them enjoyed the messiness or the feel of the clay. No wonder the children "didn't like it." Even though they had not expressed verbally to the children their dislike for clay, they had convinced the children that something was wrong with the experience.

USE OF PROPER MATERIALS

Because the small muscles of young children are underdeveloped, they should be provided with materials which will enable them to best express themselves. Large sheets of paper encourage the use of large muscles. Large brushes and crayons are easier for the children to hold. Materials should be appropriate to the developmental level of the children. They enjoy making

large, free arm movements. They need opportunities to develop eye-hand coordination. They are interested in the various uses of materials.

Covering the table with butcher paper or newspaper before an activity begins is a great aid at cleanup time. Simply roll the butcher paper containing the excess paint, clay, paste, or other spilled materials and place the roll in a waste container. An old shower curtain or a canvas under creative materials is also a time and energy saver.

It is important to provide materials which help to release feelings, not create frustration. Several children were sitting at a table using pegs and boards. They were enjoying the experience. Ronald came to the table and began using the materials. He was not as adept as the other children in using his small muscles, and he soon became discouraged. Then he became frustrated and pushed the pegs and boards onto the floor. Painting at the easel or playing in the block area would have better met his needs.

PLACEMENT OF MATERIALS

The placement of equipment for self-expression is most important. It should be near a water supply, in an area which is well lighted, and out of the traffic pattern. How discouraging it is to a child to be interrupted by others who are passing by.

Materials should be placed on low shelves or cupboards so that the children can have ready access to them and be able to exhibit their independence. Seeing materials often encourages their use.

Children can and should be encouraged to help with "clean up." Good work habits can be taught. If materials are near the washroom or sink, children can help to tidy the area. Many teachers think it is their responsibility to clean up when the children have finished in a certain area. The real value of letting the children help clean up is that they actually find it as stimulating as using materials.

Provide a place where the art work can be hung. A portable drying rack serves the purpose adequately. Since most children like to take their creations home with them, a place should be provided where the art work can dry. If space is limited, a folding wooden clothes rack can be used and then folded out of the way.

CONCERN FOR THE INDIVIDUAL

Each child comes from a different background and has had various experiences. To one child the feel of finger paint has a different meaning than to another child. Meet the child at his own level and then help him to further his experiences with the various materials. He may be hearing double standards— one at home and one at school. One of the limits of the preschool is that children are not allowed to climb on the furniture. Perhaps a child says, "At home I can climb on the furniture." Then the teacher explains, "Maybe your mother lets you climb on the furniture at home, but at school, we climb on the jungle gym, boards, and boxes." A child can understand that we do different things in different settings. He needs time to internalize and evaluate. He needs emotional support in respect and understanding.

As the child expresses himself with creative materials, the teacher can encourage the child to discuss his work by such honest statements as, "I like the colors you are using," or "This is an interesting design," but her comments should be with the child in mind rather than filling her own needs to be busy or feel important. From conversation the teacher can gain insight into the child's ideas and feelings.

The teacher should emphathize on the child's level. Judging a child's work on an adult level tends to make one critical. It is understanding that the child needs.

USE OF ENRICHING EXPERIENCES

When a young child draws, he sometimes eliminates an important part of the subject, such as a body, when he is drawing a person or an animal. He draws things as they appear to him. His firsthand experiences have been rather limited, and so some things have great importance for him. In order for him to clarify some of his misconceptions or omissions, the wise teacher will provide things which stimulate improving his expressions. For instance, if a rabbit with huge ears, a small body, and no legs appears in the child's drawing, it would be appropriate for the teacher to bring a rabbit into the nursery school and let the child see it and learn about it firsthand rather than trying to explain verbally the parts of a rabbit.

Some teachers are concerned that all children do not enjoy the materials and experiences which are provided for them. If enough interest and thought go into the preparation of such experiences, it is possible to provide an atmosphere which will radiate and draw children like a magnet. The same experiences day after day would tend to discourage participation by the children even though they like some repetition. On the other hand, using some experiences two or three days in a row could encourage their use.

GOALS AND OBJECTIVES

In order for a creative experience to be meaningful, it should be well-planned and executed. Using it just to consume a block of time is unacceptable. Goals and objectives should be clearly defined and within the reach of the children. Providing materials too advanced for the particular children involved detracts from the experience and might even discourage future participation.

AVAILABILITY OF TEACHER

A teacher should always be nearby to supervise the activities. Many times when she does not actively participate, she lends support by her presence. She is there to help, not to hinder. If given the opportunity, most children can solve their problems without the interference of an adult.

A teacher may initiate an activity and then watch for the appropriate time to withdraw to the sidelines so that the children can carry on. It is as important to know when and how to step out as it is to know when and how to step in.

LIMITS

Limits should be clearly defined and consistently maintained. Each head teacher may designate different limits; so it is necessary for all teachers to become aware of the limits of their individual group. One teacher had the children confine their finger painting to paper while another teacher permitted her children to finger paint on the table tops or the glass in the sliding doors.

CONCERN FOR PROCESS OR PRODUCT?

In a society as complex as ours, it is possible to become too product- and time-conscious. Too often we hear parents outwardly encourage their children to "make something" so they can account for part of their time.

One child had received direct urgings from her mother for a period of time and so, upon entering school one morning, walked directly to the easel, grabbed a brush, dipped it in red paint and made two large lines across the paper. As she left the easel, she remarked: "There, I've made a picture for Mother and now I can do what I want!"

One preschool was having difficulty with some of the parents over this subject. Parents were pressuring the children—and the school—into making something for the children to take home each day. The teacher recognized that the children were not enjoying the use of the materials as they had previously. She therefore arranged for the children to finger paint directly on the tops of tables. On another day, a large piece of butcher paper was placed on the floor, and the children had the experience of making a group mural. (What conversation and cooperation!) When it came time to go home, the children had no products. Explaining to the parents helped them understand what had occurred, and the children again enjoyed using the materials without feeling they had to make something.

CONCERN ABOUT PATTERNS, STEREOTYPED CUTOUTS, COLORING BOOKS

Patterning of any kind should be eliminated from the experiences of young children. It stifles creativity rather than encourages it. Children draw things as they see them. Lines made by others are meaningless to children. Requiring a young child to stay inside lines created by someone else is not within the ability of the young child.

Coloring books may provide teachers with good sources for visual aids, but should never be used with young children.

One mother was called to school for a conference with a kindergarten teacher because her child "refused to color anything" which was given to him by the teacher. The things which were provided were stereotyped and provided no interest for the child who had been encouraged to draw his own pictures.

CONCLUSION

As stated by Hoover in *Art Activities for the Very Young:* "Our objective is to provide experiences which will expand their horizons of understanding and manipulative skills. But, most important of all, we are developing the creative potential which we know exists within each one of our children." (p. 60.)

It is the responsibility of the teacher to provide materials, attitudes, and an atmosphere conducive to self-expression. Benefits from such expression are endless.

For an easy and quick overview of the activities presented in this chapter and for values to be gained by the children, see the chart on page 39.

BLOCKS

For some time the use of blocks with young children has been questioned, but gradually a greater number of teachers are becoming aware of the many values which blocks have to offer. See chart on page 39.

A student teacher in a preschool was anxious to promote block play with a group of four-year-old children. The floor space was very limited; so she moved out the domestic equipment. The first day after the equipment was moved, the children all asked, "Who took our stove?" "Where did the refrigerator go?" They wandered around as if they were lost. The second day they began to improvise by using blocks. By the end of the week, they had experienced many joys from using blocks. They made equipment for the domestic area. They worked cooperatively and came up with some ingenious ideas. The use of blocks was no longer a problem.

VALUES OF SPECIFIC ACTIVITIES FOR PRESCHOOLERS

Key: ● Best ■ Average ▲ Least

ACTIVITIES / VALUES	SENSORY EXPERIENCE	EXPLORATION	SATISFACTION & ENJOYMENT	SELF-EXPRESSION	MANIPULATION	EMOTIONAL RELEASE	EXERCISE IMAGINATION & INITIATIVE	GOOD WORK HABITS	LEARNING EXPERIENCE	SKILL & CONCENTRATION	EYE-HAND COORDINATION	HARMONY, RHYTHM & BALANCE	INSIGHT INTO OWN FEELINGS	DEVELOPS LARGE MUSCLES	DEVELOPS SMALL MUSCLES
BLOCKS Large	▲	●	●	■	■	●	▲	▲	▲	■	■	●	●	●	▲
BLOCKS Small	■	●	■	■	■	▲	▲	▲	■	■	●	■	■	▲	●
CHALK	▲	▲	▲	▲	▲	▲	▲	■	▲	▲	■	▲	▲	▲	■
CLAY	●	●	■	●	●	●	●	●	■	■	■	▲	●	●	■
COLLAGE	●	●	●	●	●	●	●	●	■	■	■	▲	■	▲	●
CRAYONS	▲	▲	▲	▲	▲	▲	▲	■	▲	▲	■	▲	▲	▲	■
CUTTING & PASTING	■	■	■	■	■	■	■	●	■	●	●	▲	▲	▲	●
DOMESTIC AREA	■	●	●	●	■	●	●	●	●	■	■	▲	●	■	■
PAINTING Easel	■	●	■	■	●	■	■	●	■	■	■	▲	■	●	■
PAINTING Finger	●	■	●	●	■	●	■	●	■	▲	■	▲	●	■	■
PAINTING Sponge or Block	■	●	■	■	●	■	■	●	■	■	■	▲	■	■	●
PAINTING Miscellaneous	■	■	■	■	■	■	■	●	■	■	■	▲	■	■	■
SAND	●	■	■	●	●	●	●	●	●	■	■	▲	●	●	■
STRINGING	▲	▲	■	▲	■	▲	■	■	▲	●	●	■	▲	▲	●
WATER	●	●	●	●	●	●	●	●	●	■	●	■	●	●	●
WOODWORKING	●	●	●	●	●	●	●	●	●	●	●	■	●	●	■

ROLE OF THE TEACHER

Physical Arrangements

Because of the nature of the material involved, it is imperative that plenty of space and time are allotted to the children. If a preschool does not have adequate space, it may be necessary to move some of the equipment into another area or room so that there will be sufficient floor space for using the blocks.

The children are on the floor a great deal when using blocks; because of this and the noise the blocks might create, it is suggested that blocks be used on a rug or carpet if at all possible. This also protects the blocks from damage when they tumble down.

Blocks should be out of the way of the traffic pattern. It is discouraging to be building a structure only to have someone accidentally knock it down because it was too near an entrance or intermingled with another activity.

A unit of time should be allowed so that the children can utilize the structures they make. It is rather discouraging to spend time building when one cannot enjoy the creation. The teacher should be aware of the time and warn the children far enough in advance to be ready to terminate the activity at the appropriate time. Simply by being told, "It's almost time to pick up the blocks," or "It will soon be juice time," the children can somewhat prepare themselves. If possible, leave the structure up for later play.

Good planning should go into the purchasing of blocks. Green and Woods, in *A Nursery School Handbook*, tell us: "All blocks should be designed to fit together mathematically, each size twice as long or wide as the preceding size. Not only will they serve better purposes in building, but they will stack compactly when not in use. All types of blocks should be either shellacked or waxed. This finish will be more practical than paint." (p. 5.)

Blocks play an important role in the preschool curriculum. Their omission would be like attempting to use nails without a hammer.

Supervision

When children are using blocks, a teacher should be nearby, but she does not have to actively participate with the children. Her verbal support may be enough to sustain activity in this area.

When structures begin to get too tall or wobbly, a suggestion from the teacher can direct the activity into constructive channels. Statements such as "Build as high as your nose," or "It's time to start another stack" give suggestions in a positive manner and are usually readily accepted by the children.

To interest children in the block area, it may be necessary to provide a "pace-setter" which merely attracts the children to the area. It should not be an elaborate structure but just an eye catcher. The teacher should avoid patterning with blocks and telling children how to build. Let them use their own imaginations. Perhaps a clarifying suggestion would be appropriate.

The teacher should indicate to the children what the limits are for the particular area. Blocks are to be used for building. Hollow blocks should be handled carefully. The area in which to operate and the size of the structure should have the safety of the children in mind. The teacher should use positive statements in her interaction with children, showing appreciation for a structure but avoiding overemphasis and never giving the children the idea that they must make certain structures in order to gain approval.

Children should be involved in cleanup. If the shelves are low and near the building area, it is easy to encourage the children to help. A teacher might say, "You pick up that size and I'll pick up this size," which gets the cleanup under way. To bring a child back from another area to help pick up blocks is not the most effective idea. Watch the children; as their interests begin to diminish, suggest putting away the blocks. When children take many blocks off the shelf at one time, the task of replacing them can look insurmountable to them. Here the teacher should use her initiative and wisdom in directing the children.

In the fall, Charles delighted in getting all the blocks off the shelves. He actually played with them very little. What he waited for was a teacher to tell him it was time to put them back on the shelves. To him this was the signal to run. Sometimes he would wait for other children to build structures; then he would knock them over and run. At first, because of their inexperience and feeling of helplessness, the teachers would run after him and bring him back. He would wait for his chance and then escape. Again, he would be captured and returned. He thrived upon this, but the teachers became very discouraged.

The teachers decided upon a plan which they thought had merit. Charles was seeking attention; why not give him positive attention so that he would not need to seek it in undesirable ways? They worked very diligently with him and were sometimes encouraged and sometimes discouraged. By spring, Charles began to respond. They were rewarded because of their perseverance. In the sight of the other children, he changed from the child they least wanted to play with to the child they most wanted to play with.

BIBLIOGRAPHY FOR BLOCKS

BOOKS

Green, Marjorie, and Elizabeth Woods. *A Nursery School Handbook.* Sierra Madre, California: Sierra Madre Community Nursery School Association, 1963.

Hartley, Ruth E. *Understanding Children's Play.* New York: Columbia University Press, 1967.

Hoover, Francis L. *Art Activities for the Very Young.* Worcester, Massachusetts: Davis Publications, 1967.

ARTICLES

Cartwright, Sally. "Blocks and Learning." *Young Children*, March 1974.

Rudolph, Marguerita, and Dorothy H. Cohen. "The Many Purposes of Block-building and Woodwork." *Young Children*, October 1964.

PAMPHLETS

Antin, Clara. *Blocks in the Curriculum.* New York: Early Childhood Education Council of New York City, 51 West 4th Street, 1969.

Franklin, Adele. *Blocks—A Tool of Learning.* #86. Bank Street College of Education, 69 Bank Street, New York 14, New York.

Starks, Ester B. *Block Building.* Washington, D.C.: EKNE, 1965.

CHALK

See discussion under Crayons and Chalk, pages 47-48. For values see chart on page 39.

CLAY (OR DOUGH CLAY)

For values, see chart on page 39.

USE OF MATERIAL

When earth clay is used, the child should freely use his hands in order to fully appreciate the media. Cookie cutters, rollers, and other objects detract from the sensory experience.

With dough clay, however, the child may use cookie cutters and rollers because this media more closely resembles cookie dough, and the child grows in an experience which is "realistic."

Clay is a media ruling out the need for failure. A child can express his own ideas through rolling, pounding, pinching, or doing whatever he desires. He can either retain or destroy his creation. The experience can be solitary or social.

Dough should not be used as a substitute for clay, but as an additional material. It provides sensory and manipulative experience, but it does not stimulate as much creativity as clay. Earth clay must be prepared in advance of its use. (See p. 43 for recipe.) The children may assist here; they delight in helping prepare earth clay. Some teachers feel that a school cannot be successfully operated without a large bucket of earth clay readily available for experimentation and release of feelings.

ROLE OF THE TEACHER

Again the teacher is urged to refrain from patterning for the children. She may manipulate materials, encourage conversation, and support the children, but should take a minor role. The conversation of the children when they use earth clay is most enlightening and interesting, and the teacher can learn valuable things about the way the children think.

To stimulate the interests of the children in the clay area, one teacher discussed building a bird's nest and then helped the children gather leaves, twigs, string, and other materials. They took these materials to the clay table, and there learned a great deal by making birds' nests. One objection to this is that the clay is not reusable because the other material has been added.

Again, children should be encouraged to aid in cleanup. When clay is left on the table for a period of time and allowed to dry, it is often difficult to remove. But a tongue depressor turned lengthwise removes clay quite easily. Covering the table in advance with paper facilitates cleanup.

It is important that limits are understood by the children. One teacher reported that children were putting clay on her arms, her face, and even in her hair. If she had defined the limits for the children, there should have been no problem. Sometimes we expect too much of children, and they do not know what the limits are.

If materials are to be reused, proper storage is essential. Earth clay should be stored in a covered earthen jar or metal container. The clay can be molded into a large ball and covered with damp paper towels or cloths if it is to be used again soon. If longer storage is desired, make impressions with your thumb and fill them with water. Too much water causes the clay to become moldy. Dough clay should be stored in airtight containers and will keep for several days. Clay can be an inexpensive item and can last for a long period of time if it is cared for properly.

RECIPES

Earth Clay. (Powder sold inexpensively at art supply stores, potteries, or play equipment companies.) Proper storage is essential.

Method 1. Put desired amount of water in earthen jar. Gradually add clay powder, stirring until it reaches the consistency of sticky bread dough. Let stand overnight. Knead powder into clay until desired consistency.

Method 2. Knead water into powder with hands, using only enough water to moisten. Mold into balls and leave exposed to air until pliable but not too sticky.

Method 3. Place powder in cloth sack. Tie firmly. Place in pail, covering with water. Remove clay next day and mold into balls.

Dough Clay

 # 1 Flour-Salt Dough

2 cups flour
1 cup salt

(A small amount of liquid oil keeps dough from drying out.) Use enough water to work flour and salt into a dough. To color it, add food coloring to water. Consistency is like cookie dough.

 # 2 Flour-Salt Dough

2½ cups flour
½ cup salt
3 T corn oil
1 T alum
2 cups boiling water

Put in bowl in order given. Stir. (Add food coloring if desired.) Store in covered dish.

 # 3 Flour-Salt Dough

1½ cups flour
½ cup salt
½ cup water
¼ cup vegetable oil

Mix flour and salt; slowly add water and oil. (Coloring is optional.) Knead well. Store in refrigerator in closed container or plastic bag. Can be baked at 225° F for 2 hours. Color or decorate if desired.

Cooked Clay

1 cup flour
½ cup cornstarch; blend with cold water.
4 cups boiling water; add 1 cup salt.

Pour hot mixture into cold. Put over hot water and cook until clear. Cool overnight. Knead flour in until right consistency. Coloring may be added with the flour. Keep in airtight container. If dough becomes hard, add more water as needed.

Cornstarch Dough

#1 Cornstarch Dough

2 T cornstarch
4 T boiling water
4 T salt

Mix cornstarch and salt. Add color if desired. Pour on boiling water; stir until soft and smooth. Place over fire until it forms soft ball. If material crumbles, add a little boiling water. Fingers may be dusted with cornstarch if mixture sticks to hands. Wrap in waxed paper.

2 Cornstarch Dough

1 cup cornstarch
2 cups salt
1 1/3 cups cold water

Mix salt and 2/3 cup water in pan and bring to a boil. Stir cornstarch and remaining water thoroughly. Add mixtures together and knead well. Store covered in refrigerator.

3 Cornstarch-Salt Dough

1 cup salt
½ cup cornstarch
½ cup boiling water

Mix together and heat until thick. Mixture thickens quickly. Color may be added. If fragrance is desired, add oil of clove or cologne.

Sawdust Clay

1 Sawdust Clay

6 cups sawdust
5½ cups flour
2 tablespoons salt

Gradually add small amounts of boiling water. Blend thoroughly until mixture resembles stiff dough. Store in cool place in damp cloth or aluminum foil. Keeps about a week.

2 Sawdust Clay

2 cups sawdust
1 cup plaster of paris
½ cup wallpaper paste
2 cups water

Mix ingredients thoroughly.

3 Sawdust Clay

Add 1 cup of paste to 2 cups of sawdust. Mix with hands until mass can be formed into a ball and not cling to the fingers or hand.

Papier-Mâché

Tear 4 to 5 double sheets of newspaper into small pieces. Soak overnight in hot water. Knead well. Gradually add 1 cup water to ½ cup flour and bring to boil over low heat. Stir until thick and glossy. Stir into paper mixture.

BIBLIOGRAPHY FOR CLAY

BOOKS

Green, Marjorie, and Elizabeth Woods. *A Nursery School Handbook.* Sierra Madre, California: Sierra Madre Community Nursery School Association, 1963.

Knudsen, Estelle H., and Ethel M. Christensen. *Children's Art Education.* Peoria, Illinois: C. A. Bennett Company, 1971.

Vermeer, Jackie, and Marian Lariviere. *The Little Kid's Craftbook.* New York: Taplinger Publishing Company, 1973, pp. 51-59.

COLLAGE

For values, see chart on page 39.

Webster defines collage as "An agglomeration of fragments such as matchboxes, bus tickets, playing cards, pasted together and transposed, often with relating lines or color dabs, into an artistic composition of incongruous effect. It is a type of abstraction."

In order to stimulate the imagination of children and increase their awareness and interest in the feel of different textures, try a collage.

Gigi, four, exercised her ingenuity with materials provided by using straws for arms and legs, a sponge for a head, heavy twine for hair, and different fabrics for a blouse and skirt. She used small pieces of foam for shoes. Such imagination!

ROLE OF THE TEACHER

The teacher's role is similar for this activity as for previous ones.

The teacher provides a number of different things which the child may use as his imagination dictates. The number of different materials supplied at one time will depend upon the ages and development of the children involved. Young children can adequately handle three or four materials, while older children delight in a larger selection from which to choose.

SOME SUGGESTED TEACHING AIDS

Building Materials	*Food Products*
bark	beans
fiber board	cereals
popsicle sticks	egg shells
sand	macaroni, spaghetti
sawdust	popcorn
screen	rigatoni
shavings	rice
tongue depressors	salt (colored)
wood	seeds—fruit and vegetables
wire	shellroni

Plastic

doilies
egg cartons
flowers
foam
food containers
hair rollers
straws
styrofoam
toothpicks

Fabrics

burlap
chiffon
corduroy
cotton
denim
felt
fur
knits
leather
muslin
net
organdy
pellon
rug yarn
satin
shagbark
silk
taffeta
velvet
wool
yarn

Sewing

beads
buttons
elastic
ribbon
ric-rac
sequins
spools
string
tape
yarn

Paper and Paper Substitutes

aluminum foil
blotters
boxes (small)
cardboard
    boxes
    corrugated
    food containers
    shirt cardboard

catalogs
cellophane
construction
cups from candy box
doilies
egg cartons
gift
greeting cards
gummed stickers
magazines
plates
reinforcements
sandpaper
stamps
straws
tissue
towels
tubes
wallpaper
waxed

Miscellaneous

acorns
bottle caps
cans
clothes pins
corks
cotton balls
excelsior
feathers
flowers
glitter
hair pins
jars
jar lids and rings
leaves
net sacks
packing materials
paper clips
pebbles
pipe cleaners
Q-tips
shells
shoe laces
sponges
toothpicks
twigs, sticks

Junk can be made into beautiful pictures. Have lots of boxes, tubes, and materials of all kinds and sizes. Provide appropriate cutting tools. Have good strong ways to attach objects (glue, staples, and other materials). Color and embellish the product. Through this kind of creative play, children learn skills, dexterity, scale, and balance. What they learn in the process is what's important—not what they make.

- Materials can be placed between two sheets of waxed paper and then pressed with a warm iron. It seals the design (especially good for crayon and leaves).
- Materials can be pasted on cloth or wallpaper instead of paper for a different experience.
- Applying colored tissue paper (with liquid starch as the moisture) on nonwaxed paper plates creates an interesting experience involving color.
- Using heavy paper and strong glue, let children make a collage with noodles, corn flakes, and similar materials.
- Glue small boxes (match, food, or other) together for an interesting design.

BIBLIOGRAPHY FOR COLLAGE

BOOKS

Hoover, Francis L. *Art Activities for the Very Young.* Worcester, Massachusetts: Davis Publications, 1967.

Vermeer, Jackie, and Marian Lariviere. *The Little Kid's Craftbook.* New York: Taplinger Publishing Company, 1963, pp. 43-50.

CRAYONS AND CHALK

See chart on page 39.

The value of crayons for young children is debatable. If small crayons are supplied, it is difficult for children to grasp them because their small muscles are not well developed. In using crayons, the child must use considerable pressure, and he often finds this expenditure of energy tiring before he has had ample opportunity to express himself. Large crayons are easier for young children to hold. Large pieces of paper are necessary so the child can have free arm movement. Paint brushes offer a much better experience for young children. Standing at an easel, the child can have full use of his body.

Some teachers advocate that children should use only whole crayons with the wrapping still in place. There are advantages to using smaller pieces of crayons. The child can manage a shorter piece easier. If the crayon is turned on its side, another method of creation is available—a crayon twist, made by twisting the crayons on the paper to make a design.

Placing crayon shavings between two sheets of waxed paper and then pressing with a warm iron offers another interesting experience involving color.

Another way to use crayons is to make a "crayon melt." Heat a frying pan to warm. Place a piece of aluminum foil in the bottom. Have the child make a picture with a crayon on the foil in the pan. Then apply a piece of newsprint or construction paper over the drawing and press gently. The paper will absorb the crayon design. Wipe off remaining paint from foil and you're ready for the next child to make his design.

Place a flat object (leaf, screen, popsicle stick) under newspaper. Color over it with crayon.

Chalk provides many of the same experiences as crayons. Because of the dryness of chalk, it has a tendency to rub off. When it is used on paper, it can be made more permanent if it is dipped into cool buttermilk or if the paper is rubbed lightly with buttermilk before the chalk is applied. It brings out the color in the chalk and acts as a fixative.

Give the child some blank sheets of paper or paper combined into a booklet. Tell him he can make his own book. He makes the pictures, and you add the text as he dictates it. Use at storytime.

SOME SUGGESTED TEACHING AIDS

Burlap
Cardboard, light weight
Construction
Cotton fabrics
Fabrics
Manila paper
Newspaper want-ad section
Newsprint
Oilcloth, back side
Poster paper
Sandpaper
Screen
Wallpaper
Window shades
Wood

BIBLIOGRAPHY FOR CRAYONS AND CHALK

BOOKS

Knudsen, Estelle H., and Ethel M. Christensen. *Children's Art Education.* Peoria, Illinois: C. A. Bennett Company, 1971.

CUTTING AND PASTING

See chart on page 39.

RECIPES FOR PASTE

Some teachers prefer to make their own paste. Some recipes are included.

Method 1

1 cup flour
2¼ cups boiling water
¾ tsp. oil of wintergreen
1 cup cold water
1 tsp. powdered alum

Mix flour with cold water; stir until smooth. Add boiling water, stir. Cook in double boiler over low heat until smooth. Add alum, stir until smooth. Remove from heat; add oil of wintergreen when mixture is cooling. Store in covered jars in a cool place.

Method 2

Mix 1 cup of flour with 2 cups of cold water. Stir until free of lumps. Add 1 teaspoon powdered alum, and 1 tablespoon table salt. Stir into 1 quart of boiling water. Cook until it changes from a milky mixture to one that is clearer.

Method 3

1 cup sugar
1 qt. water
30 drops oil of cloves
1 cup flour
1 tsp. powdered alum

Mix ingredients and cook in double boiler until thick. Stir to keep smooth. Remove from heat. Add oil of cloves. Store in covered jar.

Method 4

Combine 1 cup flour and ½ cup water. Mix until creamy and smooth. Cover when not in use. The same ingredients can be used to make a more durable paste by using boiling water.

SOME SUGGESTED TEACHING AIDS

- Color dry salt with powdered tempera. Brush paste on paper; then sprinkle salt over paste. A salt shaker makes a good container.
- Take very absorbent egg cartons. Tear into small pieces. Use for pasting.
- Take black sheet of construction paper. Cut holes in various sizes, shapes, and places. Paste tissue over holes.
- Get fabric samples from decorator or remnants. Paste objects on them. Beautiful wall hangings.
- Cut designs from paper on fabric. Paste on cans or jars. Nice gifts.
- Tear or cut strips from magazines. Let children paste them.
- Fold paper. Cut or tear designs in it.
- Take strips of magazines or colored catalogs (about 2" wide). Snip about 1½" deep every ½" or 1". Roll strips and tie or glue uncut edge. Makes unusual hanging object.
- Make a mural of the community, letting children make and cut out their homes, churches, and other important landmarks.
- Provide scraps of paper and paper bags. Children can make paper bag puppets or masks.
- Paste objects on paper plates.
- Use various materials such as those listed for collage.

BIBLIOGRAPHY FOR CUTTING AND PASTING

BOOKS

Vermeer, Jackie, and Marian Lariviere. *The Little Kid's Craftbook.* New York: Taplinger Publishing Company, 1973, pp. 31-42.

DOMESTIC AREA

VALUES FOR CHILDREN

See chart on page 39.

Children who engage in dramatic play often reenact what they see or hear at home, but to them it is realistic living. It helps them understand the adult world. Anything is possible: a child can be the mother, father, baby, street sweeper, engineer, doctor, or whatever he likes.

With adequate time and space, children play out what is important to them. They are making a trial run for the future. A very essential part of their growth, development, and understanding, play should be encouraged rather than discouraged.

Most young children enjoy this area of creativity. When interest begins to dwindle, it may be necessary to include a few props: cereal boxes, dress-up clothes, or extra utensils. Rearrangement of the available materials will add interest. A store can be built with blocks, boxes, and boards.

ROLE OF THE TEACHER

The teacher provides a wholesome atmosphere and encourages children to enjoy fully this activity. She participates in a passive rather than an active role.

Child-size furniture is a must. When children try to climb into beds intended for dolls, they become very frustrated when the beds keep collapsing. Play has been stimulated when small cots are provided and the children use them as they are intended to be used.

A teacher can encourage dramatic play when she provides two similar things, such as two telephones or two buggies. Similar props encourage socialization, dramatic play and problem solving. For example, a quiet child can be invited to "talk in the phone" with another child, encouraging the quiet child to participate and calming a boisterous child.

Children often express ideas or use words which they have seen or heard in the home. John and Ann were playing in the domestic area. Ann handed a block to John and told him to go to work. He did so. Shortly she called to him and told him it was time to come home. Dutifully he returned only for her to throw her arms around him and say, "Oh darling, I'm so glad you're home." John was startled by her reaction, dropped the block—his lunch bucket—and said, "Let me out of here." With that, he ran to another area to participate. This was a familiar reaction on Ann's part, but it was foreign to John.

Appropriate pictures placed in the domestic area may be the added stimulation some children need. Listen to what transpires; it can be refreshing and revealing.

SOME SUGGESTED TEACHING AIDS

- Stove, refrigerator, cupboard (either purchased, homemade, or from boards, boxes, or blocks), ironing board and iron
- Dolls, doll clothes, crib, buggy, bed, high chair
- Dishes, pots and pans, silverware, measuring cups and spoons
- Dress-up clothing (masculine, feminine and/or occupational): hats, scarves, gloves, purses, wallets, ties, vests, belts, bandanas, shoes of all varieties, large pieces of colored fabric, ribbons, lace, girdles, jewelry, eyeglass frames, rubber boots, jackets, caps or special props (doctor and/or nurse bags, stethoscopes, fireman equipment, Indian jewelry and headdresses), suitcases, trunks, and others
- Water opportunities: dishes, cleaning, washing clothes, pouring and measuring, pouring spout, a large tub, bucket, and others
- Cans, cartons, plastic bottles
- Food stuffs occasionally
- Mirrors
- Telephones
- Add variety to this area by using only part of the equipment at a time, by rearranging the equipment, or adding something special.
- Cover an easel with flannel or felt and provide colors, shapes, or figures out of fabric for exploration and/or dramatic play.
- Occasionally prepare food for lunch or snack in this area.
- Put emphasis on self-discovery. Include imaginative (dress-ups and props) and real experiences (hospital—so that children are no longer afraid of the equipment or experience; bathing baby—a change from being on the receiving end of the experience; wash day—materials and tasks are real).
- Provide two or more of the same object (telephone, doll, whatever) to encourage interaction.

- Cover the jungle gym or another structure for privacy. Include a flashlight.
- Move the equipment outside.
- Put real flowers on the table.

BIBLIOGRAPHY FOR DOMESTIC AREA

BOOKS

Axline, Virginia. *Dibs—In Search of Self: Personality Development in Play Therapy.* Boston: Houghton Mifflin Company, 1964.

Hartley, Ruth E., and L. M. Goldenson. *The Complete Book of Children's Play.* New York: Crowell, 1957.

Hartley, Ruth E., Frank Lawrence, and Robert Goldenson. *Understanding Children's Play.* New York: Columbia University Press, 1952, Chapters 2, 3, 4, and 5.

Hildebrand, Verna. *Introduction to Early Childhood Education.* New York: The Macmillan Company, 1971, pp. 212-29.

Leeper, Sarah H., Rugh J. Dales, Dora Sikes Skipper, and Ralph L. Witherspoon. *Good Schools for Young Children.* New York: The Macmillan Company, 1974, pp. 329-50.

Read, Katherine. *The Nursery School.* Philadelphia: W. B. Saunders, 1971, pp. 354-66.

Spodek, Bernard. *Teaching in the Early Years.* Englewood Cliffs, New Jersey: Prentice-Hall, 1972, pp. 199-217.

ARTICLES

Almy, Millie. "Spontaneous Play: An Avenue for Intellectual Development." *Young Children,* May 1967, pp. 265-76.

Bender, Judith. "Heavy You Ever Thought of a Prop Box?" *Young Children,* January 1971, pp. 164-69.

Cornelius, Ruth. "What Did You Do Today? We Played." *Childhood Education,* 32 (1960): 302-3.

Davis, David C. "Play, A State of Childhood." In Mills, Belen (ed.) *Understanding the Young Child and His Curriculum.* New York: The Macmillan Company, 1972, pp. 142-46.

Dennis, Lawrence. "Play in Dewey's Theory of Education." *Young Children,* March 1970, pp. 230-35.

Fowler, William. "On the Value of Both Play and Structure in Early Education." *Young Children,* October 1971, pp. 24-35.

Hymes, James. "Why Play is Important." New Paltz, New York: State Teachers College, n.d.

Lieberman, J. Nina. "Playfulness and Divergent Thinking." *Journal of Genetic Psychology,* December 1965, pp. 219-21.

Nicolaysen, Mary. "Dominion in Children's Play—Its Meaning and Management." *Young Children,* October 1966, pp. 20-29.

Noecker, Albertine. "A Doll Corner Upstairs." *Young Children,* December 1969, pp. 102-5.

Riley, Sue Spayth. "Some Reflections on the Value of Children's Play." *Young Children,* February 1973, pp. 146-53.

Rosecrans, C. J. "Play—The Language of Children." In Mills, Belen (ed.) *Understanding the Young Child and His Curriculum.* New York: The Macmillan Company, 1972, pp. 117-25.

Scarfe, N. V. "Play Is Education." In Mills, Belen (ed.) *Understanding the Young Child and His Curriculum.* New York: The Macmillan Company, 1972, pp. 126-31.

Sutton-Smith, Brian. "The Role of Play in Cognitive Development." *Young Children,* September 1967, pp. 361-70. Also in Mills, Belen (ed.) *Understanding the Young Child and His Curriculum.* New York: The Macmillan Company, 1972, pp. 131-41.

Van Camp, Sarah. "How Free Is Free Play?" *Young Children,* April 1972, pp. 205-7.

Weininger, Otto. "Unstructured Play as a Vehicle for Learning." *OMEP,* 4 (1972): 63-69.

PAMPHLETS

Play—Children's Business: Guide to Selection of Toys and Games. Washington: Association for Childhood Education International, 3615 Wisconsin Avenue N.W. 75¢.

PAINTING

Because there are different ways in which painting may be done, this section will be divided into separate areas: Easel, Finger, Sponge or Block, and Miscellaneous.

See chart on page 39.

EASEL PAINTING

Materials

Brushes

½" to 1" width of bristle
Good quality
Handle approximately 10" to 12" long

Paper

Butcher paper
Cardboard
Cartons
Construction paper
Corrugated paper
Fingerpaint
Magazine
Newspaper
Newsprint
Paper sacks
Paper towel
Wallpaper

Other Surfaces or Materials

Clay

Fabrics

Burlap
Cotton
Leather

Nylon
Oil cloth
Plastic
Vinyl

Rocks

Sea shells

Wood

Boxes
Branches
Scraps

Easel

Sturdy
Wood or metal construction
Place for paint jars
Clip for holding paper
Correct height
Out of traffic pattern
Sometimes indoors and sometimes outdoors
Good lighting
Close to sink, washroom, or sponges
Easily cleaned
Two easels side by side encourage cooperation and participation.

Paint

Shake dry powder paint and water together in screw-top jar. (Red and orange paint mix best when warm water is used.) Add a small amount of wheat paste to prepared paint (thickens the paint to better consistency). A pinch of salt will keep paint from going sour in warm room. Extender may be added.
Let the children help prepare the paint.
Keeps indefinitely if tightly covered and kept in cool place.
Stir well before using.
Primary colors are most appealing. White and black should be offered occasionally.
Use two to four colors.
A small amount of liquid detergent facilitates easy clean-up.

Jars

Use pint glass jars or half-pint jars. Lids are available for storage.
Baby food jars
Quart milk cartons washed out and cut off
Frozen juice cans (6-oz. size).
Paper cups

Clothing

A protective covering should be worn (smock, old shirt on backwards, or apron).

53

Techniques

Using one brush for each color keeps the colors true but does not provide much opportunity for the child to explore. Sometimes use one brush for each color and sometimes allow for exploration and experimentation.

Wipe end of brush on top of jar.

Children should be encouraged to refrain from tasting the paint. While most paints are nontoxic, a consumed quantity can produce intestinal difficulties.

If easels are unavailable, place paper on floor. Put paint in muffin tins and flat containers.

Cleanup

Children should be encouraged to:

Wash out brushes

Cover jars containing paint

Hang pictures where they can dry. If space is limited, use large wooden clothes drying frame. Folds out of way.

Wipe up spills on tray, easel, and floor. A cover placed on floor prior to painting aids in cleanup.

FINGER PAINTING

Finger painting is a good emotional release. A child can express his many moods: his joys, his concerns, his interests, his sorrows. He can even show his fears and then quickly wipe them away.

Finger painting also provides an excellent sensory experience. Adding different substances to the finger paint, such as sand, glitter or paper, can change the experience.

Materials

Finger paint (see recipes which follow)

Surfaces: Paper (butcher, shelf, hard surfaced wrapping), oil cloth, table top, wood, wallpaper, cardboard, glass, plastic, vinyl.

Sponges to spread water on the paper or table and for cleanup

Water to dampen paper, wash hands, and for cleanup

Protective covering for children

Rack for drying paintings

Procedure

Define limits for children and teachers.

Have pan of water and sponges nearby for cleanup.

Dampen table and paper with sponge.

Spread paper smoothly on table

Put a heaping tablespoon of finger paint on the paper. (Colorless finger paint may be used; then the teacher can sprinkle powdered tempera on paper for child. If child sprinkles tempera, cans become messy and hard to hold.)

Finger painting can be done directly on table tops.

Encourage children to clean up.

Add variety of music during the activity.

Mention to the children that they can also make designs with fists, knuckles, palms, and fingernails.

Bon Ami or glass wax can be used on windows.

Recipes

Finger paint can be purchased commercially or can be made by any of the following recipes:

■ *Method 1*

One 12 oz. box of cold water starch
An equal amount of soap flakes
Powder paint for coloring
2 cups cold water

Mix together the starch and soap flakes. Slowly add the water while stirring. Mix and beat until it reaches the consistency of whipped potatoes. Add tempera. Dark colors show up more effectively than light colors.

- *Method 2*

  Moisten 1 cup laundry starch with 1 cup cold water, add 2 cups hot water and cook until thick. Remove from heat and add 1 cup soap flakes and a few drops of glycerine.

- *Method 3*

  Mix together in double boiler one cup flour, one teaspoon salt, and three cups cold water. Cook until thick, beating with an egg beater or electric mixer.

- *Method 4*

  Paste method 4 (p. 49) in equal amount with liquid laundry starch.

Cornstarch Finger Paint

Dissolve ½ cup cornstarch in cold water. Add to 4 cups boiling water and stir. Let mixture come to boil again. Cooling causes paint to thicken slightly.

Wallpaper Paste Finger Paint

Put amount of water you desire into pan. Sprinkle flour on top of water, a small amount at a time. Stir in a circular motion until all lumps are gone. Add more flour until desired consistency (should be similar to liquid laundry starch).

Starch and Soapflake Finger Paint

½ cup linit starch
1½ cups boiling water
½ cup soap flakes
1 tablespoon glycerine (optional but makes it smoother)
Food coloring

Mix starch with enough cold water to make smooth paste. Add boiling water and cook until glossy. Stir in soap flakes while mixture is warm. When cool, add glycerine and coloring. (The addition of 1½ cups salt will make the texture more grainy.)

Soap Flakes

Put soap flakes into mixing bowl and add water gradually while beating with egg beater or electric mixer. Consistency should be about the same as stiffly beaten egg whites. Add color.

Salt and Flour Finger Paint

Stir 1 cup flour and 1½ cups salt into ¾ cups water. Add coloring. The paint will have a grainy quality.

Starch Finger Paint

Combine and cook until thick:
One 1 lb. box of gloss starch
1 cup soap flakes
½ cup talcum powder
4 quarts warm water

For preservation and fragrance, add cologne, oil of cloves, or wintergreen.

Liquid Starch Finger Paint

Pour liquid starch on wet surface. Add color, if desired.

Starch-Gelatin Finger Paint

Combine ½ cup laundry starch and ¾ cup of cold water in saucepan. Soak 1 envelope unflavored gelatin in ¼ cup cold water. Add 2 cups hot water to starch mixture and cook, stirring constantly, over medium heat until mixture comes to a boil and is clear. Remove from heat and blend in softened gelatin. Add ½ cup soap flakes and stir until mixture thickens and soap is thoroughly dissolved. Makes about 3 cups.

Pudding Finger Paint

Instant or cooked pudding may be used for a different experience. Danish dessert offers yet another texture. (It does stain some surfaces.) When food stuffs are used in this manner, define for children "today we're finger painting with _____ . Another day we will have it for a snack." All finger paints should be stored in tightly covered jars and in a cool place.

BIBLIOGRAPHY FOR FINGER PAINTING

BOOKS

Green, Marjorie, and Elizabeth Woods. *A Nursery School Handbook.* Sierra Madre, California: Sierra Madre Community Nursery School Association, 1963.

Haupt, Dorothy, and Keith D. Osborn. *Creative Activities.* Detroit: Merrill-Palmer School, 1966.

Hoover, Francis L. *Art Activities for the Very Young.* Worcester, Massachusetts: Davis Publications, 1967.

Knudsen, Estelle H., and Ethel M. Christensen. *Children's Art Education.* Peoria, Illinois: C. A. Bennett Company, 1971.

Shaw, Ruth. *Finger Painting.* Boston: Little, Brown & Company, 1934.

SPONGE OR BLOCK PAINTING

Materials

Sponges. Cut in small pieces. A spring clothespin makes an excellent handle.

Paint. Should be quite thick. Place in staggered cups of a muffin tin. Sprinkle a small amount of wheat paste over the paint in the container. It thickens the paint.

Paper. Butcher paper is best. Absorbent paper can also be used.

Other objects: cork, pieces of wood, spool, potatoes, string, potato masher, etc. (Designs can be carved in potatoes or other firm fruits or vegetables such as carrots, turnips, lemons, apples). A sink stopper makes an interesting design. Leaf: paint it and then print it onto paper.

Procedure

Dip sponge or other object into thick paint and then make print on paper.

MISCELLANEOUS PAINTING

Towel Painting

Paint design on formica table top or similar surface. Take a paper towel and press on wet surface over the painted design. Remove towel and allow to dry. This can also be done over a finger painting.

Painting can be done directly on paper towel with brush and easel paint.

Ink Blots

Fold paper in half—reopen paper. Place a few drops of paint on one side of the paper and refold. Press paper together firmly. Reopen paper and a symmetrical design has been produced. Newsprint is best for this experience.

Dry Powder Painting

Dip wads of dry cotton into dry powder paint and apply to damp paper.

Painting with Water

Let children paint with clear water, using large brushes on boards, sidewalks, and other large surfaces that water will not damage. They can carry a small pail with them.

Painting on Different Materials

Provide cloth, paper towels, smooth paper, sponge, glass, plastic, leather, linoleum, egg cartons, aluminum foil, cone-shaped spools, corrugated paper, mailing tubes, paper bags, pleated muffin cups, waxed paper, tissue paper, metal, stone, rocks, wallpaper, and other materials.

Murals

Provide children with a long sheet of butcher paper, paint, and encouragement. They will do the rest.

Crayon and Paint

Child makes design on paper with crayon and then paints over it. The paint will not cover the crayon marks. Child discovers uses of materials, textures, and designs.

Vinyl Painting

Apply vinyl to wall or roll out on floor. Children paint on it and then wipe it off.

String Painting

Dip long string into paint. Arrange it on half a piece of paper. Fold other half over string and press. Pull string out. Design is on both halves of sheet. Use different colors of paint.

Bubble Painting

Put liquid soap and water in bowl about 8" across top. Add coloring. Give child a straw and encourage him to blow as many bubbles as he can. When bubbles rise over top of the bowl, take piece of absorbent paper and place over bowl. The paper breaks the bubbles and the design is printed on paper with top of bowl as border.

Doily Painting

Take a piece of butcher paper larger than a paper (or plastic) doily. Place doily on paper. With brush and tempera paint, paint over doily. Lift doily and you have a design. Doily can be printed onto another paper, too.

SAND

See chart on page 39.

Most young children delight in playing in sand. Running their hands through it, smoothing out roads and constructing tunnels and ditches are but a few of the ways in which they use sand. It is an interesting medium for children.

Whether sand is used in a large area on the playground or in a sand box matters little as long as there is plenty of room in which to explore. Props such as trucks, shovels, buckets, sifters, measuring spoons and cups, and containers tend to stimulate the imagination of young children. The addition of sea shells to sand makes an interesting and life-like experience. Water changes the consistency of sand, and it becomes easier to manipulate.

Definite limits should be set up such as: "Keep the sand in the sand area," "Shovels, hoes, and rakes stay close to the ground," "Sand is for building, not throwing." This will give the children ideas as to how the sand is to be used.

During the wintertime sand can be used in a sand box inside the school; however, some floors are easily scratched by it. Canvas, plastic, or newspapers could be spread on the floors to protect them.

In the summertime, a running hose in the sand can provide enjoyable creativity for children. Sand should be dampened for cooking and molding. See that a board is nearby for dumping cakes and products.

Socialization is another important aspect provided by sand. Children discuss, share ideas and materials, participate in collective monologue, and learn to cooperate as members of a group.

It is advisable to store sand toys near the sand area, separating them from other toys. Trucks, cars, measuring cups, sifters, jello molds, and so on, are best stored on low shelves; it is better for buckets and shovels to be hung on low hooks or nails. A messy storage area discourages children from using the equipment.

BIBLIOGRAPHY FOR SAND

BOOKS

Winslow, Marjorie. *Mud Pies and Other Recipes.* Riverside, New Jersey: The Macmillan Company, 1961.

ARTICLES

Elder, Connie Z. "Miniature Sand Environments: A New Way to See and Feel and Explore." *Young Children*, June 1973, pp. 283-86.

PAMPHLETS

Water, Sand & Mud as Play Materials, Washington, D.C.: NAEYC, 1834 Connecticut Avenue N.W.

STRINGING

See chart on page 39.

Stringing is another small muscle developer. It is good to encourage the use of small muscles. Some children lack the control which would make this experience pleasurable, while others thrive on it.

- Allow plenty of time for children to experiment.
- If needles are used, make sure they are large enough for the children to grasp.
- Use a double thread so needle will not slip off. Yarn may be better.
- If needles are not used, make ends of string or yarn firm by covering with scotch tape, dipping in paste or wax and allowing to dry.
- Make a large knot in the end of the string by using a bead or piece of macaroni to keep objects from slipping off.
- A shoelace makes an acceptable "string" because of the hard tip.
- If colored macaroni is used, color the dry macaroni with water and food coloring rather than with alcohol. Children like to eat the macaroni, and it may be harmful if alcohol is used. Although alcohol colors and dries rapidly, it is not worth the risk with young children. When coloring with food coloring, place small amount of water and enough coloring in small bowl. Let macaroni stand in solution until it is the desired color. Remove macaroni from bowl with a fork and place on paper towels. When the excess moisture has been removed, spread individual pieces of macaroni on sheets of waxed paper and let them remain overnight. If not spread out, macaroni will dry in clusters.

SOME SUGGESTED TEACHING AIDS

Aluminum foil
Beads: large, wooden
Breakfast cereals
Colored straws cut in ½" lengths
Cranberries
Fabric
Foam packing materials
Lifesavers
Macaroni, plain or colored
Paper
Small spools

WATER

See chart on page 39.

Children need to have water experiences. Water has a soothing effect. It gives way to the motion of one's hands. School is a good place for children to explore the possibilities of water. Basins and sinks should be low and available to children. Water can be used daily or just for special occasions.

One preschool teacher had a difficult time accepting the fact that there was value in water play. From her background, she had gained the concept that water was for drinking and washing only. In her particular group were several children who never went past the water to the other areas. As the children measured, spilled, poured, and experimented with water, the teacher intensified her dislike for it. After a considerable length of time, she realized that the experience had a therapeutic effect upon the children, and she began to recognize the many other values connected with it.

SOME SUGGESTED TEACHING AIDS

- Give children a bucket of clear water and a large brush and let them "paint" anything that will not be damaged by water.
- Make a concentrated solution of soap and provide straws for children. Coloring may be added. Give each child some solution in a small bowl or fill a water table for group experience.

- Let children bathe dolls.
- Have a box of water toys readily available for use in water table.
- Encourage water play in the domestic area.
- During summer, have hose running in sand area.
- During summer, let hose run down slide. Children should wear swimming suits.
- Have a wading pool during summer months.
- If other sources of water play are not available, cut a tire in half and fill with water, and you have two places for children to explore; or use a thermos jug, a large tub, or a large five-gallon plastic jug with a spout.
- Encourage children to help water a garden, plants, or animals.
- Talk about the characteristics of water and evaporation.
- Let children wash doll clothes.
- Talk about weather which involves rain, snow, ice.
- Involve children in cleanup which requires the use of sponges and water.
- Provide containers and spouts for measuring and exploring water. Plastic squirt jars filled with water are fun for outside use.
- Introduce new terms and characteristics of water (recycling, buoyance, incompressibility, reaches own level, and others). Let children experiment.
- See also ideas about water on pages 72, 110-111, 119.

   For additional ideas about water, see "Theme 3: I Love Water" in *When I Do, I Learn* by Barbara J. Taylor, pp. 99-109 and 168-71.

- Enjoy water yourself!

BIBLIOGRAPHY FOR WATER

ARTICLES

Guillaume, Jeanette. "Water, Water, Everywhere." *Parent's Magazine*, August 1959, p. 50.

PAMPHLETS

Water, Sand and Mud as Play Materials. Washington, D.C.: National Association for Education of Young Children, 1834 Connecticut Avenue, N.W., 20009.

WOODWORKING

See chart on page 39.

Woodworking is an excellent experience for young children, but it requires very close supervision. It can be one of the booby traps of the school if left unattended. Woodworking had been enjoyed by a group of children. When they left the work table, the tools were not put away. Later, a distressed youngster passed the table and began to get ideas. He picked up a hammer and threw it through a large panel of glass. This would not have happened if teachers and children had exercised caution to see that the tools were returned to their proper storage place.

Very young children enjoy pounding and banging. Preschool children can obtain satisfaction from the actual use of tools and wood. Their first experiences are likely to be of an exploratory nature. They like to build simple structures and should be left free to use their imaginations. Patterning, as in other areas, has no place in woodworking.

When a child says that he has constructed a certain thing, you accept his comments without indicating to him that it looks like something else, needs some additions or changes, or is poorly done. To him, it is the real thing.

Woodworking is for girls as well as for boys. Too often we convey the idea that certain materials are masculine or feminine. Preschool children really fluctuate from maleness to femaleness to animals to inanimate objects and back again. This characteristic is often lost with the increase of years.

Limit the number of children who can work in the area based on space, supervision, abilities of children, tools available, and time allotted; but see that all children who want to participate are given the opportunity.

An enjoyable but inexpensive idea (especially when tools and equipment are lacking) is to get pieces of fiber board, cellotex, or acoustical tile and let the children hammer small nails into it.

EQUIPMENT

Workbench

A workbench can be either purchased or made. Proper height is important.
It should be a little shorter than half the child's height and can be made from a kitchen table which has the legs cut off.
Sawhorses with a sturdy plank may also be used.

Hammer

The claw hammer is the most practical for general use.
It should be well balanced, should have a broad head, and should weigh seven to thirteen ounces.
It should be made with the same careful workmanship and the same durable materials as regular carpenter tools.
A toy hammer is unsatisfactory.

Saw

Provide both ripsaw and crosscut saws. Know the use of each.
An eight- to ten-point crosscut saw, twelve to twenty inches in length, is desirable.
Hold saw gently and use long, even strokes.
By drawing the saw towards you on the first stroke, you initiate a groove that makes sawing easier.
Saw on downward motion.

Nails

Roofing nails are good because they have large heads.
Four-penny, six-penny, eight-penny, and ten-penny nails may also be used.
A variety of nails creates interest.
Nails 1¼" or 1½" are best.

Wood

Soft woods are easier for children to use (yellow pine, white pine, poplar).
Orange or apple crates are also good.
Wood of various sizes and shapes stimulates imagination.
A local lumberyard or carpenter will usually give you pieces of scrap wood.
Different kinds of wood create different colors of sawdust.
Dowels may be used for smokestacks, handles, and other things.
Wheels also add interest.

Plane

Many types and sizes are available. The block plane is best for young children.
Always plane in an uphill direction of the grain.

Vise

A vise mounted on the workbench holds the wood securely and allows the child to use both hands in sawing or hammering.
Several vises may be mounted on the workbench.

Brace and Bit

A 6" sweep is desirable for young children.
Children may need help in using this tool.
Several different bits may be provided. Recommended sizes are # 3, # 4, # 8, # 12, and # 16.

Sandpaper

Use a variety of sizes: fine 2/0, medium 1/0, coarse 2 and 3.
Sandpaper mounted on a wood block makes it easier for the children to use.

Other General Tools and Materials

Screwdriver, 4" to 6" long; ¼" blade
Rasp
Iron clamps, 4" or 6" mouths
Pliers
Square
Ruler
Paper
Fabrics
Spools
Tongue Depressors
Carpenter's pencil
Paint
Brushes
String
Wire
Cans
Leather
Yarn
Rubber

BIBLIOGRAPHY FOR WOODWORKING

BOOKS

Green, Marjorie, and Elizabeth Woods. *A Nursery School Handbook.* Sierra Madre, California: Sierra Madre Community Nursery School Association, 1963.

Haupt, Dorothy, and Keith D. Osborn. *Creative Activities.* Detroit: Merrill-Palmer School, 1966.

Patrick, Sara Lyman. *Tools for Woodworking in the Elementary School.* New York: The Arts Cooperative Service, n.d.

Vermeer, Jackie, and Marian Lariviere. *The Little Kid's Craftbook.* New York: Taplinger Publishing Company, 1973, pp. 97-109.

Gregg, Elizabeth. *What to Do When "There's Nothing to Do."* Dell Publishing Company, 1967, pp. 136-38.

ARTICLES

Brandhofer, Marijane. "Carpentry for Young Children." *Young Children,* October 1971, pp. 17-23.

Riley, Carole. "Carpentry in the Nursery School." *Young Children,* October 1964, p. 25.

Rudolph, Marguerita, and Dorothy H. Cohen. "The Many Purposes of Block-building and Woodworking." *Young Children,* October 1964, p. 40.

PAMPHLETS

Moffitt, Mary W. *Woodworking for Children.* New York: Early Childhood Education of New York City, 196 Bleecker Street.

Ramey, Marion. *Working With Wood.* Leaflet # 5. Creating with Materials for Work and Play. Association for Childhood Education International, 1969.

MISCELLANEOUS SENSORY EXPERIENCES

FEEL OR TEXTURE
- In a table used for water or sand, use substances such as flour, corn meal, rice, beans, or wheat.
- Place various textures on a table and let children feel them. (Wool, silk, cotton, corduroy, velvet, oilcloth, felt, screen, paper, sawdust, shavings, fur.)
- Dip colored yarn into thick wheat paste mixture. Shape it on waxed paper, let it dry. Makes interesting designs.
- Place various objects in a box or paper sack. Let the children feel them and try to identify them before seeing them.
- Ask the children to walk around the room and touch objects which are similar (wood or metal, smooth, cold).
- See "Feel Box" on page 132.
- Paint on different materials. See page 58.

SMELL
- Place small amounts of common liquids that have odors in containers and let the children smell them (extracts, perfume, vinegar, household commodities, and others).
- Show children pictures of things and ask them to describe what they think they would smell like.

TASTE
- In small bowls, place staples which look alike but have different tastes (white sugar, salt, flour, powdered sugar, soap flakes, tapioca, coconut).
- In small bowls, place staples which bear the same name but have different characteristics (white sugar, brown sugar, raw sugar, powdered sugar, sugar cubes, and others).

SOUND
- Fill various containers; let the children shake them and try to guess what is inside.
- Have duplicate containers whose contents are not visible. See if the children can correctly match them by shaking them.
- Play a record or tape and see if the children can identify the sounds. You can have pictures or replicas that go with the sounds. See if the children can match them.
- Make "telephones" with two empty juice cans and string 10'–20' long. Poke hole in bottom of can, put string through bottom, and tie a knot (inside the can). Hold string taut. Let the children talk and listen to each other.

SIGHT
- Have the children look at various objects; ask them to describe how the objects would feel before they touched them (hard, smooth, cold, etc.).
- Have the children look at a picture; ask the children to "act out" the scene.
- Have the children act out their favorite game or activity. See if the other children can guess it.

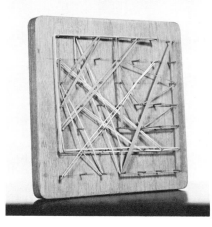

MISCELLANEOUS IDEAS FOR SMALL MUSCLE DEVELOPMENT

- Peg boards
- Small colored cubes
- Snap blocks
- Small plastic blocks representing bricks
- Puzzles (commercial or made)
- Tinker toys
- Miscellaneous table toys (card games).
- Take a piece of wood (almost any size but preferably about 4" x 6" or 5" x 8"). Hammer small nails into it about ½" apart. Give the child some small colored rubber bands and let him create his own design by stretching the bands over the nails.

- Picture lotto games
- Make mobiles using coat hanger, string or yarn, and variety of objects (purchased or made).
- Spool knit (purchased or made).

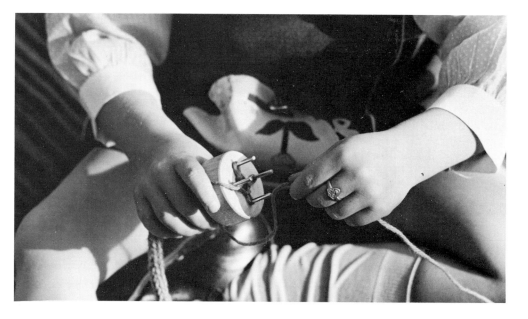

- Sewing cards (purchased or made)
- Sewing on burlap or rubberized burlap (stiffer).
- Plastic objects which fit together (Multi-fits, Knoppers, etc.)

ESPECIALLY FOR PARENTS

It isn't necessary for your child to attend a preschool group in order to enjoy creative experiences. You can provide such experiences at home—either in personal interaction with your child or by supplying the necessary materials for his enjoyment.

It seems only logical that if you take interest and pride in some of the child's accomplishments, he will also. Let's get practical for a moment. Don't you think that your child would take better care of his room or his toys if he had something invested in them? For example, if he made something to enhance the beauty of his room or to keep his toys together, doesn't it follow that he would be more interested in them? These ideas need to be simple yet praiseworthy. Suppose you had an empty gallon (or larger) ice cream container, and the child had the opportunity to decorate it for his room. Wouldn't he enjoy using it as a wastebasket or storage container for some of his toys? If he had boxes he had decorated (and perhaps had labeled with an appropriate picture), wouldn't it be easier for him to keep toys picked up or separated?

Parents need to look at creative activities with an artistic and appreciative eye. This is not the place to chastize the child for messiness, imperfect products, or lack of skills. The child learns many things through expressing himself creatively, and he should be encouraged in his pursuit.

True, you don't have all the time, money, or materials that are available in the preschool, but let's go back through the activities presented in this chapter and find a few ways you could use them in your home. The values, techniques, and goals of the preschool group would be similar to those of the home. The child's work needs to be appreciated and displayed in both places. Help him to feel that something made by him is valued.

BLOCKS

Most commercial blocks are quite expensive. To avoid the expense, you could buy just part of a set, or you could make some. Many lumber yards or carpenters will cut them for you if you don't have the equipment and skills at home. Your child can help sand and paint the blocks. Not only will you have blocks, but you will have involved other creative experiences as well—woodworking and painting.

Cardboard boxes, empty metal cans, spools, and other items can be used for building purposes. Look around your house and see how many ideas you can come up with. (How about letting him help arrange your food shelves?)

CHALK

Small blackboards (portable or wall hung) are inexpensive. They can be adjusted to the height of the child for many hours of enjoyment. They may also be used for family purposes (leaving notes, games, and other things). The child could be responsible for keeping the board and eraser clean.

Chalk could be used on paper or other materials, but because of its small size and limited qualities, the child may find this medium less satisfying than others.

CRAYONS

Crayons have some characteristics in common with chalk. If you purchase crayons for your child, make sure they are large in circumference because they will be easier for him to hold. While you are at the store, get a large pad of plain paper so that he can create his own designs, use his large muscles, and draw to his heart's content. Coloring books stifle the creativity of a young child.

For dinner soon, or for some special occasion, let the child draw some of his original designs on some paper napkins or paper towels for place mats. These have different textures than drawing paper and should be fun. Don't make this an experience where you demand perfection or require the child to stay for a long period of time. Let him be the artist.

CLAY

Clay provides many possibilities but does not require special care. It is useless, however, when stored improperly. Commercial clay is available, but any of the recipes in the chapter could be made easily by the parents and the child.

If the child has many food experiences (rolling cookies, kneading bread, making pie crust), clay may be less interesting to him than something he can actually consume. What is important is the actual experience.

The child could have his own bag of clay, his own utensils, and his own place to work. This should stimulate verbalization even if it isn't related to the clay experience.

COLLAGE AND CUTTING AND PASTING

Many parents actually have a work cupboard or drawer where children have access to paper, scissors, and other materials. If the parent and the child agree that he can use whatever is in the drawer (within established limits), he may spend many hours with these materials.

He needs to have good tools (scissors that actually cut, glue that comes out of the tube and sticks), time to work, and a place where he will be undisturbed.

For a gift or for special occasions, he could decorate a can or bottle. He could make something for a family gathering (place mats or decoration, or he could cut pictures of a certain topic from magazines or catalogs). Together with your child, design a holder for gadgets, shoes, clothes, or toys for his room.

You could make it out of plastic, burlap or other fabric. Let the child cut and paste pictures or fabric designs to help him remember what goes in each pocket.

If you purchase goods where you receive stamps or coupons, the child could stick them in a book for you.

DOMESTIC AREA

Many children do not have equipment their size at home for dramatic play, but they do have some real family experiences. The child may play with mother's pots and pans (or have some of his own out in the sand). He may not have a sink his size, but he can stand on a stool and help mother with the dishes, play with water in the tub or washbasin, or dramatize actions he sees at home. This is his way of learning various roles; he sees them and needs to try them.

With little or no cost, dress-up clothes could be available. Clothes that older brothers or sisters have outgrown are sometimes better than discarded adult clothes for young children. Something that makes this activity special is having someone to play with.

On a boring or rainy day, try covering a card table with a sheet or blanket for renewed interest. A flashlight and perhaps even a little treat brighten up almost any youngster.

If there is a baby in the family, let the child help you, or let him do similar activities for a doll.

Involve the child in food preparation and other household chores, such as setting the table, using the vacuum, or watering plants.

EASEL PAINTING

Most homes do not have an easel. If they have a blackboard or chalk board, it could be covered for the child to use when painting. The child seems to have better control over his painting if he is standing or working on the floor rather than on a table top (which is generally too high, and he has to kneel on a chair). For good weather, a wooden frame could be made to hang on a fence.

Usually parents feel it is too much trouble to allow a child to paint at home. Adequate precautions could be taken so that this would not be the case. Covering the floor, giving the child a protective covering, and establishing limits often eliminate many of the difficulties. However, it may be easier and may fulfill the same purpose if you give the child a brush and a bucket of water and turn him loose outside.

FINGER PAINTING

Here is another experience that many parents avoid. They don't know how to make the necessary preparations for the child to have a satisfying experience and for the parents to remain calm. One mother makes a finger paint out of soap, puts her children in the bathtub, and lets them go to it. When they are through, she washes off the children and rinses out the tub, and everybody is happy.

Finger paint can be obtained commercially or can be made from any of the recipes in this chapter. It does provide a satisfying experience that many other activities do not provide. Some paints stain; so be sure to protect surfaces.

An activity your child can do at home is finger painting on a large sheet of paper, letting it dry, and using it for wrapping gifts.

Another idea is to let the child finger paint on a hard surface, blot his design onto absorbent paper, let it dry, then make a colored frame for it and hang it in his room.

SPONGE OR BLOCK

The child can help mix some paint, or it can be purchased. For this purpose, it needs to be thicker than regular easel paint (can be thickened with wheat paste, extender, or less water). An old muffin tin works well for dipping.

Cut small pieces of a sponge and attach them to popsicle sticks, small wooden dowels, or old handles. The easiest way is to use spring clothes pins. Sponges can be easily cleaned for another time.

You and the child can look around the home for things which would make interesting designs. A member of the family could make some block designs from wood, potatoes, and corks. Invite the whole family to participate—not in a competitive manner but in one of exploration and communication. When you involve others, they will be interested in collecting novel and fun items to use.

Sponge or block designs can be used for greeting cards, decorative hangings, table decorations, gift paper or just for an enjoyable activity.

MISCELLANEOUS

Any of the ideas listed under this heading earlier in the chapter (and many more that you can think of) will work equally well in the home as in the school.

Also provide your child with a variety of surfaces to paint on (plastic, vinyl, fabric, wood, many papers).

Help him to know where and upon what he can paint. Set up the limits as you plan the activity with him rather than wait until he does something that offends you.

SAND

If possible, provide a sand area outside that is large enough for the child to move around in. If this is not possible, substitute a large tub or box. Provide some way to cover it from animals and debris. Occasionally add water and props (cars, measuring cups and spoons, molds). Sand is a soothing media and should be provided for children when possible.

Many parks and playgrounds have sand areas. If you take your child there, he may have an opportunity to interact with other children. The area "belongs to all." Take your child or gather up some of his friends, neighbors, or relatives. For some reason, sand stimulates interaction and cooperation.

STRINGING

This may be an activity that is tedious for young fingers. Give the child some chances to develop his small muscles and eye-hand coordination, but be flexible and understanding. (Refer back to ideas in the chapter.)

Give the child opportunities to lace his (or others') shoes. Winding laces around hooks on boots may be interesting to him.

Perhaps Dad has something he'd like strung on wire (tools, washers).

Check with the paint store or interior decorator to see if they have some paint chips, fabric samples or formica samples that could be strung on a chain.

Using heavy twine, ask the child to string your jar rings (keeps them neat, and it's a worthy task).

Using a needle and thread, let the child string buttons.

Encourage the child to make a necklace for someone (wooden beads, beads, breakfast cereal, lifesavers, straws, spools).

If you have access to some old tires or tubes, the child can string them on rope. Rather than a small muscle activity, this involves the large muscles, and he would be using his whole body.

WATER

Most parents don't have to look for water experiences for their children; they are attracted to them. But aside from household uses like washing people, animals, dishes, cars, and clothes; watering plants and lawns; and food preparation, consider some of the following ideas:

- Uses of steam (cooking, pressing, and others)
- Community resources: lake, river, pond, fountain
- Occupations relying upon water (fishing, logging, boating)
- Weather and seasons
- Vocabulary related to water (evaporate, buoyance, recycling)
- Clothing related to water (seasonal, waterproof, and others) See also, "Theme 3: I Love Water," in *When I Do, I Learn* by Barbara J. Taylor, pp. 99-109, 168-71.
- Let your child watch you or help you repair a leaking tap.
- Take him swimming or wading.
- Take him to the carwash or let him help wash the car.
- Take him to the fire station and have the fireman explain how water helps put out fires.
- If possible, take him to where they are irrigating crops.
- Show him the plumbing and explain how it works.
- Visit a ship yard, dock, river, lake (or learn about them through using books, pictures, replicas).
- Take him fishing or boating.
- Let him watch the water wagon wash the streets.

WOODWORKING

If you don't have a place at home for this activity, there are often community centers, hobby shops, schools, and other places that you can visit. They may, however, have restrictions on children using the equipment and materials.

Children should have good quality tools. It's a waste of money to buy poor imitations that don't work, don't last, and don't even resemble the real tools. (See information on pages 62-64.)

As in a school setting, children need to be supervised when using potentially dangerous tools. Go over the limits with your child and be sure that he fully understands them and why he must abide by them.

Here are some things your child might do with woodworking in the home:

- Help repair something (handle, chair, toy, other things)
- Help make some blocks for his use
- Have his own tools and kit
- Make some simple objects (boats, airplanes)
- Learn the names and uses of different tools (saw, hammer, brace and bit, pliers)
- Work on a project with an adult
- Make holes in lids for insect jars
- Sort nails into jars for future use
- Learn how to care for and replace tools

BIBLIOGRAPHY FOR CREATIVE MATERIALS

BOOKS

Carmichael, Viola S. *Curriculum Ideas for Young Children.* Pasadena, Calif.: 1886 Kinneola Canyon Road, 91107.

Cole, Ann, Carolyn Haas, Edith Bushnell, and Betty Weinberger. *I Saw a Purple Cow.* Boston: Little, Brown & Co., 1972.

Fiarotta, Phyllis. *Sticks and Stones and Ice Cream Cones.* New York: Workman Publishing Co., 1973.

Gaitskell, Charles D. *Children and Their Art.* New York: Harcourt & Brace, 1970.

Hartley, Ruth E., Lawrence K. Frank, and Robert M. Goldenson. *Understanding Children's Play.* New York: Columbia University Press, 1967.

Haupt, Dorothy, and Keith D. Osborn. *Creative Activities.* Detroit: Merill-Palmer School, 1966.

Hildebrand, Verna. *Introduction to Early Childhood Education.* New York: Macmillan Co., 1971, pp. 102-35.

Hoover, Francis L. *Art Activities for the Very Young.* Worcester, Mass.: Davis Publishing Co., 1967.

Knudsen, Estelle H., and Ethel M. Christensen. *Children's Art Education.* Peoria, Ill.: C. A. Bennett Co., 1971.

Landreth, Catherine. *Preschool Learning and Teaching.* New York: Harper & Row, 1972, pp. 93-103.

Leeper, Sarah H., Ruth J. Dales, Dora S. Skipper, Ralph L. Witherspoon. *Good Schools for Young Children.* New York: Macmillan Co., 1974, pp. 351-86.

Lowenfeld, Viktor, and W. Lambert Brittain. *Creative and Mental Growth.* 4th edition. New York: Macmillan Co., 1964.

McFee, June K. *Preparation for Art.* San Francisco: Wadsworth Publishing Co., 1970.

Moore, Shirley, and Sally Kilmer. *Contemporary Preschool Education.* New York: John Wiley & Sons, 1974, pp. 121-38.

Pile, Naomi F. *Art Experiences for Young Children.* Threshold Early Learning Library, Vol. 5. New York: Threshold Div., Macmillan Co., 1973.

Read, Katherine. *The Nursery School.* Philadelphia: W. B. Saunders Co., 1971, pp. 189-244.

Shaw, Ruth F. *Finger Painting.* Boston: Little, Brown & Co., 1934.

Spodek, Bernard. *Teaching in the Early Years.* Englewood Cliffs, N.J.: Prentice-Hall, 1972, pp. 177-89.

Taylor, Barbara J. *When I Do, I Learn.* Provo, Utah: Brigham Young University Press, 1974, pp. 121-29.

Todd, Vivian E., and Helen Heffernan. *The Years before School.* Toronto: Macmillan Co., 1970, pp. 451-77.

Vance, Barbara. *Teaching the Prekindergarten Child.* Monterey, Calif.: Brooks/Cole, 1973, pp. 219-40.

Vermeer, Jackie, and Marian Lariviere. *The Little Kid's Craftbook.* New York: Taplinger Publishing Co., 1973.

ARTICLES

Auerbach, Aaron J. "The Biosociative or Creative Act in the Nursery School." *Young Children*, October 1972, pp. 27-31.

Crase, Dixie, and Nancy Jones. "Children Learn from Recycling." *Young Children*, January 1974, pp. 79-82.

Grossman, Marian. "Art Education for the Young Child." *Review of Educational Research* 40 (June 1970): 421-27.

Margolin, Edythe. "Conservation of Self-Expression and Aesthetic Sensitivity in Young Children." *Young Children*, January 1968, pp. 155-60.

Seefeldt, Carol. "Boxes Are to Build . . . A Curriculum!" *Young Children,* October 1972, pp. 5-11.

Sparling, Joseph J., and Marilyn C. "How to Talk to a Scribbler." *Young Children,* August 1973, pp. 333-41.

PAMPHLETS

Art for the Preprimary Child. National Art Education Association, 1201 Sixteenth Street N.W., Washington, D.C., 20036.

Association for Childhood Education International. *Art for Children's Growing.* # 64. Washington, D.C.

Biber, Barbara. *Children's Drawings.* New York: Bank Street Publishers, 69 Bank Street.

Lowenfeld, Viktor. *The Meaning of Creative Expression.* New York: Bank Street Publishers, 69 Bank Street.

U. S. Government Printing Office. *How Children Can Be Creative,* # 12. U. S. Dept. of Health, Education and Welfare, Washington, D.C.

Winsor, Charlotte. *Creative Activities for Young Children.* New York: Bank Street Publishers, 69 Bank Street.

CHAPTER 3

LANGUAGE, STORIES, AND BOOKS

It is important that you ask yourself the questions: Why such a heavy emphasis on language? What am I teaching with language, stories, and books? Why am I teaching with them? How am I teaching with them? What are some helpful techniques for a story period? When are language, stories, and books most effective? What criteria should be used in selecting stories and books for young children? Are there some available sources which can aid in the selection of literature for young children?

WHY SUCH A HEAVY EMPHASIS ON LANGUAGE?

Evidence exists that a child understands language before he can speak, but it is the acquisition of language that adds depth to that understanding. People, objects, activities, and all things in the environment have labels. The child learns to communicate first with a single word or idea. Then, through increased experience with language, he is able to communicate on more complex levels and with more complex ideas.

Too often, adults do not take opportunity to listen to a preschool child. They could learn about him and his concerns merely by listening to him. He deserves to be heard. In planning a learning experience for a child, an adult may have a certain goal or activity in mind. If the child were allowed to take the raw materials or ideas, he could arrive at his own idea. The teacher should sincerely say, "That is a good idea!" "You thought of a different way to do it!" "I like your idea!" In this way, the child will be encouraged to think and do things creatively.

There should be many times during the day for the preschool child to listen and to speak. One objective of group concept teaching is to stimulate the child to ask and answer questions as well as to make comments. During free play, for example, he has opportunities to talk about materials, ideas, or relationships with others, and snack time is an especially good time for relaxation and conversation. Prestory activities, too, often involve verbal participation by the children.

A child learns about himself through language. He tries out his ideas, expresses his concerns, learns about his environment, initiates activities, learns social techniques, and communicates with adults and peers. The way others respond to him will either reinforce his verbalizing or will frustrate his verbal attempts.

A shy child may need special attention in order that he might be heard; he may be hesitant to speak or perhaps his voice is so quiet that it is difficult to hear what he is saying. Encourage his verbalizing with peers and teachers.

Topics for conversation are limitless. Something that is stimulating and exciting brings forth refreshing comments from children. Language is such an important tool in our society that it needs to be cultivated. If spontaneous conversation is not a part of the preschool program, the teacher should introduce some ways of encouraging children in this important aspect of their development. Try some of these suggestions:

- Make a large cardboard TV set. Slip different pictures into its "window" and ask children to tell about them. This encourages language and dramatic play.
- Bring some new and/or unusual object. Let the children handle it and ask and answer questions.
- Use a "think box" (see page 143).
- Show pictures and ask the children to act out the scene.
- Pose certain situations and ask the children what they would do.
- Have some children role play and have others guess what they are doing.
- Begin a story, then let each child add an event (could use pictures or no visual stimulation).
- Ask a child to tell something he has done or will be doing.
- Record conversation of children. Play it back and see if they can guess who was talking.
- Using a favorite storybook, have a child tell the story to others.

WHAT AND WHY AM I TEACHING WITH LANGUAGE, STORIES, AND BOOKS?

Following are some purposes for including literature in the curriculum of young children:

- To enrich or supplement firsthand experiences of children.
- To build correct concepts, clarify ideas, present information, and stimulate new ideas.
- To build social relations through sharing experiences.
- To foster appreciation of aesthetic things and to stimulate creative expression.
- To provide literary experiences and to acquaint the child with another way of learning about his world.
- To encourage verbal communication with other children and adults.
- For the enjoyment which stories provide as a period of quiet activity, a change of pace, a repetition of a favorite book, or an opportunity for physical closeness to a teacher.
- To encourage a positive attitude toward caring for and using books and towards reading.

HOW AM I TEACHING?

The teacher must have firmly rooted in her mind not only what she is teaching but how she will accomplish her goals. If she is providing a story period merely to occupy a block of time, she should stop and do some thoughtful reevaluating.

How can books and stories be used to provide a worthwhile experience for children? One answer is that there should be a place where a few books can be attractively displayed on a rack or table to beckon children to them. A small space, a cluttered area, too many books, or a reading area located in a traffic pattern can soon discourage children from finding enjoyment.

The teacher selects books which are well written and contain correct concepts because she is aware of the inability of young children to distinguish between reality and fantasy (Taylor, 1973). Through the use of books she can provide information to children and have the books available for their browsing every day.

An abundance of children's books are on the market today. An adult must be selective and keep standards high when selecting books for young children. Most books purchased are those chosen by adults, some of whom seem disappointed if children do not appreciate the stories they themselves enjoyed when they were children. However, story preferences differ from one person to another, and it is important that the adult find the interest of the child, then select the book.

The teacher uses time as an aid in her teaching by providing large blocks of it for various activities. Children like to sit quietly, undisturbed, while they look through books or have a story read to them individually or in a small, intimate group.

She arranges the books attractively to stimulate the interest of the children. She varies the types of books. She knows the needs and interests of the children in her group and provides books for individual children.

She stimulates the interest of the children by varying the location for reading stories—sometimes indoors and sometimes outdoors. She provides for the possibility of informal story time with one child or a group of children.

Several children at a preschool were playing with some plastic dinosaurs. They began asking the teacher questions. Knowing there was a book about dinosaurs on the shelf, she took it down. She and the children spent quite a while looking at the book and discovering things about dinosaurs.

The attitude and feelings of the teacher herself will greatly influence the children's interest in the story. One teacher felt sure the children would not enjoy the story she had prepared one day; she was right. They picked up her attitude about the story. On another day the same teacher was very excited about the story she had prepared. She conveyed this to the children, and the story time went very well, surprising her that she could influence the children. They had reacted to her mood and feelings.

Story time not only provides enriching experiences for the children in the group, but it also benefits the teacher. Through story-telling experiences, she can become better acquainted with the children, thus building a better relationship with them.

Sometimes, too, a teacher wants to teach a new topic when examples of the real objects are not available. Rather than give up the idea, she provides a book which has excellent pictures and factual text to help her. She goes over the concepts carefully with the children, listening to their comments and questions and making sure their understanding is accurate.

The teacher herself grows and develops in patience and understanding through planning and executing a story experience, for she has many factors to consider. The length of time, for example, should not be definitely predetermined. The teacher takes her cues from the children: if they are restless, the story period should be fairly short; if they are extremely interested, the story period can be longer. At any rate, story time should be leisurely and should provide a relaxed atmosphere. The size of the group can vary, but the setting should be informal. Most children are comfortable sitting on the floor.

It is imperative that the teacher know her story well in order to avoid unpleasant experiences. A teacher planned a day around chickens and eggs, for example. She had pictures, ideas, and materials to support the concepts she was presenting. She brought in an incubator with some chicken eggs about ready to hatch. At snack time the children had stuffed eggs. The day had been well planned. As the teacher started for the story room, however, she found that her book about eggs was missing. Frantically she searched for it. Not finding it, she went to the bookshelf to see if it had been replaced.

She did not find it but found another one, "All about Eggs," by Millicent Selsam. Somewhat relieved to find a book on the subject even though she was not familiar with its contents, she sat down and began her story. It told about many different kinds of eggs—chickens, fish, turtle, bird, and so on.

She had begun to feel comfortable with her quick selection when she turned the page and read, "A dog has babies, but where are the dog's eggs?" With a puzzled look on her face, she turned the page and continued: "You don't see them but they are there just the same. Hidden away inside the mother dog is a special sac; a warm, safe place where the dog's eggs change into little puppies." Her face began to turn a light pink. She tried to hurry through the rest of the book by turning a number of pages at a time. With each turn, she felt a little more uneasy.

Finally she turned to a page which showed a woman, and she read the story. "You too, grew from a tiny egg inside your mother." Now her face was a dark crimson. Quickly she closed the book and said, "I think we had better go outside."

This could have been an excellent book if she had been teaching about sex education or reproduction, but because she was unprepared to teach either, she was embarrassed. Had she been familiar with the book, she could have selected the pages that would have applied to her lesson about eggs.

TECHNIQUES FOR TEACHERS

A great deal of satisfaction derives from having discovered a way of guiding children in a positive, acceptable manner. Following are some helpful techniques in teaching with literature:

It has been debated as to whether or not a child receives value from participating during the actual story. For some children participating is a method whereby they can clarify concepts related to the story, for the story may remind them of something else. A skillful teacher who has the story group well under control can accept such interruptions. If deviation from the story is carried beyond a comment or two, however, the other children in the group lose interest, and it may be necessary for her to say, "We can talk more about that after the story."

Mentioning the name of a child who is becoming distracted can be one technique for regaining his interest.

Sometimes it is necessary to casually separate two children so that each can benefit more from the experience. A teacher may say, "I would like to sit by _____ and _____ today." Then she does so.

A teacher can move closer to a child who is uninterested, and by putting her hand on his shoulder or hand, she can return his interest to the story.

Sometimes a child finds it extremely difficult to be in a story group. If this happens, it may be a better experience for him to sit quietly in another area with a teacher and perhaps one other child and have a story there. After a period of time he may be ready to have a story experience with the group.

When children are uninterested, examine each child for possible reasons. Perhaps he has had many story experiences and has an interest elsewhere. Perhaps he has had so few story experiences that it is difficult for him to see value in it. Many reasons exist for a child's lack of interest. Look for them; then plot a course of action.

If the story time is inviting and interesting enough, children will want to be there.

Lap sitting sometimes becomes a problem. It is true that there are not enough teachers for each child to sit on a lap. To save confusion and hurt feelings, it would be wise for all teachers and children to sit directly on the floor. There is no question that children enjoy sitting in an adult's lap and listening to stories, but this activity could be reserved for very small, informal story-reading times.

At least two teachers should participate in each story time. While one teacher is giving the story, the other teacher (or teachers) can support her by giving their attention to children who need it and to those distracting others from the story.

MOST EFFECTIVE USE OF LITERATURE

A teacher can use books and stories effectively if she takes her cues from the children. When a child shows an interest in a frog, the teacher can provide a book about a frog in the reading area or she can use a story about a frog during story time.

Books are helpful to children, too. They need time to assimilate the many facts thrown at them, for example, and casually looking through a book may help them develop some concrete ideas pertaining to the world about them.

Poetry can also be very useful. Most teachers have committed to memory simple poems pertaining to the everyday world of young children. When the children find a bird or notice a rainbow or a worm, a wise teacher quotes a short poem related to the experience.

All children will not be interested in the same things at the same time, however. The teacher must provide a variety of ideas with individual children in mind.

A teacher, like the one in the following incident, should take advantage of many teachable moments. One day after a heavy snow storm, the teacher told the children about the many things she had observed on the way to school. It sounded like a story. One child said, "Tell it again teacher." Brad, a five-year-old, noticed two large icicles hanging off the corner of a building and remarked, "It looks like a pair of men's pants!"

CRITERIA FOR SELECTION OF STORIES AND BOOKS FOR YOUNG CHILDREN

In order to receive the most value from children's literature, a teacher should establish criteria for selecting books and stories.

- First, the material should be realistic and accurately reported. A child of this age has much difficulty in distinguishing between what is real and what is fantasy. Avoid ascribing human characteristics (talking, dressing) to animals, objects, or things. A child needs help in clarifying, rather than confusing, concepts. After he has mastered concepts, stories of fantasy can begin. This is usually following his fifth birthday.

  The question of telling fairy tales to preschoolers always arises. Again, these are not within the understanding of young children. Many fairy tales produce fear and deal with advanced concepts. These are better left until the school years (Read, 1971; Arbuthnot, 1972; Leeper, 1974).

  Another avenue of inquiry concerns the use of Mother Goose rhymes. Usually these are acceptable because of the rhyme and rhythm, the humor, the suspense, and the repetition, but they should be used discriminately.

- A second criterion for selecting stories and books for children is that they should be entertaining and humorous. Children enjoy an element of surprise or suspense. Often they do not appreciate adult humor.

- A third criterion for children's literature is that it should promote the child's learning by supporting firsthand experiences which he has had and will be having.

- Fourth, the length of the story or poem should depend upon the interest of the individual child. Usually three-year-olds sit quietly for a shorter time than four-year-olds, but there is great variation even within a single age group. If the children grow restless, eliminate parts of the story which are not entirely essential. If interest seems to be very keen, on the other hand, you may even add to the story.

- Fifth, the effect of the story on the child needs consideration. If it contains familiar elements and helps to promote sound concepts, it is generally acceptable. If it contains fear, fantasy, or morals, it is best left for later years. Nightmares, poor social relationships, or emotional upsets can be results of such elements.

- Sixth, the literature should have literary value including plot, interesting word sounds or plays on words (catch phrases, repetition of incidents or ideas), and words which are simple, descriptive, and within the understanding of the child. A great amount of direct conversation adds interest.

- Seventh, know the children for whom the story is selected. Their needs, interests, attention span, and maturity level will be good indicators as to whether or not the story will appeal to them.

- Eighth, illustrations should closely represent the written text. Children enjoy colorful pictures, but some of their favorites are done in black and white or with one or two colors. The important thing is how well the pictures are portrayed. Many unnecessary details detract from the picture. Photographs can be useful, especially when accompanying factual material, by showing the comparison of sizes between the different elements represented.

  Two awards for children's books are given each year: the John Newberry Award for the best literary contribution to children's literature and the Caldecott Award for the outstanding picture book published during the previous year. They are not always awarded to a book for preschool children. If either is, however, it can be an indication of the quality of the book.

WRITING ORIGINAL STORIES

The criteria previously listed for selecting stories and books for young children would apply equally here. When it is difficult to obtain a story on a certain subject, originate one, using the criteria listed.

Some of the values for a teacher in writing original stories are that she gains self-confidence, develops creativeness, and becomes more flexible in her teaching.

USE OF POETRY

As you listen to the conversation of children, it is truly poetic. The play on words, the fun sounds, and the humor are delightful. Too often adults think that poetry has no place in the lives of young children. How wrong they are. An excellent introduction to poetry is a priceless experience for a child.

There are many excellent authors and sources from which to choose, and almost every subject has been explored. Sometimes it is difficult to select a poem because there are so many available. (See Prestory Activities, pp. 139-141).

The attitude of the teacher toward poetry will be influential. It is important that the teacher enjoy and appreciate the poetry she selects and that she share it enthusiastically with the children. Poetry spontaneously recited has great value.

A part of that value is that poetry helps children to listen carefully and stimulates their minds to creativity. It would be well for a teacher to jot down the poems of children—their newly learned words and their ways of expressing their feelings.

As with stories, it is desirable to have different types of poetry available: poems related to children's everyday experiences at home or at school, nonsense verses for fun, poems which bring melody and rhythm to the ear, poems which have special meaning to individuals, and poems which stimulate and encourage exploration. Through repetition, not through rigid memorization, children will learn and enjoy poetry.

ESPECIALLY FOR PARENTS

Parents would be wise to review the criteria for selecting books on pages 81-82. Sometimes we hurriedly choose a book for a child, influenced by time's pressure or by attractive pictures in the book or by some insignificant

83

thing rather than by sound reasoning. Remember that the books we make available to our children will have a definite influence upon their later reading and their enjoyment of books.

Consider the following story:

It was a beautiful Saturday afternoon as the Morrill children merrily climbed into the car for their weekly trip to the library. Excited voices filled the air. Lisa, seven, said, "I'm going to look for a book that has a princess. Yes, a very beautiful princess with lots of pretty clothes. I love fairy tales."

"Well, I hope I can find a book about a trip to the moon. I think going to the moon would be super—just like on TV," commented Kevin, five.

"And I want a book with some animals in it like the ones we saw at the circus," added Larry, not wanting to be left out of any experience or conversation even though he was only three.

The trip to town was short, and the three bubbly children scampered into the children's library. From time to time, one of them would consult mother for advice as each child formed a pile of books. Soon they had selected and checked out their books for the week.

The following Saturday they were back to repeat their literary exchange. As Mrs. M. sat there each week, she noticed another mother with her children—about six and three. The mother engaged in a power struggle with first the older child and then the younger one. Everyone in the library would stop reading periodically to observe the difficulty.

On the third Saturday as the Morrill children selected books, Mrs. M. noticed that the power struggle between the woman and her children was even more violent today than on previous Saturdays. Finally, in embarrassment, the woman sat down by Mrs. M. "Why do my children have to act this way in public?" she began in utter frustration, half talking out loud to herself and half directing her comments to Mrs. M. "I keep telling them going to the library is exciting and fun—and do you know what? I almost have to carry them inside to get them near the books!" She continued, "Every night when we sit down to read a fairy tale like "The Three Pigs" that I liked to read when I was a child, they get so fussy—they wiggle and make faces at each other and hit and finally end up going to their rooms crying. I keep telling them they are going to learn to like books no matter what the cost!"

Mrs. M. sat in utter disbelief. Why, her children had enjoyed hearing stories since they were very young. And going to the library was a privilege, certainly not a punishment! She responded to the woman's puzzled inquiries and excited overtones as her children either returned books to the shelf or added them to their growing take-home pile.

Now it was the woman who sat in disbelief. Her curiosity became so aroused that she couldn't remain silent. Half apologetically she said, "My name is Mrs. Ray. The last few weeks I have been watching you with your children as they select books. They seem so happy and excited. And look at mine. They are still sitting on the floor, absolutely refusing to choose some books so that we can go home. Well, believe me, I am willing to out-wait them today. They have made a fool out of me for the last time at the library. See, I have brought my knitting and will sit here all day if necessary. But, I must admit that your children actually seem to enjoy the library. Out of curiosity, how do you *make* them act that way?"

With a chuckle in her voice, Mrs. M. answered, "Oh, I don't *make* them act that way. We have given them some good experiences with stories, books, and poetry, and they can hardly wait for their weekly trip to the library. In our home, reading times are very special. We have times when we read to each child, and sometimes we all hear the same book or story. My husband and I enjoy reading, too."

Now, let's analyze the library scene and Mrs. M's approach:

- Her children had a positive, enthusiastic attitude about books and reading.

- Her children were encouraged to look for and select books for their own interest and need.
- She had a fair understanding of the developmental abilities of each child.
- She reads for pleasure and also for knowledge about raising happy children.
- In the home, reading is either for the individual or for the family.

You can follow the pattern of either Mrs. M. or Mrs. Ray, but chances are very good that if you follow Mrs. M.'s example, you will all be a lot happier, and your children will develop good reading habits. (By the way, libraries have more than books. Ask about filmstrips, movies, picture sets, and story hour.)

Language is more than books; it is talking and listening and observing. Sometimes we are so busy giving commands that we don't stop to explain or listen. We expect instant obedience. That is a short-range goal; whereas, if we explain why certain things are as they are, or have to be, or should be, the child will begin to develop some cause and effect ideas, will be able to reason later things for himself, and will find a variety of solutions to problems. You might even find, when you try to explain your request to a child, that it is unreasonable because there is no valid support for it.

Another thing about language: talking *with* a child is one thing; talking *about* him is another. If you can say something honest, positive, and complimentary to him in the presence of others, this treatment is upbuilding. But never criticize him before others; criticism is degrading.

Sincerely listening to your child is not only a courtesy; it is a necessity. How are you going to find out what he thinks (accurately or inaccurately) if you don't listen? He often has very good ideas and sincere questions. He deserves your undivided attention.

Careful observation of your child will help you plan some meaningful experiences for him. How does he respond when stories are suggested? How much time does he spend with books? Is he starting to recognize written symbols (letters and/or numbers)? Does he ask questions about signs?

Nonverbal language (gestures, actions) is also an important factor. In fact, some authors say that it is much more influential on the behavior or attitudes of children than verbal language. You may not be aware of the actual messages you are sending to your children. If you say, "Have some of this delicious broccoli" with a sick look on your face, how do you expect the child to respond? If you are counting on the words, you will be disappointed. Be consciously aware of the model you are displaying for your child.

Here are some things you might try at home to help your child develop good language and reading habits (be selective with your child and the situation):

- Read with him often—books that he enjoys in a comfortable setting.
- Take him to the library often.
- Discuss ideas with him instead of lecturing to him.
- Provide books for him to look through.
- Help him to find out about things of interest by using books.
- *Tell* (rather than always read) stories. You might have some continued stories with always a new episode to consider about some fictional character or about factual events about family members.
- Help him select some *good* TV programs.
- Provide some listening experiences (records, tape recorder).
- Help him make up some games so that he takes part in establishing rules.
- Encourage him to tell stories to other family members or to friends.
- Let him participate in a family gathering (with a poem, a song, an idea).
- Give him some sheets of paper (or a booklet) and let him draw a story while you write down his comments.
- Play a game with him like "What would you do if . . . ?"
- Help him to write a poem (think of rhyming words).

- Help him write a letter to someone.
- When he is interested and ready, have some alphabetical cards or letters for his exploration.
- Show him how to write his name (starting with a capital and then lower case letters), family names, and others upon his request.
- Assign a family member to record the family conversation at dinner one night (who talks the most; do members share in the discussion or talk only about personal interests; how much time is spent in pleasant conversation). A tape recorder can be used if available. Discuss the conversation.
- Increase his vocabulary by introducing and defining appropriate words and terms.
- See *When I Do, I Learn* by Barbara J. Taylor, pp. 129-33, 138-39.

BIBLIOGRAPHY FOR LANGUAGE, STORIES, AND BOOKS

BOOKS FOR TEACHERS AND PARENTS

Arbuthnot, May H. *Children and Books.* Chicago: Scott, Foresman & Company, 1972.

Hartley, Ruth E., and Robert M. Goldensen. *Understanding Children's Play.* New York: Thos. Y. Crowell, 1967.

Leeper, Sarah H., Ruth J. Dales, Dora Sikes Skipper, and Ralph L. Witherspoon. *Good Schools for Young Children.* New York: The Macmillan Company, 1974, pp. 172-232.

Read, Katherine. *The Nursery School.* Philadelphia: W. B. Saunders, 1971, pp. 209-13.

Sawyer, Ruth. *The Way of the Storyteller.* New York: Viking Press, 1967.

Spodek, Bernard. *Teaching in the Early Years.* Englewood Cliffs, New Jersey: Prentice-Hall, 1972, pp. 59-85.

Taylor, Barbara J. *When I Do, I Learn.* Provo, Utah: Brigham Young University Press, 1974, pp. 129-34.

Todd, Vivian E., and Helen Heffernan. *The Years before School: Guiding Preschool Children.* Toronto: The Macmillan Company, 1970, pp. 420-50.

ARTICLES

Cazden, Courtney B. "Children's Questions: Their Forms, Functions, and Roles in Education." *Young Children*, March 1970, pp. 202-20.

Engelmann, Siegfried. "The Structuring of Language Process As a Tool of Thought." In *Understanding the Young Child and His Curriculum*, edited by Belen Mills, pp. 292-303. New York: The Macmillan Company, 1972.

Margolin, Edythe. "Conservation of Self-Expression and Aesthetic Sensitivity in Young Children." *Young Children*, January 1968, pp. 155-60.

Mattick, Ilse. "The Teacher's Role in Helping Young Children Develop Language Competence." *Young Children*, February 1972, pp. 133-42.

Paige, Marjorie L. "Building on Experiences in Literature." *Young Children*, December 1969, pp. 85-88.

Reid, William R., Rose C. Engel, and Donald P. Lucker. "Language Development for the Young." In *Understanding the Young Child and His Curriculum*, edited by Belen Mills, pp. 369-77. New York: Macmillan Company, 1972.

Rich, Dorothy. "Spurring Language Creativity in Young Children." *Young Children*, January 1968, pp. 175-77.

Smith, Grace. "On Listening to the Language of Children." *Young Children*, March 1974, pp. 133-40.

Taylor, Barbara J. "The Ability of Three-, Four-, and Five-Year-Old Children to Distinguish Fantasy from Reality." *Journal of Genetic Psychology* 122 (1973): 315-18.

Wickens, Elaine. "Please Don't Tell the Children." *Young Children*, October 1967, pp. 15-18.

PAMPHLETS

Adventures in Literature with Children, #92. Washington: Association for Childhood Education International.

Bibliography of Books for Children. Washington: Association for Childhood Education International.

Children's Books for $1.25 or Less, #36. Washington: Association for Childhood Education International.

Books for Children—a Selected List. New York: Bank Street Publication, 69 Bank Street.

Books in Preschool, compiled by Louise Griffin. #121. 48 pp. Washington: ERIC-NAEYC Publication, 1834 Connecticut Ave., N.W., 20009. 1970. $1.75.

Multi-Ethnic Books for Young Children. 80 pp. Washington: ERIC-NAEYC Publication, 1834 Connecticut Avenue, N.W., 20009. $2.00.

Horn Book, Inc., 585 Boylston Street, Boston, Mass. 02116

Hunnicutt, C. W. *Answering Children's Questions*. New York: Bureau of Publications, Teacher's College, Columbia University.

Hymes, James L. *Teacher Listen. The Children Speak*. New York: National Association for Mental Health, 10 Columbus Circle, 1949.

Lewis, Claudia. *Deep As a Giant*. New York: Bank Street Publication, 69 Bank Street.

Lewis, Claudia. *Language as an Art*. New York: Bank Street Publication, 69 Bank Street.

Van Ripper, C. *Helping Children Talk Better.* Chicago: Better Living Booklet, 57 West Grand Avenue, pp. 7-37.

If at all possible, go to a local bookstore and read the books before you purchase them. If that is not possible, below are listed some of the publishers you can write to for an annotated catalog of books. An age guide is listed; but remember this is only a guide. Some books listed for preschool children are too advanced, and some books cover such a wide age range (preschool—grade 2) that they may not meet the needs or interests of younger children. Books are expensive. Well-used books are worth the money, but inappropriate books are a waste.

Atheneum Publishers
Books for Children
122 East 42 Street
New York, New York 10017

Bradbury Press
2 Overhill Road
Scarsdale, New York 10583

Thos. Y. Crowell Co.
Dept. of Books for Children and Young People
666 Fifth Avenue
New York, New York 10019

E. P. Dutton & Co.
Library and Education Dept.
201 Park Avenue South
New York, New York 10003

Harper & Row, Publishers
Library Dept.
10 East 53rd Street
New York, New York 10022

Little, Brown & Co.
Children's Books
34 Beacon Street
Boston, Mass. 02106

Prentice-Hall
Children's Book Dept.
Englewood Cliffs, New Jersey 07632

The Seabury Press
Books for Young People
815 Second Avenue
New York, New York 10017

The Viking Press
School and Library Dept.
625 Madison Avenue
New York, New York 10022

BOOKS FOR CHILDREN

The following are some selected books for preschoolers (also see books listed at end of chapters 4, 5, and 10). Select each book for its *individual merits rather than by author or title only.*

Author	Name of Book	Publisher
Adelson, Leone	*All Ready for Winter*	David McKay, 1956
Barry, Katharine	*A Bug to Hug*	Harcourt, Brace & Co.
Baum, Arline and Joseph	*One Bright Monday Morning*	Random House, 1962
Beim, Jerrold	*Andy and the School Bus*	Wm. Morrow & Co., 1947
Bendick, Jeanne	*A Fresh Look at Night*	Franklin Watts (N.Y.)
Berg, Jean H.	*Baby Susan's Chickens*	Wonder Books, 1951
Blair, Mary	*The Up and Down Book*	Golden Press, 1964
Bond, Gladys B.	*Patrick Will Grow*	Whitman, 1966
Bradfield, Joan and Roger	*Who Are You?*	Whitman, 1966
Brenner, Barbara	*Somebody's Slippers, Somebody's Shoes*	W. R. Scott, 1957
Bright, Robert	*I Like Red*	Doubleday, 1955
Brown, Margaret W.	*The Important Book*	Harper, 1949
Budney, Blossum	*A Kiss Is Round*	Lothrop, Lee, 1954
Burton, Virginia Lee	*The Little House*	Houghton Mifflin, 1942
Carroll, Ruth	*Where's the Bunny*	Oxford Univ. Press, 1950
	Where's the Kitty	Henry Walck, 1962
Cleary, Beverly	*The Real Hole*	Wm. Morrow, 1960
Clifford, Eth and David	*Your Face Is a Picture*	Seale (Indianapolis), 1963
Cole, William	*Frances Face-Maker*	World, 1963
Conklin, Gladys	*We Like Bugs*	Holiday House, 1962
	I Like Butterflies	1960
Cook, Bernadine	*Looking for Susie*	Young Scott, 1956
	The Curious Kitten	Young Scott, 1956
	The Little Fish that Got Away	Young Scott, 1956
Cooper, Marjorie	*Jeepers the Little Frog*	Rand McNally, 1965
Dugan, William	*The Ball Book*	Golden Press, 1964
	The Truck & Bus Book	Golden Press, 1966

Duvoisin, Roger	*The House of Four Seasons*	Lothrop, Lee & Shepard
Duncan, Lois	*The Littlest One in the Family*	Dodd & Mead, 1960
Earle, Vana	*The Busy Man and the Night Time Noises*	Lothrop, Lee & Shepard, 1954
Emberley, Ed.	*The Wing on a Flea* (a book about shapes)	Little, Brown & Co., 1961
Ets, Marie Hall	*Play with Me*	Viking Press, 1955
Evers, Alf	*Open the Door*	Franklin Watts, 1960
Flack, Marjorie	*Angus* (series)	Doubleday
	New Pet	Doubleday, 1943
	Wag-Tail-Bess	Doubleday, 1933
Freeman, Don	*Come Again, Pelican*	Viking Press, 1961
	Mop-Top	Children's Press, 1955
Gay, Zhenya	*What's Your Name*	Viking Press, 1955
Gibson, Morrell	*Hello Peter*	Doubleday, 1948
Goudey, Alice E.	*The Good Rain*	Aladdin Books, 1950
Green, Mary M.	*Everybody Has a House*	Wm. R. Scott, 1961
	Is It Hard? Is It Easy?	1960
	Everybody Eats	1950
Gustavson, Harry M.	*Up Goes the House*	Oxford Univ. Press (N.Y.), 1947
Harrison, David L.	*The Boy with a Drum*	Golden Press, 1969
Howell, Virginia	*Who Likes the Dark*	Howell, Soskin, 1945
Ivens, Dorothy	*The Long Hike*	Viking Press, 1956
Iwasaki, Chihiro	*Momoko's Lovely Day*	London: Bodily Head, n.d.
	A Brother for Momoko	1970
	Momoko and the Pretty Bird	1972
Jackson, Kathryn	*Wheels*	Golden Press, 1952
Jones, Mildred G.	*The Little Cowboy*	Reilly & Lee, 1955
Kaufman, Joe	*The Toy Book*	Golden Press, 1965
Keats, Ezra	*Peter's Chair*	Harper & Row, 1967
Konkle, Janet	*The Kitten and the Parakeet*	Children's Press, 1952
Krauss, Ruth	*The Birthday Party*	Harper & Bros., 1957
	The Bundle Book	Harper & Bros., 1951
	The Growing Story	Harper & Bros., 1947
Leaf, Munro	*Boo*	Random House, 1948
Lenski, Lois	"Small" series	Henry Walck
	"Little" series (*Little Farm, Little Fire Engine*, etc.)	
Livingston, Myra C.	*Whispers* (poetry)	Harcourt, Brace, 1958
Marino, Dorothy	*Goodbye Thunderstorm*	J. B. Lippincott, 1958
Martin, Dick	*The Apple Book*	Golden Press, 1964
	The Sand Pail Book	Golden Press, 1964
	The Fish Book	1964
Mayer, Mercer	*A Boy, A Dog, and A Frog*	Dial Press, 1967
McCaffery, Wm. A.	*How to Watch a Parade*	Harper & Bros., 1959
McClosky, Robert	*Blueberries for Sal*	Viking Press, 1966
	Make Way for Ducklings	1966
	Lentil	1964
Meeks, Esther	*In John's Backyard*	Follett Pub., 1957
Moore, Lilian	*Too Many Bozos*	Golden Press, 1960
Nodset, Joan	*Go Away, Dog*	Harper & Row, 1963
Parsons, Virginia	*Homes*	Garden City Books, n.d.
	Night	1958
Paul, Grace	*Come to the Country*	Abelard-Schuman, 1965
	Freddy the Curious Cat	Doubleday, 1958
Petersham, Maud & Miska	*The Box with Red Wheels*	Macmillan, 1969

Pfloog, Jan	*The Bear Book*	Golden Press, 1965
	The Cat Book	1964
	The Dog Book	1964
	The Fox Book	1965
	The Squirrel Book	1965
	The Tiger Book	1965
Provensen, Alice and Martin	*Roses Are Red, Are Violets Blue?*	Random House, 1973
Rice, Inez	*A Long, Long Time*	Lothrop, Lee & Shepard, 1964
Ryland, Lee	*Gordon and the Glockenspiel*	Whitman, 1966
Schlein, Miriam	*How Do You Travel?*	Abingston Press, 1954
Schurr, Cathleen	*Cats Have Kittens—Do Gloves Have Mittens?*	Alfred A. Knopf, 1962
Skaar, Grace	*All about Dogs, Dogs, Dogs*	Wm. R. Scott, 1957
	Nothing but Cats, Cats, Cats	1957
	What Do They Say?	1950
Slobodkina, Esphyr	*Caps for Sale*	Wm. R. Scott, 1947
Smith, Eunice Y.	*The Little Red Drum*	Albert Whitman, 1961
Steiner, Charlotte	*Kiki* series	Doubleday
	Where Are You Going?	1946
	My Bunny Feels Soft	Alfred A. Knopf
	What Do You Love?	Alfred A. Knopf
Taylor, Barbara J.	*I Can Do*	Provo, Utah: BYU Press, 1972
Thompson, Eleanor	*What Shall I Put in the Hole That I Dig?*	Whitman Pub.
Wagner, Peggy	*Hurrah for Hats*	Children's Press, 1962
Wildsmith, Brian	*Brian Wildsmith's Birds*	Franklin Watts, 1967
Wright, Betty R.	*Good Morning Farm*	Whitman, 1964
Wright, Ethel	*Saturday Ride*	Wm. R. Scott, 1952
	Saturday Walk	1951
	Saturday Flight	1954
Yashima, Taro	*Umbrella*	Viking Press, 1958
Zaffo, George J.	*The Big Book of Real Trains*	Grosset & Dunlap, 1963
Zion, Gene	*All Falling Down*	Harper & Bros., 1951
	Hide and Seek Day	1954
	Really Spring	
	The Summer Snowman	1955
	Harry the Dirty Dog	1956
	The Plant Sitter	1954
	No Roses for Harry	1962
	Dear Garbage Man	1957
Zolotow, Charlotte	*One Step, Two . . .*	Lothrop, Lee & Shepard, 1955
	Someday	1965
	Over and Over (about holidays)	Harper & Row, 1957

CHAPTER 4

MUSIC, MOVEMENT, SOUND, AND RHYTHM

What are the values for young children in being exposed to music, movement, sound, and rhythm? What role does the teacher play? What are some suggested uses of (a) music, (b) movement, (c) sound, and (d) rhythm?

VALUES FOR CHILDREN

Children have various feelings which need expression. Music is but one of the constructive ways in which they can give vent to their feelings. To ride a stick horse rhythmically around the play yard, to move vigorously to music, to beat on a drum, to be engrossed in listening to a short excerpt from a favorite classic, or to sing wholeheartedly—all these help a child to cope with everyday problems.

An appreciation for music which will be lifelong can be the result of a child's pleasant introduction to it. On the other hand, forcing a child to listen to music against his will can produce the opposite effect.

Music can be introduced in many different ways. To capitalize on firsthand experiences and enrich them with music increases the possibilities of a child's expression. When a child comes to preschool with a very limited background in music and its values and uses, it may be necessary to give him some firsthand experiences upon which he can build.

This is not difficult to do; music is everywhere. A child may pick up the rhythmic dripping of a tap and incorporate it into his play, whereas this same sound may be annoying to an adult. A child may notice the swaying of the trees as the wind blows. He may comment on the movement of a familiar play-yard pet. Often children are much more observant in this way than the adults who are teaching them. Much can be gained from being with and listening to children.

It is possible, too, for a child to exhibit his creativeness by originating songs as he moves about in his familiar setting. It would be well to listen to and to record the songs of young children.

Another benefit of music is that a child can develop physically through his many exposures to it. He can be encouraged in large or small muscle activities. Sometimes, for example, the incorporation of music in his activities will change his tempo or his mood or his expression. One day a group of children were seated at the finger-painting table when they heard a quiet, melodious waltz from the music room. Unconsciously, they began to sway with the music. Then the record was changed to a loud, booming march, and the children immediately changed from their tranquil expression to one of heavy pounding.

Moreover, children can increase their immediate knowledge by expressing it through music. How does a duck walk? A horse? A rabbit? What sounds are made in the preschool setting? The wood in the fireplace? The popcorn in the pan? The clock on the wall? By helping the children to be observant to the many things around them, they can incorporate this attribute into their lives to help them increase their awareness and appreciate many things which ordinarily go unnoticed.

A child can learn about different types of instruments such as string, woodwind, and percussion. He can further this knowledge by exploring and expressing himself through their use.

Another plus for music is that a child gains concepts of rhythm through experiences with it. Maturity is the contributing factor as to whether or not a child can keep time to music, but practice helps him in his singing ability. (Read, 1971.)

A shy child can often be helped to express himself to music along with other children if he has had the opportunity to observe them until he feels comfortable. At no time should an adult force a child to participate or indicate to him how he should move. Both of these things can be detrimental to the child.

With the aid of music in teaching, the goal is to help the child express himself rather than to get him "to move" to music.

THE ROLE OF THE TEACHER

One of the most important roles of the teacher is to discover the developmental stage of each child in the group and then to plan experiences which will be beneficial. A teacher who tries to introduce skipping, for instance, to children who are not physically mature enough for this step would be inviting frustration for the child rather than release. She must discover from the children what their interests, concepts, and abilities are. It may be necessary to bring certain things to the attention of the children. For example, a chicken raises its head to drink water while a dog laps it up with his tongue. She should help the children gain as much as possible from their firsthand experiences.

A wise teacher also has a wide repertoire of songs upon which she can call when the moment is right. She sees that musical experiences are provided often for the children. Music in some form should be included each day. Much more important than having a trained voice is that a teacher enjoy music with children. One teacher kept maintaining that she could not "carry a tune in a bucket." But through years of encouragement, she finally began to feel more comfortable in a musical setting. One day in the nursery school she sang a song to the children. How great was her joy when a child said enthusiastically, "Oh, teacher, sing it again!"

A good teacher encourages use of music through spontaneous expression—both indoors and outdoors. She further encourages expression through use of pictures, stories, poetry, and ideas. Ann liked to have a teacher watch her as she slid down the slide. She asked a teacher to go with her, which the teacher willingly did. Ann slid down once and then looked at the teacher. She slid down again and glanced at the teacher with a puzzled look. Finally, after her third trip down, she disgustedly turned to the teacher and said, "Well, when Miss M. stands by the slide, she always sings!" Ann had noticed how fun it was to slide as the teacher sang about her activity. She appeared troubled when the gaiety was missing.

A teacher picks up the rhythmic movements of the children rather than expecting them to conform to set tempos. She encourages the use of movement by providing opportunities for children to express themselves. She is flexible in the use of rhythm instruments, realizing that at the first exposure to these instruments, children need time to explore them. She repeats this experience so that children can become acquainted with the use of instruments. She encourages the children to be creative rather than to follow a stereotyped procedure by saying something like this to the children: "I'm going to play some music and when you feel like playing your instrument, you do so." Some will participate; others will watch.

Teaching songs to preschool children is done through repetition. The teacher may say, "I am going to sing a new song for you today. You listen." She sings the song and then says, "I am going to sing it for you again." She repeats it. The next time she may say, "This time when I sing the song, you may sing along with me if you wish." She sings it again, and some of the children may participate. She may repeat it once or twice more if some of the children are interested. Then she sees that it is used still again soon so that the children will have another exposure to it. Visual aids are useful in teaching music because they create interest and further expose the children to the song through words and pictures. If the task of learning a new song is labored, the children will lose interest.

The teacher values the individual child and plans accordingly. She does not require a child to remain in the musical setting if the child is not willing to do so. Instead, she provides a quiet activity for him so that he will not distract others from the experience. She also incorporates music into other activities—creative art, dramatic play, free play, or snack time—in order to create new interest and ideas. Note that an activity takes on a new light when music is added.

She is selective in the use of musical records, by providing only those which have value to children: marked rhythms, quality, variety, introduction of various instruments, or participation. Often she uses music so that the children have a chance to get better acquainted with it through repetition. She calls the musical selections by name to familiarize the children with them. Upon entering the preschool one morning, a four-year-old asked: "Teacher, will you put on the Nutcracker Suite so we can dance to it?" She could also call other selections by their proper names.

If the teacher is not musically inclined, she arranges for another teacher to help with this activity rather than eliminate it.

A perceptive teacher invites a guest to bring an instrument to the school for the children to enjoy. In providing this experience, she plans carefully with the guest so that both know what to expect. The children will enjoy the experience more if they are told something about the instrument, how it is tuned, what makes it play, and so on. They will want to hear familiar tunes rather than those that exhibit the skill of the guest.

From time to time it may be necessary for the teacher to provide props which will encourage creative expression, such as long, full skirts, crepe paper streamers, scarves, or balloons.

The teacher provides experiences which will help children to release their feelings constructively, whether the feelings be of anger and hostility or of joy and excitement. She shows interest and enthusiasm in the children's activities and encourages them. She knows of the variation in interest span of young children and plans accordingly.

In sum, an experienced teacher knows of the many values of music and includes music of some kind in her daily planning. She realizes that in order to be effective, some experiences must be structured, not to the point of excluding creative thinking, but to the extent that a specific time or activity is planned. When the experience is to be a group activity, it necessitates more planning than if it is to be incidental. And, of course, a teacher sets up and maintains necessary limits in teaching with music.

SOME SUGGESTED TEACHING AIDS

MUSIC

- Informal singing time in which songs are used that pertain to the everyday lives of children—animals, people, situations.
- Using an autoharp—either indoors or outdoors.
- Using appropriate records to increase singing or participation.
- Listening to short excerpts of familiar classical selections.
- Having a guest demonstrate and play an instrument.
- Beating rhythms with drums or finger cymbals or by clapping.
- Placing a record player where children can have access to it.
- Using music during activities such as free play, creativity, dramatic play, snack time.
- Taking children to a rehearsal of a band or an orchestra if it is located nearby.
- Playing music outside on the play yard.
- Dancing with flowers (real or plastic).

A MINI-PLAN INVOLVING MUSIC (see also page 17)

Theme: Cello

Behavioral Objectives: At the end of the experience, the child will be able to:

1. Give the proper name of the instrument.
2. Name at least four parts of the instrument.

3. Tell the classification of the instrument (woodwind, string, or percussion).
4. Pantomime the way the instrument is played.
5. Sing familiar songs with the accompaniment of the cello.

Learning Activities:

If a teacher does not play this particular instrument, a guest cellist will be invited to the group. Discussion will include the way the instrument is stored when not in use, the different parts and names of the instrument, the reason why it is called a "string" instrument, and the way it is played. Familiar songs will be played on the cello, and the children will be invited to sing along. Children will be given another opportunity to ask questions and make comments. The teacher will go over the main objectives with the children to make sure they have learned the correct concepts.

MOVEMENT

- Picking up rhythms of children by using a drum or finger cymbals or by clapping.
- Helping children to see movement in everyday things such as animals, people (community helpers, professionals), or objects (clocks, taps, cars, trains).
- Suggesting ideas to children and letting them express their individual ideas (colors, moods, holidays).
- Talking about movement as we walk, skip, run, jump, climb. (Some interesting ideas, music, and references can be found in Rosanna R. Saffran's *First Book of Creative Rhythms.* New York: Holt, Rinehart and Winston, 1963. It is written for school-age children but some of the ideas can be adapted for preschool use.)
- Having children use their own imaginations. "How would you move if you were a puppet on a string?" "How would you move if you were popcorn in a hot pan?" "How would you move if your shoe were stuck on a large piece of chewing gum?"

- Getting a parachute (small size, if possible, works better with pre-schoolers).
  Marshmallow: Hold parachute waist high. On signal throw arms and chute as high as possible. Let it float down softly.
  Waves: Gently wave chute up and down and observe rippling motion.
  Cover-up: Hold chute waist high. Upon signal extend arms upward and while still holding onto chute turn around; then squat on ground. Chute covers children.
  Bouncers: Place two yarn or other small balls in center of chute. Try to keep them bouncing by shaking chute up and down.
  Catchers: Space teachers, boys, and girls around outside of chute. Slowly move chute up and down. On count of "three" the teacher calls either "boys" or "girls." The called group runs under chute, and others try to "catch" them.
      Make up your own actions.

A MINI-PLAN INVOLVING MOVEMENT (see also page 17)

Theme: Creative Movement

Behavioral Objectives: At the end of the experience, the child will be able to:

1. Express through movement the way at least three different pictures make him feel.
2. Verbally express his feeling about the pictures.
3. Move his body in different ways and at different tempos.

Learning Activities:

A group of well-selected pictures will be shown to the children. They will include different colors and children involved in various activities (a child sitting on a hill while the wind blows her hair, a child riding a horse, a child playing on the sand at the ocean, two children running through a meadow, a boy climbing a tree, a boy pulling a girl in a wagon, a child swinging, children riding stick horses, a child playing in a puddle of water, a child wrestling with a dog, a bird flying). The children will be encouraged to verbalize their ideas and feelings about the pictures and then to express them physically. All ideas and movements are accepted. Do certain activities encourage more conversation and participation? Are some colors more stimulating? Are some children more verbal while others are more physical? Can the children mesh verbal and physical activities?

SOUND
- Encouraging children to listen to sounds around them, both indoors and outdoors.
- Providing a variety of sounds which are familiar to children, either through use of the objects or with a tape recorder. Let the children try to identify the sounds.
- Letting children record and listen to their own voices or sounds they desire to record.
- Setting up experiences which help children clarify concepts. For example, an electric clock sounds different from a grandfather clock.
- Talking about and making sounds of different transportation vehicles (trains, buses, cars, boats, airplanes).
- Talking about and making sounds of different animals (dogs, cats, rabbits, horses, chickens, turtles).
- Talking about and making sounds the children heard on their way to school today.

- Talking about how different sounds make them feel (train whistle, cow moo, wind, rain, thunder, animal sounds, music, household appliances).
- Using various pictures for stimulation.
- Making various musical instruments (horns, drums).

A MINI-PLAN INVOLVING SOUND (see also page 17)

Theme: Sounds Around Us

Behavioral Objectives: At the end of the experience, the child will be able to:

1. Identify four out of six sounds.
2. Tell who is most likely to be making that particular sound.
3. Imitate at least three sounds that he heard at home this morning.

Learning Activities:

A tape of familiar sounds will be played while the children listen. The tape will be based on normal home activities. (Sounds of an alarm clock; brushing teeth; going downstairs; preparing breakfast: running water, egg beater or electric mixer, setting table; baby crying; pet wanting to eat; radio or TV; telephone ringing; door bell; door opening and closing; typewriter; car.) Rather than a lot of unrelated sounds, they are arranged so as to be in a logical sequence and could easily be used as part of a story. The second time the tape is played, it is stopped after each sound while the children discuss it. They may come up with even better ideas than the original ones. The children will be encouraged to make sounds they heard earlier in the day and let the other children guess what made the sound.

RHYTHM

- Clapping to the rhythm of the individual children's names.
- Providing rhythm instruments for exploration and enjoyment.
- Using records which portray various rhythms.
- Talking about the rhythm of the body in running, walking, skipping, and stretching. (Some interesting ideas, music, and references can be found in Rosanna R. Saffran's *First Book of Creative Rhythms*, page 176.)
- Picking up the rhythm of activities in which children are involved.
- Talking about the rhythmic movement of animals as they walk.
- Talking about the rhythmic movement of poetry.
- Stimulating children to express their ideas about rhythm.
- Using pictures which portray rhythm.
- Using a metronome.
- Demonstrating and talking about vibration (elastic bands, string instruments).
- Making a burlap or felt container for instruments. Put outline of instrument on each pocket. Children can replace instruments correctly.
- Making a rhythm game with the children. Example: Say, "Show me what you can do with your hands." The children will demonstrate. Then ask same about feet, head, body. Do the actions suggested. Then starting with two or three actions, say, "We can make some signs that would tell us what to do." On board or large sheet of paper, draw a symbol to represent a hand (a mitten, perhaps). ("This tells us when to clap.") Draw a symbol to represent a foot (a shoe perhaps). ("This tells us when to stamp.") Draw a symbol for standing and sitting (a chair perhaps). ("This tells us when to stand up and sit down.") Draw a few symbol patterns on the board. As individuals or as a group, do as the symbols indicate. Some more advanced children will want more symbols and can "write" their own rhythms.

A MINI-PLAN INVOLVING RHYTHM (see also page 17)

Theme: Rhythm Instruments

Behavioral Objectives: At the end of the experience, the child will be able to:

1. Name the different instruments.
2. Demonstrate how each instrument is played.
3. Follow the varying rhythms played on the piano with at least two different instruments.
4. March around the room to the varying rhythms played on the piano, sometimes using an instrument and sometimes not.

Learning Activities: The teacher will introduce the instruments one at a time, calling them by name and placing them in view of the children. After all instruments are out (several of each kind), the children each select one. They are given time to explore and experiment with it. The teacher then begins the rhythm experience by clapping hands in a slow, steady manner, asking the children to play their instruments to the clapping rhythm. Then the piano is played with a slow, steady rhythm changing to a fast, steady rhythm. The children are encouraged to change to a different instrument, and the procedure is repeated. When the children feel comfortable with the instruments and varying rhythms, they are asked to march around the room, still listening to the rhythms. Instruments are then used while the children are marching. Instruments are exchanged several times so that each child has an opportunity to use different instruments. (Be patient and don't expect too much of the children.)

ESPECIALLY FOR PARENTS

Children who have parents with musical talents are indeed fortunate. Those things which parents enjoy are shared with their children. A father who sings, sings with his children. A mother who plays the piano, plays it for her children. Parents who appreciate good music play it around the home and attend concerts. Children pick up these attitudes.

But what of the child who does not have musical parents or opportunities to hear good music? Some parents may have had a negative early musical experience; others may have had no musical exposure; while still others may have had musical opportunities. It is possible that none of these parents sees the real value in music as either enjoyment or physical and emotional release. Here is an excellent opportunity for parents and child to learn together. Even busy or musical parents can learn things with their children.

Here are some ideas to try at home or with your children (select those which are appropriate, or design better ones):

- Activities:
  - If possible, have a record player (one that the children can use) and a variety of records (classical, popular, waltzes, marches). Help the child to learn proper care of the player and the records and also to identify the records by their names ("Grand Canyon Suite").
  - If no record player is available, turn on the radio during musical programs.
  - Help your child make some simple musical instruments (oatmeal boxes for drums, cans or paper tubes with various objects in them (rice, rocks) for shakers, waxed paper over a comb.

101

- Listen to sounds (animals, transportation) and ask him to reproduce them.
- Encourage him to move like things in nature (trees, animals).
- Clap various rhythms for him and see if he can reproduce them.
- Make sounds and have him do the action—then change roles.
- Make a game. Show him a picture of an instrument, and have him imitate the way it is played. Then you imitate the instrument and have him find the picture of it.
- Learn some simple, fun songs with him.
- Dance with him, using a variety of rhythms.
- Imitate household sounds (dripping water, motors, clocks).
- Record the child telling an important incident or story. Play it for the family.
- Use ideas throughout this chapter.
- See *When I Do, I Learn* by Barbara J. Taylor, pp. 116-21, 134-35.

- Community Resources:
  - Take your child to the local music store and ask the clerk to demonstrate some of the instruments.
  - Take him to a concert in the park (it's usually easier for him to sit there than in a formal concert).
  - Take him to a school where a band or an orchestra is playing.
  - Go for a walk and find out how many different sounds you can hear.
  - Take him to the library where you can listen to records.
  - Visit a friend who plays an instrument.
  - Visit a dance studio.

BIBLIOGRAPHY FOR MUSIC, MOVEMENT, SOUND, AND RHYTHM

BOOKS

A. Containing songs and/or music

Andrews, Gladys. *Creative Rhythmic Movement for Children.* Englewood Cliffs, New Jersey: Prentice-Hall, 1954.

Buttolph, Edna G. *Music Is Motion.* Cincinnati: The Willis Music Co., # 6918.

Caines, Gracia. *Happy Songs for Children.* Cincinnati: The Willis Music Co., # 6250.

——————— . *Happy Songs for Children, Book Two.* Cincinnati: The Willis Music Co., # 6923-31.

Dalton, Arlene, Myriel Ashton, and Erla Young. *My Picture Book of Songs.* Chicago: M. A. Donohue & Co., 1947.

McConathy, Osbourne, Russell V. Morgan, James L. Mursell, Marshall Bartholomew, Mabel E. Bray, Edward B. Birge, and W. Otto Miessner. *Music for Early Childhood.* New York: Silver, Burdett, 1952.

Mursell, J. L., and Gladys Tipton. *Music for Living Through the Day.* Morristown, New Jersey: Silver, Burdett, 1962.

Pitts, Lilla Belle, Mabelle Glenn, Lorrain E. Watters, and Louise G. Wersen. *The Kindergarten Book.* Boston: Ginn, 1959.

Renstrom, Moiselle. *Tune Time.* Salt Lake City: Pioneer Music Press, 1957.

——————— . *Rhythm Fun.* Salt Lake City: Pioneer Music Press, 1957.

——————— . *Merrily We Sing.* Salt Lake City: Pioneer Music Press, 1962.

Seeger, Ruth. *American Folk Songs for Children.* Garden City, New York: Doubleday & Co., 1948.

Walker, Mary L. *Songs for Young Children.* New York: Paulist/Newman Press, 1865 Broadway, New York, 10023, 1973.

Wilson, Harry, Walter Ehert, Alice M. Snyder, Edward J. Hermann, and Albert A. Renna. *Growing with Music* (series). Englewood Cliffs, New Jersey: Prentice-Hall, 1963.

Wood, Lucille F., and Louise B. Scott. *Singing Fun.* St. Louis: Webster Publishing Co., 1954.

——————— . *More Singing Fun.* St. Louis: Webster Publishing Co., 1961.

B. Information about Music, Movement, Sound, and Rhythm

Aronoff, Frances W. *Music and Young Children.* New York: Holt, Rinehart, and Winston, 1969.

Burnett, Mollie. *Melody, Movement, and Language.* San Francisco: R and E Research Associates, 4843 Mission Street, 1973.

Doray, Maya. *See What I Can Do.* Englewood Cliffs, New Jersey: Prentice-Hall, 1972.

Gerhardt, Lydia A. Moving and Knowing: *The Young Child Orients Himself in Space.* Englewood Cliffs, New Jersey: Prentice-Hall, 1972.

Green, Marjorie M., and Elizabeth L. Woods. *A Nursery School Handbook for Teachers and Parents.* Sierra Madre, California: Sierra Madre Community Nursery School Association, 1963.

Haupt, Dorothy, and Keith D. Osborn. *Creative Activities.* Detroit: Merrill-Palmer School, 1966.

Landreth, Catherine. *Preschool Learning and Teaching.* New York: Harper & Row, 1972, pp. 103-14.

Leeper, Sarah H., Ruth J. Dales, Dora S. Skipper, and Ralph L. Witherspoon. *Good Schools for Young Children.* New York: Macmillan Co., 1974, pp. 374-86.

Moore, Shirley, and Sally Kilmer. *Contemporary Preschool Education.* New York: John Wiley & Sons, 1974, pp. 141-53.

Read, Katherine. *The Nursery School.* Philadelphia: W. B. Saunders Co., 1971, pp. 228-35.

Sheehy, Emma D. *Children Discover Music and Dance.* New York: Teachers College Press, Columbia University, 1968.

Sinclair, Caroline B. *Movement of the Young Child: Ages Two to Six.* Columbus, Ohio: Charles E. Merrill Pub. Co., 1973.

Spodek, Bernard. *Teaching in the Early Yeras.* Englewood Cliffs, New Jersey: Prentice-Hall, 1972, pp. 189-97.

Taylor, Barbara J. *When I Do, I Learn.* Provo, Utah: Brigham Young University Press, 1974, pp. 114-21.

Todd, Vivian E., and Helen Heffernan. *The Years Before School.* Toronto: Macmillan Co., 1970, pp. 478-503.

Vance, Barbara. *Teaching the Prekindergarten Child.* Monterey, California: Brooks/Cole, 1973, pp. 285-339.

ARTICLES

Bacon, F. D. "Music and the Young Child." *OMEP* 5 (1973):128-30.

Foster, Florence P. "The Song Within: Music and the Disadvantaged Child." *Young Children,* September 1965, p. 373.

Kuhmerker, Lisa. "Music in the Beginning Reading Program." *Young Children,* January 1969, pp. 157-63.

Myerson, Edith S. "Listen to What I Made! From Musical Theory to Usable Instrument." *Young Children,* December 1970, pp. 90-92.

Stecher, Miriam B. "Concept Learning Through Movement Improvisation: The Teacher's Role As Catalyst." *Young Children,* January 1970, pp. 143-53.

PAMPHLETS

Barrett, Mary. *Living Music with Children.* Washington: National Assoc. for the Education of Young Children, 1834 Connecticut, N.W.

Buttolph, Edna G. *Music Without the Piano.* Brooklyn, New York: Early Childhood Education Council of New York, Bedford Avenue and Avenue H. (c/o Brooklyn College), December 1958.

_____. *Music with Young Children* (# 14). New York: Bank Street College of Education, 69 Bank Street.

Jones, Elizabeth. *What Is Music for Young Children?* # 107. Washington: NAEYC, 1834 Connecticut, N.W., 1969.

Proudzinski, John, and Stanley Roth. *It's a Small, Small World, But Larger Than You Think.* Reprinted by DCCDCA, 1974, # 140. $2.00.

Rosenberg, Martha. *It's Fun to Teach Creative Music.* New York: The Playschools Association, 120 West 57th Street, 1963.

RECORD SOURCES FOR YOUNG CHILDREN

See your local record dealer or write to the following for catalogues and/or information:

Bomar Records, 622 Rodier Drive, Glendale, California, 91201.

Children's Music Center, 5373 West Pico Blvd., Los Angeles, California, 90019.

Children's Record Guild, a division of American Recording Society, 27 Thompson Street, New York, New York.

Educational Record Sales, 157 Chambers Street, New York, New York.

Folkways Records, Children's Catalog, 165 West 46th Street, New York, New York, 10036.

Kimbo Educational Records, P. O. Box 246, Dial, N. J., 07723.

Young People's Records, 100 Fifth Avenue, New York, New York.

BOOKS FOR CHILDREN

Author	Title	Publisher
Avery, Kay	*Wee Willow Whistle*	Knopf, 1947
Brown, Margaret W.	*The Little Brass Band*	Harper, 1955
Harrison, David L.	*The Boy with a Drum*	Golden Press, 1969
Horwich, Frances R.	*Here Comes the Band*	Golden Press, 1956
Lacey, Marion	*Picture Book of Musical Instruments*	Golden Press, 1956
McCaffery, William A.	*How to Watch a Parade*	Harper, 1959
Ryland, Lee	*Gordon and the Glockenspiel*	Whitman, 1961
Smith, Eunice	*The Little Red Drum*	Whitman, 1961
Steiner, Charlotte	*Kiki Dances*	Doubleday, 1949
	Kiki Loves Music	Doubleday, 1949

CHAPTER 5

SCIENCE

Often when the word "science" is mentioned, the hearer thinks of chemistry, biology, physics, and other related subjects, and the question often is, "What can preschool children learn about those subjects?" The answer to that is, "They can learn a great deal." They are observant, interested, and easily stimulated. Concepts may need to be simplified and words defined, but most preschoolers are deeply interested in science. It is all around us. We need but to adapt it to the level of the children with whom we are working.

The question, "When do you teach science during the day?" is often asked. And the answer is: use it whenever it fits best into the schedule. It could be part of the creative experience, the prestory activity, the story, the music, or freeplay—or it could be in lieu of any of these activities. Work it in at a time most meaningful for the children. Allow time for questions and exploration.

VALUES FOR CHILDREN

Following are some of the main benefits children derive from having experiences with science:

1. Gaining necessary firsthand experiences.
2. Developing basic concepts.
3. Increasing their skill of observation.
4. Receiving opportunities to use tools, equipment, and familiar materials.
5. Receiving aid in problem solving.
6. Stimulating their curiosity, and their desire for exploration and discovery and receiving an increase in their basic knowledge through answers to their questions.
7. Developing their sensory, physical, emotional, intellectual, spiritual, and social characteristics.

ROLE OF THE TEACHER

As with other areas of curriculum, the teacher's role in science is very important; she must see that the children's experiences with science are of value and interest to them.

Her attitude and feelings about science must be wholesome, and she must feel secure and comfortable about preparing and presenting scientific materials, testing each presentation before presenting it. If any of the children fear certain animals, she should avoid using them in her presentations. Overcoming fear takes patience and requires that a child have several pleasant experiences with the animal he fears.

The teacher should take time to enjoy surroundings with the children. Exploration of natural phenomena can help one develop aesthetic appreciation. As the children explore their surroundings, she should be able to clarify, explain, reinforce, and discuss with them their many questions. If they fail to ask questions or make comments about the world in which they live, it is the responsibility of the teacher to motivate them to become more sensitive. She can do this through the use of pictures, songs, stories, or planned incidents. One teacher stimulated a group of children by bringing a turtle to school and suggesting to them that they find food to feed the new pet.

Another role of the teacher is to supply accurate information, using a vocabulary on a level with the understanding of the children, but not hesitating to introduce and define certain scientific terms in order to increase the vocabulary of the children. Being able to clarify concepts on a preschool level is sometimes difficult, but it is possible. If a child asks a question and the teacher is unable to supply an immediate answer, this does not excuse the teacher from saying, "I am not sure. Let's find out." Then she finds out—perhaps not on that day, but in the immediate future—and conveys the information to the child. Sometimes they find out together.

The teacher also sets limits for the children to explore safely. She determines what limits are necessary and then lets the children have freedom within these guidelines. Science is a matter of exploration.

Another responsibility of the teacher is to make sure the experiences she plans are simple, not dangerous, kept to a minimum indicated by the children's needs and interests, and planned around familiar things. She always relates the *unknown to the known* in order to increase the existing knowledge of the children.

She also nurtures the child's curiosity about living things: animals, insects, plants, and various aspects of reproduction. Having containers of these living things and making opportunities available for the children to see them will stimulate them to participate.

Moreover, the teacher should become more aware of the many possibilities in science (physical, biological, social) to meet the needs of the children. She should be continually on the lookout for ideas and visual aids. Through art experiences, she teaches about such things as color, shape, texture, rhythm, balance, and harmony. This can be done through ideas, experiences, and materials. Through musical experiences, she teaches about sound, rhythm, tones, movement, variations, tempos, and so forth. (See Chapter on "Music, Movement, Sound, and Rhythm.")

The teacher provides a wide variety of experiences but takes cues from the children. Their interests are vital. From participating with and listening to young children, she will increase her own observational powers.

Promoting social contact by providing an experience in which two or more children can share, the teacher plays a passive role rather than an active one in order that the children may explore together. And although she takes the opportunity to encourage spontaneous scientific experiences, she also provides some planned ones, taking every possible opportunity to help children get clear, basic concepts.

The children should be involved in the scientific experiences as they take place; firsthand experience has no substitute. Many children may be reluctant to enter into the activity, but with the assistance of an understanding teacher, they may gain confidence in themselves and in their exploration.

A CHILD GOES FORTH

NEW
REVISED, ENLARGED
EDITION

BARBARA J. TAYLOR

Some kind of follow-up or feedback should follow every scientific experience to test whether the children have learned correct concepts. A preschool teacher had planned the day around the weather, hoping to familiarize the children with the principle of the way in which rain is formed. She readied her equipment and gathered the children around her, then placed a pan of water on a hot plate and waited for it to boil. Next she took a small pyrex custard cup filled with ice and held it over the steam from the pan. Moisture began to collect on the outside of the bowl, and soon drops of water fell as she told the children about the principle of rain. The children sat very attentively until after the demonstration; then without question or comment they went outside to play. She assumed the experiment had been a success. The next morning when a mother brought her mature four-year-old to nursery school, she said, "Would you be interested in the comments Mala Ree made about the science experience you had yesterday?" Of course, the teacher wanted to hear what the mother had to relate. "Mala Ree reported 'Mother, God doesn't make the rain; I learned how to make it at school.' " Without this vital feedback, the teacher would have assumed that the children had gained correct concepts from the experience. She made certain that this child, and the others, understood the "rain" concept.

Because science can be approached from many angles, this section will be divided into three general areas: physical, biological (animals, humans, plants, and food), and social. The bibliography at the end of this section is lengthy; therefore, only suggested teaching aids will be listed here.

Regardless of the scientific experience presented, it should be a good learning experience for each child involved. Songs, pictures, records, poetry, audio-visual aids, experiments, and excursions can be valuable in teaching science to young children.

PHYSICAL SCIENCE

Suggested Teaching Aids

Use the real object whenever possible. If not available, use the next best possible aid. Pictures are good stimulators. Many excellent ones are available.

- Making a game. Have the child focus on one dimension (color). When he knows this, add another dimension (shape). When he understands these, look for something that contains both. Add another dimension (density: thick, thin). Have the child look for something that includes all three. Then add another (size) and look for all four. ("Look for something that is red, square, thin, and large.") Use only as the child is ready to combine dimensions.
- Observing machines at work (dump truck, street sweeper, steam roller, garbage truck, derrick, steam shovel).
- Obeying signals while crossing the street.
- Talking about various methods of communication: telephone, telegraph, radio, television, newspaper, magazine, post office, letter.
- Discussing various fuels and methods of heating: coal, oil, gas, electricity, steam.
- Familiarizing children with gravity by placing a car on an inclined board or a wagon on a slope. A pulley or pump could also be used.
- Talking about balance through use of blocks, teeter-totter, weights.
- Using a magnifying glass to examine various materials and objects.
- Discovering the use of a magnet—things which are attracted and things which are not. Introduce, define, and experiment with new terms—attract and repel, for example. Sprinkle pepper or lightweight visible material over the water. It floats. Dip small piece of soap into the water, and the material goes away from soap (repelled). Sprinkle sugar into the water. The material floats to the sugar (attracted).

- Exploring the uses of household tools and appliances (mixers, vacuums, egg beater).
- Performing simple experiments—dissolving salt or sugar in water.
- Exploring light and shadows by using a flashlight. (Use Robert Louis Stevenson's poem, "My Shadow.")
- Discussing friction.
- Investigating water. It evaporates, cleans things, changes things (rocks, sand), comes in different forms (liquid, gas, solid), and is used for many purposes (mix paint, drink, play). It can be an excellent emotional release. Following are some suggestions for its use:

Siphoning from one container to another.
Floating objects (soap, toys, wood, metals) on it, showing effects of size and weight.
Observing reflections.
Blowing soap bubbles (air and water).
Washing and drying doll clothes (principle of evaporation).
Building dams and canals.
Feeling the force as it comes from the tap.
Building a snowman. Making snow "angels."
Freezing ice and watching it melt. Using ice cubes to set jello.
Evaporating water. (In a pan of water, mark the level and observe each day.)
Stretching various materials over can and pouring water over it. Showing that water goes through some things better than others (fabrics, plastic, paper, rubber).
Watering plants.
Discussing wearing apparel for water (boots, umbrella, apron).
Cleaning up for school.
Observing moisture on glass of ice water on a hot day.

Boiling water to produce steam.

Pouring water through a funnel or from one container to another.

Preparing creative materials.

Drinking.

Preparing food and cooking it.

Changing the consistency of materials such as sand and flour.

Playing with it in a basin or tub.

Using it to wash or bathe.

- Observing shapes (round, square, oblong, free-form, triangle, hexagon, octagon) and things that are these shapes.
- Mixing colors and observing the changes.
- Observing things nearby that are not alive (rocks, soil, liquids, air).
- Discovering the use of a lever.
- Discovering the use of wheels: aid in our work and play, wheels in the home (sewing machine, clocks, motors, pulleys, roller skates, toys).
- Providing substances and their opposites: wet and dry, long and short, hard and soft, hot (or warm) and cold, sweet and sour, rough and smooth.
- Exploring the weather: seasons, time of day, changes, temperature.
- Observing and discussing the weather: fog (watch it move, lift); mist; rain (moisture, wearing apparel, sky, temperature); sun (warmth, light); frost, hail; snow; appropriate wearing apparel for different types of weather.
- Talking about the changes in the sky: sun, moon, and stars.
- Observing cloud formation, movement on windy or rainy days.
- Investigating the characteristics of snow: taste, feel, sight.
- Making a simple chart which shows snow, rain, sun, and wind. An arrow could be turned to indicate the weather for the current day.
- Discussing wind using kites, pinwheels, or balloons; watching smoke; observing dry leaves when wind blows; watching a weather vane or wind sock; discussing how hard the wind is blowing.
- Exploring air: movement made by fan, occupies space, unseen. (Use paper bag, balloon, pinwheel, whistle, parachute, weather vane, tire pump.)
- Observing the difference in temperature in the shade and the sun, or in different seasons of the year.
- Using woodworking tools and materials.
- Making crystals.
- Preparing a mineral garden: Mix 8 teaspoons salt, 8 teaspoons water and 2 teaspoons household ammonia in a pint of water. Pour into a shallow pan. Paint a clinker a variety of colors with water paint; put it into the mixture. Watch it grow. As the water evaporates, it will leave the salt crystals behind.
- Preparing a clinker or coal garden: This garden grows in a hurry. Wash four or five small pieces of coal or clinkers and arrange them in a pan or bowl. Mix together: 1 cup tap water, 6 tablespoons table salt, and 4 teaspoons bluing. Pour over coal or clinkers, letting it drip over each piece. Set the pan in the sunlight. If color is desired, drop one drop of any color of food coloring on each piece. Crystals will form in a few hours, but the larger ones will take several days to grow.
  Note: If a chemical garden using water glass (sodium silicate) and metallic crystals is used, *extreme caution* should be exercised. Water glass is lye, and some of the crystals are poisonous.

111

A MINI-PLAN INVOLVING PHYSICAL SCIENCE
(see also page 17)

Theme: Color

Behavioral Objectives: At the end of the experience, the child will be able to:

1. Name the primary colors.
2. Tell how two other colors were made by mixing primary colors.
3. Demonstrate the combining of colors by using food coloring or cellophane.

Learning Activities:

A low table will be covered with newspaper or butcher paper. Each child will be given a white foam egg carton (with lid removed) and an eye dropper. Some of the egg sections are filled half full of clear water. Small containers of red, yellow, and blue food coloring are available on the table. The children are encouraged to make one section of each of the primary colors and then to combine the colors in any way they like. It isn't long until a child says, "I made green!" "Look at this blue! It's different" "This is purple!" "I can make orange!" The child is encouraged to tell and/or show how he made the different colors. When he has filled all the sections of the carton, they can be rinsed out, and he can explore again. Suggestions could be made to some reluctant children who have not discovered the thrill of making a new color. Also on the table have some pieces of cellophane in the primary colors. Combine these in different ways to make new colors.

Theme: Crystals

Behavioral Objectives: At the end of the experience, the child will be able to:

1. Pick out crystals when shown a variety of things.
2. Define what a crystal is.
3. Discuss the steps in making crystals at school.

Learning Activities:

The teacher will show the children different crystals and rocks. She will explain what a crystal is and what things are crystals (sand, sugar, salt). Then she will show some crystals she made previously. The children are given materials for making crystals to take home. They examine the crystals with a magnifying glass.

Materials and instructions for making crystals:

Method 1: Mix ½ cup each of salt, bluing and water and 1 T ammonia. Pour over crumpled paper towels. In one hour crystals begin to form. They reach a peak in about four hours and last for a couple of days.

Method 2: Break a brick or some charcoal briquets into small pieces. Place several pieces in the center of a bowl. Mix ¼ cup salt, ¼ cup liquid bluing, ¼ cup water, and 1 T ammonia together. Pour solution over the pieces of coal or brick. Fill a medicine dropper with food coloring and drop small amounts over the brick pile. Leave the dish alone and let the crystals grow. Because the crystals will crumble easily, don't move the dish around much. Watch and note when the first crystals appeared and how fast they developed. Crystals are formed because water is drawn into the brick, leaving the solids behind. The ammonia, bluing, and salt form a complex crystal. Use a hand lens to observe the shape. (Challand and Brandt, 1963, p. 72.) Crystals form faster if briquets are warmed first.

BIOLOGICAL SCIENCE

A. Animals

Suggested Teaching Aids

- Discussing insects and how they protect themselves (bees and wasps sting; mosquitos and fleas bite).
- Observing characteristic movement of animals: some swim, some fly, some hop, some walk, some crawl. (Spontaneous delight of children is obvious as they observe movement of animals.)
- Observing physical characteristics of various animals (flipper, wing, webfoot, claws, number of legs).
- Discussing or feeding various animals and observing what they eat (hay, grain, milk, carrots, nuts).
- Observing and discussing birth, nutrition, and habits of animals or insects.
- Observing frogs in various stages (egg, tadpole, frog).
- Bringing a pet to school.
- Discussing and observing various housing for animals (nest, hole, house, cage).
- Observing animals with their young (caring for and feeding them).
- Imitating sounds made by various animals.
- Learning the names of animal babies, male and female.
- Discussing how animals protect themselves (camouflage, hibernation, claws, odor, horns).
- Feeling the covering of various animals (shell, fur, wool, skin, feathers).
- Observing animals at work (mule, bee, ant, spider, beaver, squirrel).
- Discussing ways animals help us (work, food, clothing, protection, transportation).
- Caring for animals: cleaning cages, feeding, watering. (This increases self-reliance in child.)
- Using a heavy paper, make a chart which is a series of pictures about an animal, each picture emphasizing a different part of the animal (head, ear, feet). Make identical pictures on cards. Child matches card to chart.

113

- Discussing ways we care for animals and limits in handling them.
- Observing wild animals at a park or zoo.*
- Visiting a poultry farm.*
- Visiting a dairy and watching the cows being milked.*
- Observing eggs hatching.
- Watching and feeding birds. (Making a bird house or feeder.)
- Observing various birds' nests.
- Watching a caterpillar spin a cocoon.
- Making an ant farm.

A MINI-PLAN FOR ANIMALS (see also page 17)

Theme: Covering of Animals

Behavioral Objectives: At the end of the experience, the child will be able to:

1. Name at least three different coverings of animals.
2. Tell how these coverings help the animal.
3. Describe how each covering feels when touched.
4. Place into groups the animals having the same kind of covering when the child is given a group of pictures.

LEARNING ACTIVITIES:

If possible, the children are taken to a nearby farm to observe animals. If this is not possible, several animals will be brought to the school. The coverings stressed on this day are hair (horse), fur (rabbit), feathers (chicken or other bird), wool (lamb), shell (turtle), and scales (fish). If this seems to be too many for the children involved, use the same theme for several days, or select only a few of the animals. Discussion of each animal includes type of covering, color, how covering helps the animal, feel of the covering, how it differs from other types of covering, where the animal lives, and other facts. Have examples of the coverings for the children to feel even if real animals are brought to school. Give children time to ask and answer questions, make comments, and feel coverings. At the end of the discussion, have a group of pictures of animals with both similar and dissimilar coverings and let the children place them into groups of similar coverings.

B. Humans

Suggested Teaching Aids
- Learning about the different parts of the body (e.g. digestion, heart, tongue, hair, eyes).
- Learning about the senses: sound: listening to sounds of transportation, household, nature (recording or tape would be excellent), exploring sound and movement (see page 65 and Chapter 4); touch: feeling various textures (see page 65); smell: various odors (see page 65); taste: various flavors (see page 65); and sight: observing things which look similar but are different (see page 65).
- Observing a mother bathing, feeding, or dressing a baby.
- Making a "family portrait" by cutting pictures from magazines and pasting on construction paper.
- Observing different characteristics of people (hair coloring, eye coloring, skin coloring, height, weight, sex).

*Community resource

- Discussing ways to help keep us well.
- Discussing things the child can do now that he couldn't do when he was younger.

A MINI-PLAN FOR HUMANS (see also page 17)

Theme: Sense of Touch

Behavioral Objectives: At the end of the experience, the child will be able to:

1. Identify four objects by sense of touch only.
2. Describe four different textures using the proper terms.
3. Arrange textures from one dimension to its opposite (rough-smooth, hard-soft).

Learning Activities:

There will be objects with all the various textures on the bulletin board. The children are encouraged to feel them, describe them, and tell of their uses. Various textures will be provided at the creative table for cutting, pasting, or picture making. At the sensory table, the child will be blindfolded and given an object to feel. Then he is to find an identical object by feeling things on the table. A story is told using the everyday objects in a child's life which are of different textures (soft pillow, stiff brush, smooth water).

C. Plants

Suggested Teaching Aids

- Preparing a nature table, using small and portable objects. Change objects often.
- Providing a museum shelf to include cones, rocks, shells.
- Gathering various kinds of seeds (flower, vegetable, weed).
- Observing changes in nature.
- Discussing uses of plants for food, clothing, and shelter.
- Discussing the cycle of a tree and its uses (paper, lumber).
- Observing the growth of seeds in a terrarium: roots growing downward and stems growing upward. Plant seeds close to glass sides of terrarium.
- Caring for plants. They need air, water, sunshine, and soil.
- Exploring the growth of plants (peas growing on vine, potatoes growing on root, corn growing on stalk, and lettuce growing in leaves).
- Sprouting seeds (alfalfa, beans, others).
- Planting seeds from fruit (oranges, apples, grapes, grapefruit). Dry seeds two to three hours. Plant in soil. Water each day.
- Observe growth.
- Growing miniature garden indoors (reap, prepare, and use vegetables, fruits, or sprouts).
- Making a series of pictures about a plant (with heavy paper) and placing these on a chart, each picture emphasizing a different part of the plant (blossom, root, leaves). Making individual cards identical to chart. Child matches card to chart.
- Observing growth of vegetables in water (tops of carrots or turnips in saucer, bird seed on damp sponge, sweet potato or carrot in jar).
- Planting and caring for a garden.
- Planting bulbs in cans or cartons.
- Taking a nature walk.

A MINI-PLAN FOR PLANTS (see also page 17)

Theme: Beans

Behavioral Objectives: At the end of the experience, the child will be able to:
1. Identify bean seeds when given a variety of seeds.
2. Name three different ways we eat beans (sprouts, green, dried).
3. Describe how a bean grows.

Learning Activities:

Bean seeds, along with a variety of other seeds (beet, radish, carrot, tomato, others) will be placed on the science table. The produce itself (or a picture of it) will be with its own seeds. The teacher will help the child point out characteristics of the various seeds so that he can identify them. The various seeds will also be used for a collage. An appropriate bean dish will be served for lunch (string, chili, lima) or snack (sprouts or bean salad). Bean seeds for sprouting and planting have been soaked overnight. The children plant string beans in a terrarium (so that they can see the roots, stems, and other parts) and also in paper cups or in a garden. Seeds for sprouting are placed in a wire or plastic container. The children care for both kinds of seeds, noting the daily changes.

D. Food (See also Chapter 10)

Suggested Teaching Aids

- Discussing the different tastes of food (sour, sweet, bitter, salty, other). Also showing where taste buds are located in the tongue.
- Discussing food that grows in water (e.g. fish, shrimp, crab, oysters).
- Preparing vegetables and fruits for eating or cooking.
- Observing different colors of fruits and vegetables.
- Feeling different coverings of fruits and vegetables.
- Tasting fruits or vegetables in various forms (raw, cooked, juice).
- Experimenting with coconut (husk, shell, liquid, chunks, shredded).
- Making applesauce.
- Discussing and making butter.
- Discussing and making ice cream.
- Observing differences when heat is applied to eggs (raw, soft boiled, hard boiled).
- Making soup.
- Popping popcorn.
- Making bread.
- Making cookies.
- Making gelatin.
- Making puddings, instant or cooked.
- Providing empty food containers to stimulate interest in domestic area.
- Using basic four food chart, food stuffs, or pictures.
- Providing dishes which contain a certain food commodity in various forms, e.g. sugar (raw, refined, brown, powdered).

A MINI-PLAN FOR FOOD (see also page 17)

Theme: Apples

Behavioral Objectives: At the end of this experience, the child will be able to:
1. Tell at least three ways apples are prepared for eating.
2. Name at least two colors of apples.
3. Tell how apples are grown.

4. Name at least four parts of the apple.
5. Discuss the steps in making applesauce.

Learning Activities:

Pictures of apples in a variety of different settings are placed on the bulletin board. Nearby is a low table which has been covered with butcher paper. It contains apples of different colors and sizes. The teacher discusses the apples with the children (how grown, various colors, different ways in which we eat them, the kind of covering, whatever). Children wash their hands. Under careful supervision of the teacher, the children peel, core and cut the apples for applesauce. The apples are placed in an electric sauce pan and cooked. Applesauce is served for snack.

SOCIAL SCIENCE

Suggested Teaching Aids

- Talking about the roles of various family members (mother, father, sister, brother, baby, grandparents).
- Discussing various community helpers (policeman, fireman, doctor, nurse, baker, farmer, cook, teacher).
- Inviting one of the community helpers to the school.*
- Discussing the occupations of fathers and mothers of the children in the group.
- Asking the children what they want to be when they grow up and what they know about that occupation.
- Discussing ways we help each other.
- Providing props for dramatic play about various occupations.
- Making a mural which shows important landmarks in the community (homes of the children, schools, churches, stores, other places).
- Taking an excursion through your community (walk, car, bus), noting important landmarks.*

A MINI-PLAN INVOLVING SOCIAL SCIENCE
(see also page 17)

Theme: Park

Behavioral Objectives: At the end of this experience, the child will be able to:

1. Describe some of the activities or areas included in most parks.
2. Describe how parks are cared for.
3. Discuss why we have parks and who uses them.

Learning Activities:

If possible, take the children on an excursion to a nearby park. Let them play in the various areas and on the equipment. Take a walk with them around the park, noting the trees, shrubs, buildings, and other things. Have a story and a snack under one of the trees. Discuss with the children the importance of keeping the park clean and tidy. Ask them if they have ever been to other parks and if so, what they did there that might be either the same or different from this park.

If unable to visit, discuss parks, using visual aids like pictures and books. Ask the children how many have ever visited a park, what they did at the park, and how we care for them. Role play different situations (play, picnic).

*Community resource

ESPECIALLY FOR PARENTS

Parents, be observant of the things which are happening in your own home and community. There are so many things children can learn about science if experiences and time for exploration are provided for them. You, too, may learn some very interesting facts. As in the chapters of this book, look at the ideas to see how practical or feasible they are for you and your child. If they are good, use them. If they are inappropriate, substitute some better ones. These are suggestions only to help you become more aware of the environment and how it relates to your child.

Almost anything we do is a part of science, whether it is classed as physical, biological, or social, and young children are interested in what is going on around them. Since you are with your child much more than a teacher, you have many more opportunities to help him understand science—a fascinating subject. For example, do you know why we use salt when we freeze ice cream? Do you know what makes popcorn pop? Do you know the principle of gravity? How can heavy airplanes stay up in the air—or heavy boats keep from sinking? Don't let these simple questions frighten you away from science. If you don't know the answers, take the child to the library (or to a book) and see if you can find out together. Keep the information simple and on his level of understanding. Complicated lectures will discourage him from asking you questions in the future. You might even ask a friend who is a "scientist" to help you, a school teacher, a college student, or someone who reads and understands scientific data. There are many sources to help you; so utilize them. The bibliography at the end of this chapter has many books listed where you can find information and even books to share with your child.

Ideas abound for discovering things with your child (depending on where you live), and only a few suggestions for each of the three subareas (physical, biological, and social) will be listed here.

By all means, enjoy science *with* your child. It's really a fascinating world!

PHYSICAL SCIENCE

- Take your child to a local museum, planetarium, aquarium, or a rock show.*
- Discuss recycling of water and resources.
- Observe the stars and moon at night.
- Put your ear to the ground and listen to the activity below the soil.
- Visit a local water resource (dam, lake, fountain, storage tank).*
- Show how wheels help you daily.
- Tell your child about how you heat or cool your home, cook food, and other things.
- Tell him some of the techniques you use in your work or home (safety factors, efficient use of time and energy).
- Give him many water experiences.
- Discuss the daily and seasonal weather with him.
- Make a game: Get a piece of cardboard about twelve inches square. Divide it into four squares and color each square one of the following colors: red, yellow, blue, and white. Have your child help you cut out pictures of flowers that are each of the above colors and paste on the individual cards. Make a spinner with the four colors represented plus two more colors like green and black. Flip the spinner. If it lands on one of four main colors, take one flower of that color. If it lands on green or black, that turn is forfeited. Play until all flowers have been "won".

BIOLOGICAL SCIENCE

Animals

- Get him a pet and help him care for it.
- Take him to a zoo, a pet shop, an animal farm.*
- Visit someone who has an unusual pet or who raises animals.*
- Discuss local insects with him (bees, mosquitos, fleas).
- Discuss how and where various animals live. Visit some if possible.
- Take him to a local dairy or poultry farm.*
- Take a walk and look for birds, insects, and animals common to your community.*
- Visit a fish hatchery—or go fishing.*
- Make a bird house or bath.

Humans

- Help him learn how and why we keep our bodies clean (washing, brushing hair and teeth, resting or sleeping, eating good food).
- Help him learn about his body by discussing it with him, showing him replicas or pictures, thereby helping him to have a positive attitude toward himself.
- Give him some enjoyable, stimulating sensory experiences.
- Help him to recognize and appreciate different physical characteristics of people.
- Visit a friend or neighbor who has several children.*
- Play a game with him: "If you wanted to find out about something, what would you do?" (Feel, ask, see, smell, listen).
- Make up your own ideas to help him integrate parts of his body.
- Make an animal game like the color game under physical science.

*Community resource

Plants and Food

- Plant a garden. Provide a special area for the child.
- Go on a nature walk. Gather leaves, cones, other things.*
- Sprout seeds in your kitchen (use screen or plastic tray or flower pots).
- Get some seed tapes from variety or grocery store and plant them indoors.
- Grow herbs or seasonings in a hanging pot in the kitchen.
- Grow some vegetables in water (carrot or turnip tops, sweet potato, others).
- Grow some fruit or vegetables in soil (pineapple top, avocado pit, others).
- Plant seeds indoors in empty milk carton (cut lengthwise), muffin tin, egg shells, egg cartons, ice cube trays.
- Plant a terrarium.
- Make a bottle garden.
- Get some house plants (African violets, ferns, ornamental fruit trees).
- Plant some bulbs in glass jar. Put some bulbs with head pointed upward and some pointed downward. Observe how stem always grows upward.
- Let the child water house plants.
- At Christmastime, purchase a tree with needles (in large can) which can be decorated and then planted outside in the spring.
- Put strawberry plants in wooden or clay barrel.
- Make some hanging baskets for the porch or patio.
- Make some duplicate leaf cards and then play a game (similar to "Old Maid").
- Put a stalk of celery in water containing food coloring. Observe how the water is carried to the leaves.
- Purchase some fresh cobs of popcorn. Let dry, then make popcorn.
- Purchase and observe Indian corn.
- Observe the landscaping around your home and area.
- Go to the park.*
- Visit a seed store, plant nursery, local orchard, commercial garden, berry patch, greenhouse).*
- Purchase (or grow) squash or pumpkin. Eat the produce but save the seeds. Dry them and roast them for eating, or plant them for growing.
- Assist your child in pressing flowers and/or leaves.
- Let him arrange a vase of flowers.
- Gather a variety of weeds and help make an arrangement.
- Purchase some raw peanuts. Shell and roast them. Then make peanut butter by grinding the peanuts.
- Let him assist in grocery shopping, especially produce buying.*
- Visit a local cannery.*
- Show the child how you prepare food for storage (refrigerator, pantry, canning, bottling, freezing, drying).
- Let him assist in food preparation.
- Show him how heat changes food.
- Have a chart and show what constitutes a good diet. Let him check off the things he eats each day.
- Make a drying frame and dry some fruit (make fruit leather).

Social Science

- Take a tour around the community.* Point out various people who assist us—also interesting and important landmarks.
- Take a trip to the fire station, police station, post office, hospital.*
- Take your child to a doctor and a dentist for a check-up.*

*Community resource

- As you do daily errands, briefly tell the child how these people help us (service station attendant, cleaner, barber, baker, banker, grocer).*
- Assist him in doing something nice for a neighbor, relative, friend (a visit, a treat, an errand).
- Discuss occupations of family members with him.
- Talk about your extended family (grandparents, aunts and uncles, cousins) and visit them.
- Ask him to tell you things that make him happy and how he can make others happy. Discuss good social techniques.
- Invite guests into your home and let the child help entertain them.
- Let him entertain some of his friends.
- Take a picnic to the park.*
- Take him to church.*
- Take him to community affairs that would be appropriate.*
- Take him to an athletic event.*
- If possible, visit a local radio or TV station.*
- Go swimming at a community pool.*

BIBLIOGRAPHY FOR SCIENCE

BOOKS FOR TEACHERS AND PARENTS

Arey, Charles K. *Science Experiences for Elementary Schools.* New York: Columbia University, Bureau of Publications, Teachers College, 1961.

Brinton, Henry. *Sound.* New York: John Day Co., 1963.

Caney, Steven. *Toy Book.* New York: Workman Publishing Co., 1972.

Carmichael, Viola S. *Science Experiences for Young Children.* Pasadena, Calif.: 1886 Kinneola Canyon Road, 91107.

Challand, Helen, and Elizabeth Brandt. *Science Activities from A to Z.* Chicago: Children's Press, 1963.

Haupt, Dorothy, and Keith Osborn. *Creative Activities.* Detroit: Merrill-Palmer, 1966.

Hildebrand, Verna. *Introduction to Early Childhood Education.* New York: Macmillan Co., 1971, pp. 136-66.

Landreth, Catherine. *Preschool Learning and Teaching.* New York: Harper & Row, 1972, pp. 73-92.

Leeper, Sarah H., Ruth J. Dales, Dora S. Skipper, and Ralph L. Witherspoon. *Good Schools for Young Children.* New York: Macmillan Co., 1974, pp. 301-16.

McGavack, John J., and Donald P. LaSalle. *Guppies, Bubbles, and Vibrating Objects.* New York: John Day Co., 1972.

Moore, Shirley, and Sally Kilmer. *Contemporary Preschool Education.* New York: John Wiley & Sons, 1974, pp. 64-119.

Navarra, J. G. *The Development of Scientific Concepts in a Young Child.* New York: Columbia University, Teachers College, 1955.

Neal, Charles D. *Adventures in Science.* Racine, Wisc.: Whitman Publishing Co., 1963.

Parker, Bertha M. *Electricity.* Basic Science Education Series. Evanston, Ill.: Row, Peterson, 1944.

*Community resource

_____ . *Magnets.* Basic Science Education Series. Evanston, Illinois: Row, Peterson.

_____ . *The Air About Us.* Basic Science Education Series. Evanston, Illinois: Row, Peterson, 1941.

_____ . *Thermometers, Heat, and Cold.* Basic Science Education Series. Evanston, Illinois: Row, Peterson, 1942.

_____ . *Machines.* Basic Science Education Series. Evanston, Illinois: Row, Peterson, 1944.

_____ . *Water.* Basic Science Education Series. Evanston, Illinois: Row, Peterson, 1944.

_____ . *The Ways of the Weather.* Basic Science Education Series. Evanston, Illinois: Row, Peterson.

_____ . *Toys.* Basic Science Education Series. Evanston, Illinois: Row, Peterson, 1949.

Pine, Tillie S., and Joseph Levine. *Light All Around.* New York: McGraw-Hill, 1961.

_____ . *Heat All Around.* New York: McGraw-Hill, 1963.

Podendorf, Illa. *True Book of Pebbles and Shells.* Chicago: Children's Press, 1960.

_____ . *True Book of Weather Experiments.* Chicago: Children's Press, 1961.

Read, Katherine. *The Nursery School.* Philadelphia: W. B. Saunders, 1971, pp. 215-22.

Russell, Solveig Paulson. *Lines and Shapes.* New York: Henry Z. Walck, 1965.

Schneider, Herman and Nina. *Let's Find Out.* New York: Scott, 1946.

——————. *How Big Is Big: From Stars to Atoms.* New York: Scott, 1946.

——————. *Now Try This: A Second Let's Find Out.* New York: Scott, 1947.

——————. *Let's Look Inside Your House.* New York: Scott, 1948.

Shuttlesworth, Dorothy. *The Story of Ants.* Garden City: Doubleday & Co., 1964.

——————. *The Story of Spiders.* Garden City: Garden City Books, 1959.

Skelsey, Alice, and Gloria Huckaby. *Growing Up Green.* New York: Workman Publishing Co., 1973.

Spodek, Bernard. *Teaching in the Early Years.* Englewood Cliffs, New Jersey: Prentice-Hall, 1972, pp. 113-35 and 155-75.

Taylor, Barbara J. *When I Do, I Learn.* Provo, Utah: Brigham Young University Press, 1974, pp. 55-111.

Todd, Vivian E., and Helen Heffernan. *The Years Before School.* Toronto: Macmillan Co., 1970, pp. 306-52.

Ubell, Earl. *The World of Push and Pull.* New York: Antheneum, 1954.

Valens, E. G. *Magnet.* Cleveland: World Publishing Co., 1964.

Vance, Barbara. *Teaching the Prekindergarten Child.* Monterey, Calif.: Brooks/Cole, 1973, pp. 339-53.

Vermeer, Jackie, and Marian Lariviere. *The Little Kid's Craftbook.* New York: Taplinger Publishing Co., 1973, pp. 110-17.

Ware, Kay. *Let's Read about Butterflies.* St. Louis: Webster Publishing Co., 1957. (Webster Classroom Science Library has a great variety of science books.)

Yates, R. *Science with Simple Things.* New York: Appleton-Century-Crofts, 1940.

ARTICLES FOR TEACHERS AND PARENTS

Althouse, Rosemary, and Cecil Main. "The Science Learning Center: Hub of Science Activities." *Childhood Education,* February 1974, pp. 222-26.

Bennett, Lloyd M., Rose F. Spicola, and Marcia Vogelsang. "Preschool Children Learn Science." *Science and Children* 7 (May 1970): 10-11.

Bennett, Lloyd M. "Pre-Student Teaching Experience Using Science with Three-through Five-Year-Old Children." *School Science and Mathematics* 72 (April 1972): 301-7.

——————. "Teaching Science Concepts to Preschoolers." *School Science and Mathematics* 69 (November 1969): 731-37.

Croft, Doreen, and Robert Hess. *An Activities Handbook for Teachers of Young Children.* New York: Houghton Mifflin, 1972, pp. 61-79.

Hucklesby, Sylvia. "Opening Up the Classroom: A Walk Around the School." Urbana, Illinois: University of Illinois, ERIC Clearinghouse on Early Childhood Education, 1971.

King, W. H. "The Development of Scientific Concepts in Children." In Mills, Belen (ed.) *Understanding the Young Child and His Curriculum.* New York: The Macmillan Company, 1972, pp. 347-71.

Kluge, Jean. "What the World Needs Now: Environmental Education for Young Children." *Young Children,* May 1971, pp. 260-63.

Kolson, Clifford J., George C. Jeffers, and Paul H. Lamb. "The Oral Science Vocabulary of Kindergarten Children." In Mills, Belen (ed.) *Understanding the Young Child and His Curriculum.* New York: The Macmillan Company, 1972, pp. 380-89.

Newman, Donald. "Sciencing for Young Children." *Young Children*, April 1972, pp. 215-26.

Piltz, Albert, Glenn Blough, and Ruth Roche. *Discovering Science: A Readiness Book.* A Teacher's Guide, Columbus, Ohio. Charles E. Merrill, re. 1973 (science for the four- and five-year-olds).

Weaver, V. Phillips. "Social Concepts for Early Childhood Education." In Mills, Belen (ed.) *Understanding the Young Child and His Curriculum.* New York: The Macmillan Company, 1972, pp. 391-401.

Zeitler, W. R. "Preliminary Report on a Pre-Primary Science Program." *School Science and Mathematics* 69 (May 1969): 417-25.

PAMPHLETS FOR TEACHERS AND PARENTS

A.C.E.I. Publications, Ruth Roche, coordinator. *Young Children and Science.* 3615 Wisconsin Avenue N.W., Washington, D.C. 20016.

Bank Street Publication. *Firsthand Experiences & Sensory Learning.* New York: 69 Bank Street, New York 14, New York.

Books in the Pre-School (# 121). Washington: NAEYC, 1834 Connecticut Avenue N.W., 1970. $2.00.

Friedman, David B., and Dorothy Colodny. *Water, Sand and Mud as Play Materials.* Washington: NAEYC, 1834 Connecticut Avenue N.W.

Haupt, Dorothy. *Science Experiences for Nursery School Children.* # 103. National Association for Nursery Education, Washington, D.C.: 1834 Connecticut Avenue N.W.

Hochman, Vivienne, and Mildred Greenwald. *Science Experiences in Early Childhood Education.* New York: Bank Street Publication, 69 Bank Street, New York 14, New York.

Multi-Ethnic Books for Young Children: An Annotated Bibliography for Parents and Teachers (# 122). Washington: NAEYC, 1834 Connecticut Avenue N.W., 1970. $2.00.

Rudolph, Marguerita. *Toward Science.* New York: Early Childhood Education Council of New York City, 51 West 4th Street.

Zim, Herbert. *Science for Children & Teachers*, # 91. Washington: ACEI, 1953.

BOOKS FOR CHILDREN, TEACHERS, AND PARENTS

Physical Science

Author	Name of Book	Publisher
Aliki	*Fossils Tell of Long Ago*	Thos. Y. Crowell, 1972
	The Long Lost Coelacanth and Other Living Fossils	
Balestrino, Phillip	*Hot As an Ice Cube*	Thos. Y. Crowell
Bartlett, M. F.	*The Clean Brook*	Thos. Y. Crowell
	Where the Brook Begins	
Berkeley, Ethel S.	*Big and Little, Up and Down*	Wm. R. Scott, 1950

Branley, F. M.	*Air Is All Around You*	Thos. Y. Crowell, 1962
	The Big Dipper	
	The Beginning of the Earth	
	Flash, Crash, Rumble & Roll	1964
	Floating and Sinking	
	Gravity Is a Mystery	
	The Moon Seems to Change	1960
	North, South, East and West	1966
	Oxygen Keeps You Alive	
	Rain and Hail	
	Rockets and Satellites	
	Snow Is Falling	1963
	The Sun: Our Nearest Star	1964
	Weight and Weightlessness	
	What Makes Day and Night?	1961
	What the Moon Is Like	1963
Bulla, C. R.	*What Makes a Shadow?*	Thos. Y. Crowell, 1962
Darby, Gene	*What Is a Season?*	Benefic Press, 1959
	What Is a Rock?	
	What Is a Magnet?	
	What Is a Rocket?	
	What Is the Solar System?	
	What Is a Machine?	1961
	What Is Light?	
	What Is Air?	
	What Is Gravity?	
	What Is Weather?	
	What Is Electricity?	
	What Is Water?	
	What Is a Star?	
Friskey, Margaret	*The True Book of Air Around Us*	Children's Press, 1953
Gallant, Kathryn	*Jonathon Plays with the Wind*	Coward McCann, 1958
Gans, Roma	*Millions and Millions of Crystals*	Thos. Y. Crowell
	Icebergs	
	Water for Dinosaurs and You	
	The Wonder of Stones	
Goldin, Augusta	*The Bottom of the Sea*	Thos Y. Crowell, 1966
	Salt	
	The Sunlit Sea	
Gottleib, Suzanne	*What Is Red?*	Lothrop, Lee, 1961
Hoberman, Mary A. and Norma	*How Do I Go?*	Little, Brown, 1958
Huntington, Harriet E.	*Let's Go Outdoors*	Doubleday, 1939
Jeruchim, Cecile	*Hello! Do You Know My Name?*	Putnam's Sons, 1963
	(Book about lines and shapes)	
Johnson, Ryerson	*Upstairs and Downstairs*	Thos. Y. Crowell
Keats, Ezra	*The Snowy Day*	Viking Press, 1962
Kessler, Ethel and Leonard	*Pling, Plink Goes the Water in My Sink*	Doubleday, 1954
Miles, Betty	*What Is the World?*	Knopf, 1958
Pease, Josephine	*This Is the World*	E. M. Hale, 1960
Podendorf, Illa	*The True Book of Science Experiments*	Children's Press (E. M. Hale), 1954
	The True Book of Magnets and Electricity	Children's Press (E. M. Hale), 1961
Rinkoff, Barbara	*A Map Is a Picture*	Thos Y. Crowell, 1965
Schlein, Miriam	*Snow Time*	Whitman, 1962
	Shapes	Wm. R. Scott, 1952
Schneider, Herman and Nina	*Let's Find Out*	Wm. R. Scott, 1946
Simon, Norma	*The Wet World*	Lippincott, 1954
Showers, Paul	*In the Night*	Thos. Y. Crowell
Tangborn, W. V.	*Glaciers*	Thos. Y. Crowell

Tresselt, Alvin	*Rain Drop Splash*	Lothrop, Lee, 1946
	Follow the Road	1953
	Follow the Wind	1950
Wyler, Rose	*First Book of Science Experiments*	Franklin, Watts, 1952
Zaffo, George and Chas. Black	*Big Book of Airplanes*	Grossett & Dunlap
Zolotow, Charlotte	*When the Wind Stops*	Abelard-Schuman, 1962

Biological Science

Animals

Aliki	*My Visit to the Dinosaurs*	Thos. Y. Crowell, 1969
Bancroft, H., and R. Van Gelder	*Animals in Winter*	Thos. Y. Crowell
Branley, F. M.	*Big Tracks, Little Tracks*	Thos. Y. Crowell, 1960
Collier, Ethel	*Who Goes There in My Garden?*	Young Scott, 1963
Cooke, Ann	*Giraffes at Home*	Thos. Y. Crowell
Crawford, Mel	*The Turtle Book*	Golden Press, 1965
Darby, Gene	*What Is a Chicken?*	Benefic Press, 1957
	What Is a Butterfly?	1958
	What Is a Cow?	1957
	What Is a Frog?	1957
	What Is a Fish?	1958
	What Is a Turtle?	1959
	What Is a Bird?	1960
Dugan, William	*The Bug Book*	Golden Press, 1965
Flack, Marjorie	*Tim Tadpole and the Great Bullfrog*	Doubleday, 1934
Friskey, Margaret	*Johnny and the Monarch*	Children's Press, 1961
	The True Book of Birds We Know	1954
Gans, Roma	*Birds at Night*	Thos. Y. Crowell
	Birds Eat and Eat and Eat	1963
	Bird Talk	
	Hummingbirds in the Garden	
	It's Nesting Time	1964
Garelick, May	*Where Does the Butterfly Go When It Rains?*	Young Scott, 1961
	What's Inside?	1965
Goldin, Augusta	*Ducks Don't Get Wet*	Thos. Y. Crowell
	Spider Silk	1964
Hawes, Judy	*Bees and Beelines*	Thos. Y. Crowell, 1964
	Fireflies in the Night	
	Ladybug, Ladybug, Fly Away Home	1967
	Shrimps	1966
	Watch Honeybees with Me	1964
	What I Like about Toads	1969
	Why Frogs Are Wet	1968
	My Daddy Longlegs	1972
Humphreys, Dena	*Big Book of Animals Every Child Should Know*	Grossett & Dunlap
Hurd, Edith T.	*Sandpipers*	Thos. Y. Crowell
	Starfish	
Kaufmann, John	*Bats in the Dark*	Thos. Y. Crowell, 1972
Lerner, Marguerite	*Fur, Feathers, Hair*	Lerner Pub. (Medical Books Books for Children), 196
Mason, George F.	*Animal Sounds*	Morrow, 1948
Mizumura, Kazue	*The Blue Whale*	Thos. Y. Crowell
	The Emperor Penguins	1969
Podendorf, Illa	*The True Book of Spiders*	Children's Press, n.d.
	The True Book of Insects	1954

Schlein, Miriam	*Fast Is Not a Ladybug*	Wm. R. Scott, 1953
	Heavy Is a Hippopotamus	1954
Selsam, Millicent E.	*All about Eggs*	Wm. R. Scott, 1952
Simon and Schuster	*Golden Nature Guides—Insects, Birds, Trees, Flowers, and Reptiles*	Simon and Schuster
Skaar, Grace	*What Do They Say?*	Wm. R. Scott, 1950
Steiner, Charlotte	*Patsy's Pet*	Doubleday, 1955
Waters, John	*Green Turtle Mysteries*	Thos. Y. Crowell
Woodcock, Louise	*This Is the Way the Animals Walk*	Wm. R. Scott, 1956

Humans

Aliki	*My Five Senses*	Thos. Y. Crowell, 1962
	My Hands	
Balestrino, Phillip	*The Skeleton Inside You*	Thos. Y. Crowell
Branley, F. M.	*High Sounds, Low Sounds*	Thos. Y. Crowell, 1967
Brown, Margaret Wise	*The City Noisy Book*	Harper, 1939
	The Country Noisy Book	1940
	The Indoor Noisy Book	1942
	The Noisy Book	Wm. R. Scott, 1939
	The Quiet Noisy Book	Harper, 1950
	The Seashore Noisy Book	Harper, 1941
	Shhhh Bang! A Whispering Book	Harper, 1943
	The Summer Noisy Book	Harper, 1951
	The Winter Noisy Book	Harper, 1947

Darby, Gene	*What Is a Sound?*	Benefic Press
Goldin, Augusta	*Straight Hair, Curly Hair*	Thos. Y. Crowell, 1966
Parker, Bertha M.	*Sound*	Row, Peterson, 1952
Podendorf, Illa	*The True Book of Sounds We Hear*	Children's Press (E. M. Hale), 1955, 1971
Schlein, Miriam	*Little Red Nose*	Abelard-Schuman, 1955
Selsam, Millicent E.	*A Time For Sleep*	Wm. R. Scott, 1953
Showers, Paul and Kay	*A Baby Starts to Grow*	Thos. Y. Crowell
	Before You Were a Baby	
	A Drop of Blood	1967
	Finding Out by Touching	
	Follow Your Nose	
	Hear Your Heart	
	How Many Teeth?	1966
	How You Talk	
	The Listening Walk	
	Look at Your Eyes	
	Use Your Brain	
	What Happens to a Hamburger?	
	Your Skin and Mine	1965
Wolff, Janet	*Let's Imagine Sounds*	Sutton, 1962

Plants and Food

Adelson, Leone	*Please Pass the Grass*	David McKay, 1960
Bancroft, Henrietta	*Down Come the Leaves*	Thos. Y. Crowell
Bulla, C. R.	*A Tree Is a Plant*	1960
Darby, Gene	*What Is a Tree?*	Benefic Press, 1957
	What Is a Plant?	1960
Downer, Mary L.	*The Flower*	Young Scott, 1955
Eggleston, Joyce S.	*Things That Grow*	Melmont, 1958
Goldin, Augusta	*Where Does Your Garden Grow?*	Thos. Y. Crowell
Jordan, Helene J.	*How a Seed Grows*	Thos. Y. Crowell, 1960
	Seeds by Wind and Water	1962
Krauss, Ruth	*The Carrot Seed*	Harpers, 1945
Rothschild, Alice	*Fruit Is Ripe for Timothy*	
Selsam, Millicent E.	*Seeds and More Seeds*	Harper, 1959
	Play with Plants	Wm. Morrow
Smith, Laura and Ernie	*Things That Grow*	Melmont, 1958
Udry, Janice May	*A Tree Is Nice*	Harper, 1956
Webber, Irma E.	*Up Above and Down Below*	Wm. R. Scott, 1943
	Travelers All	1963
	Bits That Grow Big	1949

Social Science

Adorjan, Carol M.	*Someone I Know*	Random House, 1968
Anglund, Joan	*A Friend Is Someone Who Likes You*	Harcourt, Brace, 1958
Becky	*Tall Enough Tommy*	Children's Press, 1946
Berends, Polly B.	*Who's That in the Mirror?*	Random House
Berman, Rhoda	*When You Were a Little Baby*	Lothrup, Lee & Shepard, 19
Brown, Myra B.	*First Night Away from Home*	Franklin Watts (N.Y.), 1960
Bryant, Bernice	*Let's Be Friends*	Children's Press
Buckley, Helen E.	*Grandfather and I*	Lothrup, Lee & Shepard, 19
	Grandmother and I	1961
Burton, Virginia Lee	*Mike Mulligan and His Steam Shovel*	Houghton Mifflin, 1939
Dillon, Ina K.	*Policeman*	Melmont Pub., 1957
Francoise	*What Do You Want to Be?*	Scribners Sons, 1957

Greene, Carla	*"I Want to Be a . . ."* (series)	Children's Press
	Fisherman, Bus Driver,	
	Train Engineer, Animal	
	Doctor, Dentist, Postman,	
	Space Pilot, Nurse, Baseball	
	Player, and others	
Hastings, Evelyn B.	*About Postmen*	Melmont Pub., 1957
Heffelfinger and Hoffman	*About Our Friendly Helpers*	Melmont Pub., 1957
	About Firemen	
Lattin, Anne	*Peter's Policeman*	Follett Pub., 1958
Parks, Gale	*Here Comes Daddy*	Wm. R. Scott, 1951
Penn, Ruth B.	*Mommies Are for Loving*	Putnam's Sons
Puner, Helen W.	*Daddies, What They Do All Day*	Lothrop, Lee & Shepard, 1946
	Mommies, What They Do All Day	
Taylor, Barbara J.	*I Can Do*	Provo, Ut.: BYU Press, 1972
Thompson, Frances B.	*About Doctor John*	Melmont Pub., 1961
Udry, Janice M.	*Let's Be Enemies*	Harper, 1961
Watts, Mabel	*Little Campers*	Rand McNally, 1963
Young, W. Edward	*Norman and the Nursery School*	Platt & Munk, 1959

CHAPTER 6

PRESTORY ACTIVITIES

This section is called "Prestory Activities" because it contains ideas which can be used to prepare children for story time. These ideas can be used with only one child, a small group, or a large group as children assemble for any group experience.

Is there any value to having a planned activity for children as they prepare for a group experience? If the activity is planned with the children's needs and interests in mind, if it is planned on the children's level, if it encourages children to participate, if it has some learning connected with it, if it is an enjoyable experience, and if it is of short duration, the answer is "Yes." But the "ifs" are very important. All of the "ifs" might not be covered with each activity you plan, but try to include as many as possible.

Vary the activity each day to keep the interest level of the children high. They will feel that they had better get into story or group time or they might miss something. The teacher begins the activity with the arrival of the first child or children. As others complete their present activity, they join the group for an enjoyable, interesting experience. (If a teacher waits until all children are there before she begins, there is no incentive for the children to get there. "Why hurry so you can wait?")

Some Suggested Teaching Aids

- *Animal.* Have an animal concealed until group time. Then bring it into the group or take the children to the animal, whichever is more appropriate.
- *Chalk on Blackboard.* With the teacher drawing crude stick figures, the children can supply a story. It is surprising how rapidly the story content can change. Some children who do not ordinarily express themselves become verbal in such a setting. Accept the children's ideas and let the story flow freely.
- *Children Tell Original Stories.*
  A. Without props or aids
     One day a group of children was ready and waiting for story time before the teacher was ready. One child volunteered, "I'll tell you a

story." The other children agreed; so Dell moved to the place usually occupied by the teacher and told his story. It was short and to the point: "Once there was a dog." Other children wanted to have a turn. Some of the stories were familiar ones, and some of them were "make-believe" stories. It was a good experience for the children; they thoroughly enjoyed it. This type of participation was used from time to time. Children who wanted to tell a story were given the chance, but those who did not were not forced.

B. With props or aids

Using an old book (a dress pattern book, for example) with a stiff back and heavy pages, paste pictures into it (Children and/or teachers may do this). Show the pictures and let the children make up a story. (Can be used over and over.)

- *Cognitive Concepts.* If many of the activities of the day have been geared to the theme, a diversion is in order. Prestory could be a good time. Suppose you want to see how children respond to certain situations. "I want to buy some oranges. Where do I go to get them?" "Where can I go to get a new collar for my dog?" This gives the children an opportunity to think where you go for specific items. It's another experience in classification. Visual aids help here.

   Teach about prepositions by using an object in relationship to another object. "Where is the spoon?" (over, under, beside, on, in the box.) Then give the child a chance to place the object and tell its relationship.

- *Exercises.* Exercises such as "Head, shoulders, knees, and toes" help to reduce some of the tensions and physical needs of children. Of course, many exercises other than this can be used.

   Have the children sit on the floor with their legs outstretched. Have them touch the opposite knee with their fingers. Try it with an elbow. Now the nose. This is exciting for children but sometimes hard on teachers. Most preschoolers are capable of this activity.

   Have the children stand and pretend they are "rag dolls." Help them to relax by hanging their heads, then moving their arms limply, then their legs, and so on until they are on the floor.

   Have the children walk around the room as they think animals would walk, using their own creative imaginations and without patterning from teachers.

   When any type of stimulating activity is used just prior to a quiet period, it is important to provide an activity immediately following it which will relax the children. Some of the finger plays on pages 133-136 will work nicely for this purpose.

- *"Feel" Box.* Take a small cardboard box (about 16" x 8" x 8" or a size that can be easily handled by a child) and cut out one side. On each end make holes large enough for the child to place his hands inside the box. The child puts his hands in the ends and holds the open side away from him so that he can not see inside the box but the other children can. The child closes his eyes while the teacher places an object through the open side into the box. The child feels the object and tries to guess what it is.

- *Films.* If films are used, they should be very carefully selected and used infrequently. They can be used to supplement firsthand experiences, but should never be used in place of them if the actual experience is available. Evaluate each film as to length, concepts taught (including vocabulary), interest for the children, and value to be gained from the film. Consider also whether *this is the very best way to teach this particular topic.*

- *Finger Plays.* Children enjoy "doing" as well as "seeing." Finger plays should be short and of interest to the children. They can help with number concepts while the children dramatize the actions. If the other

teachers involved know the finger plays, it adds to the success of the experience. Following are some finger plays, along with some body activities for children.

Bunny Song

Here is my bunny with ears so funny,
And here is his hole in the ground.
When a noise he hears,
He pricks up his ears
And jumps in his hole with a bound.
(Right fist forms bunny, and two
fingers the ears. Left hand
closed to make a "hole.")
      —Unknown

One Little Body

Two little hands go clap, clap, clap!
Two little feet go tap, tap, tap!
Two little hands go thump, thump, thump!
Two little feet go jump, jump, jump!
One little body turns around;
One little body sits quietly down.
      —Unknown

*The Carpenter**

The carpenter's hammer goes rap, rap, rap,
And his saw goes see, saw, see;
He planes and measures and hammers
and saws
While he builds a house for me.
(The doubled-up hand makes the
hammer; the open hand, slanting

downward and moved back and
forth as in sawing, makes the
saw; the right hand, with fingers
closed, is moved back and forth
for the plane; and the measuring
is indicated by both hands as if
using a long tape or ruler. The
arms and hands over the head may
make the pointed roof of the
finished house.)
                    —Louise M. Oglevee

*The Squirrel**

These are the brown leaves fluttering
down,
And this is the tall tree, bare and
brown;
This is the squirrel with eyes so
bright,
Hunting for nuts with all his might.
There is a hole where, day by day,
Nut after nut he stores away.
When winter comes with cold and
storm,
He'll sleep curled up all snug and
warm.
(Imitate leaves with both hands;
tall tree, left hand, with fingers
outspread; right hand, the squirrel
running here and there; hole,
thumb and finger of left hand;
right hand curled up for sleeping
squirrel in branches of tree.)
                    —Louise M. Oglevee

*Touch Exercise**

I'll touch my hair, my lips, my eyes,
I'll sit up straight and then I'll rise;
I'll touch my ears, my nose, my chin,
Then quietly sit down again.
                    —A. M. Shumate

Night & Morning

This little boy is going to bed;
(First finger of right hand in palm
of left.)
Down on the pillow he lays his head;
(Thumb of left hand is pillow.)
Wraps himself in the covers tight—
(Fingers of left hand closed.)
This is the way he sleeps all night.

*Colina, Tessa, ed. *Finger Plays and How to Use Them*. Cincinnati: The Standard Publishing Company, 1952. Used by permission of the publisher.

Morning comes, he opens his eyes;
Back with a toss the cover flies;
(Fingers of left hand open.)
Up he jumps, is dressed and away,
(Right index finger up and hopping
away.)
Ready for frolic and play all day.
                    —Unknown

Going to Sleep
Some things go to sleep in such a
funny way—
Little birds stand on one leg and
tuck their heads away.
Little chickens do the same a-
sitting on their perch;
Little mice lie soft and still as if
they were in church.
Little kittens all curl up in such a
funny ball.
Sleepy children all stretch out, so
they'll grow straight and tall.
                    —Unknown

Five Little Kittens
There were five little kittens.
One little kitten went to sleep,
Two little kittens went to sleep,
Three little kittens went to sleep,
Four little kittens went to sleep,
Five little kittens went to sleep.
All the kittens were fast asleep.
(Hold left hand up; with right
hand fold the left-hand fingers
into the palm, one by one,
starting with little finger.)
                    —Unknown

My Little Kitten
My little kitten ran up a tree.
(Fingers running up arms.)
And sat on a limb to look at me.
(Hands rest on opposite shoulder.)
I said, "Come, kitty," and down he
ran,
(Fingers running down arms.)
And drank all the milk
(Hand cupped, with opposite
finger drinking from pan)
I poured in his pan.
                    —Unknown

Hands
On my head my hands I place,
On my shoulders, on my face.
On my lips, at my side;
Quickly at my back they hide.
                    —Unknown

Little Hands

Open, shut them; open, shut them;
Give a little clap;
Open, shut them; open, shut them;
Lay them in your lap.

Creep them, creep them slowly upward
To the rosy cheek;
Open wide the shining eyes,
Through the fingers peek.

Open, shut them; open, shut them;
To the shoulders fly;
Let them like the birdies flutter,
Flutter to the sky.

Falling, falling slowly downward,
Nearly to the ground;
Quickly raise them, all the fingers
Twirling round and round.

Open, shut them; open, shut them;
Give a little clap;
Open, shut them; open, shut them;
Lay them in your lap.
(Do motions as poem suggests.)
     —Unknown

The Turtle

The turtle crawls on the ground
And makes a little rustling sound.
He carries his house wherever he goes,
And when he is scared,
He pulls in his nose and covers his toes.
     —Unknown

BIBLIOGRAPHY FOR FINGERPLAYS

Colina, Tessa, ed. *Finger Plays and How to Use Them.* Cincinnati: Standard Publishing Company, 1952.

Colville, M. Josephine. *The Zoo Comes to School: Finger Plays and Action Rhymes.* Riverside, New Jersey: The Macmillan Company.

Ellis, Mary Jackson and Frances Lyons. *Finger Playtime.* Minneapolis: T. S. Denison, 1960.

Engel, Rose C. *Language Motivating Experiences for Young Children.* Van Nuys, California: DFA Publishing Company, 1969.

Fletcher, Helen J. *Finger Play Poems and Stories.* Riverside, New Jersey: The Macmillan Company.

Grayson, Marion. *Let's Do Fingerplays.* Washington: R. B. Luce, 1967.

Hogstrom, Daphne. *Little Boy Blue Finger Plays Old and New.* Racine, Wisconsin: Whitman Publishing Company, 1966.

Jacobs, Frances E. *Finger Plays and Action Rhymes.* New York: Lothrop, Lee & Shepard, 1961.

Poulsson, Emilie. *Finger Plays for Nursery and Kindergarten.* New York: Lothrop, Lee & Shepard, 1921; also, New York: Dover Publications, 1971.

Scott, Louise B. and J. J. Thompson. *Rhymes for Fingers and Flannelboards.* St. Louis: Webster Publishing Company, 1969.

Steiner, Violette J. and Roberta E. Pond. *Finger Play Fun.* Columbus, Ohio: Charles E. Merrill, 1970.

- *Guessing Games.* Say: "I'm thinking of something that is _____ (give a couple of clues). Can you guess what it is?" (Use animals, transportation vehicles, describe a child). Children can also take a turn giving clues.
- *Guest.* Often it is easier to bring a guest into the school than it is to take children on a particular excursion. By bringing the guest to the children, they can enjoy the experience in a familiar setting. This is often helpful.

A doctor, who was a father of one of the children in a particular group of preschool children, came to the school with his black bag. Rexene backed off saying, "But I don't want a shot today." She was assured by the teachers and the doctor that he had not come to give shots that day. This particular doctor happened to be a bone specialist. After showing the children all the things he carried in his bag, he asked, "Have any of you ever known someone who has broken a bone?" Some did, and some did not. He went on to explain how he helped people when they had a broken bone. He applied a cast to a teacher's arm to demonstrate for the children. How real it was to them! They expressed sympathy to the teacher—as if she really had a broken arm. After the cast was dry, the doctor removed it. Many of the children were concerned, thinking he would cut the teacher's arm off with the cast. He took care to explain away all their fears and questions. After the cast was removed, the children said how glad they were that the teacher's arm was better. The children examined the cast, tried it on, and explored it in every way. This was an excellent experience for them because the doctor had the ability to communicate with them on their level. One child commented, "My dog has a broken leg, but he doesn't have a cast on."

A carpenter also paid a visit to a group of preschool children. The visit had been prearranged and well planned. Through his conversation, he helped the children to have a better understanding about the role of a carpenter. He brought a small door which was nearly completed and let the children finish it by putting screws in predrilled holes. He explained the use of all of his tools and, upon departing, gave each child a real carpenter's pencil. How busy the woodworking table was that day!

When inviting someone into the school who plays a musical instrument, ask the guest to briefly explain about the instrument and then play tunes which are familiar to the children. The children can listen to some of the pieces, but they also enjoy singing. Although the guest may be very talented and might want to play some music which would display his or her skills, young children become easily bored and might walk out on your guest. Keep the experience simple. The length of time for the presentation can be varied according to the interests of the children.

Bringing a guest into the school can be a good learning experience for all involved. Plan wisely; then evaluate the experience afterwards.

- *Musical Experiences.* Dancing or movement to music can not only be fun but can be a good emotional release.

Often a child can just listen to music and find it very satisfying. Introduce children to some of the good classics (calling them by name), but be observant to make sure the experience isn't so long that the children get bored.

Children enjoy expressing themselves through music—verbally or physically. Free, spontaneous movement should be encouraged. Occasional honest praise helps to motivate the quiet child.

A number of records made for children encourage participation. In selecting a record, see that while ideas are given to the child, there is freedom on the part of the child to interpret what is to be done. See list of record sources on pages 104-105.

Use the piano from time to time, sometimes to accompany songs, sometimes to teach specific concepts (high and low, loud and soft, fast and slow), sometimes to encourage child participation (marching, movement to various rhythms).

Some of the ideas under "Exercises" can be used with the addition of music.

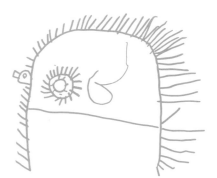

Using an autoharp with young children is also an interesting experience. Take it outside for added enjoyment. Tell the children the names of various parts, how different strings sound, and how different chords are made. Sing some favorite songs.

For other specific suggestions, see pages 96-99.

- *Number Experiences.* With the aid of a flannel board, chalk board, bulletin board, fingerplays, and others, provide some enjoyable but meaningful experiences with numbers. Many preschool children can do rote counting but still do not understand number concepts or symbols.
- *Nursery Rhymes.* Preschool children enjoy the play on words, fun repetition, and nonsense which are incorporated in nursery rhymes. Pictures add to the enjoyment. Don't expect the children to memorize nursery rhymes. Through repetition they learn the rhymes without formal training. Rigid memorization takes the fun out of them. Nursery rhymes should be selected by the same criteria as for books.

Following are some nursery rhymes familiar to most young children:

Curly-Locks	Lucy Locket
Deedle, Deedle Dumpling	Mary Had a Little Lamb
Hickory, Dickory, Dock!	Mary, Mary, Quite Contrary
Humpty Dumpty	Old King Cole
Jack and Jill	Pat-A-Cake
Jack Be Nimble, Jack Be Quick	Pease Porridge
Little Bo-Peep	Peter, Peter, Pumpkin Eater
Little Boy Blue	Rock-A-Bye, Baby
Little Jack Horner	Rub-A-Dub-Dub
Little Miss Muffett	Seesaw, Margery Daw

Simple Simon   Twinkle, Twinkle Little Star
To Market, To Market   Wee Willie Winkie

- *Original Story.* Perhaps you have written a story, or would like to, and are interested in the reactions of the children. You do not want to use it as your main story, but you do want to try it. Use it as the children are assembling for the group experience. (Maybe a parent, a friend, or someone else has written a story and would like response from a group of preschool children. Try it for them.)

  Writing for young children can be challenging. You need to know some of the characteristics of growth of young children as well as their interests and needs. Your story should be short, simple, and realistic. Writing it in poetry form is stimulating and exciting. (See page 82.)

- *Paper Bag.* Give each child a paper sack and tell him to go around the room, putting into the sack objects of certain color or shape (or other description). Examine contents with group.

  Have two sacks or boxes with identical contents. Have child "feel" in his sack and name an object in it. The second sack is handed to another child, who is requested to find the same object. Sacks are passed around until all the children have had a turn.

  Reference: Harlan, Jean D. "The Paper Bag Principle." *Young Children,* August 1973, pp. 355-57.

- *Pictures.* Select with care the pictures you use with children. They should be simply illustrated to avoid confusion and distraction.

  A teacher can hold up a picture in front of the group and stimulate responses from children by questions such as "What do you think these children are doing?" "Would you like to do this?" "What time of year is shown in the picture?" A few simple questions get the children to think about the situation, and they usually have some interesting responses.

  A bulletin board with selected pictures can also be very effective.

- *Poetry.* It is delightful to use poetry with young children. Poetry should be simple and of interest to the children. Many sources of poetry with appeal are available to the young listener. Some of the favorite authors are Rose Fyleman, A. A. Milne, Dorothy Aldis, Carl Sandburg, Polly Chase Boyden, Rachel Field, Dorothy Baruch, Robert Louis Stevenson, Kate Greenaway, Elizabeth Madox Roberts, and James S. Tippett.

  In using poetry with young children, take your cues from them. If they seem to be getting restless, perhaps only a first verse would be sufficient, or maybe the first and last verses. A good introduction to poetry when a child is young will add greatly to his future enjoyment of it.

BIBLIOGRAPHY FOR POETRY

Aldis, Dorothy. *Everything and Anything.* New York: Minton, Balch & Co., 1927.

——————— . *Is Anybody Hungry?* New York: Putnam's Sons, 1964.

Allen, Mary L. *A Pocketful of Poems.* New York: Harper, 1957.

Arbuthnot, May H., ed. *The Arbuthnot Anthology of Children's Literature.* Chicago: Scott, Foresman, 1971.

Association for Childhood Education. *Sung Under the Silver Umbrella.* New York: Macmillan Co., 1935.

Baruch, Dorothy W. *I Would Like to be a Pony and Other Wishes.* New York: Harper, 1959.

——————— . *I Like Animals.* New York: Harpers, 1933.

——————— . *I Like Machinery.* New York: Harpers, 1933.

Brewton, John E. and Sara W. *Index to Poetry for Children and Young People.* New York: H. W. Wilson Co., 1972.

Brewton, J., ed. *Under the Tent of the Sky.* New York: Macmillan Co., 1967.

Cole, Wm., ed. *I Went to the Animal Fair.* Cleveland: World Publishing Co., 1958.

Conklin, Hilda. *Poems by a Little Girl.* New York: Frederick A. Stokes Co., 1923.

Chute, Marchette. *Around and About.* New York: E. P. Dutton, 1957.

De la Mare, Walter. *Peacock Pie.* New York: Holt & Co., 1924.

Farjeon, Eleanor. *Poems for Children.* New York: Frederick A. Stokes & Co., 1951.

Ferris, Helen, ed. *Favorite Poems Old and New.* New York: Doubleday, 1957.

Field, Rachel. *Taxis and Toadstools.* New York: Doubleday, Doran & Co., 1926.

Frank, Josette, ed., *Poems to Read to the Very Young.* New York: Random House, 1961.

——————— . *More Poems to Read to the Very Young.* New York: Random House, 1968.

Govoni, Ilse Hayes, and Dorothy Hall Smith, eds. *The Golden Picture Book of Poems.* New York: Simon and Schuster, 1955.

Hopkins, Lee B. *Me!* New York: Seabury Press.

Jacobs, Leland B. *Just Around the Corner.* New York: Holt, Rinehart & Co., 1964.

Kunhardt, Dorothy. *Little Ones.* New York: Viking Press, 1935.

Kuskin, Karla. *In the Middle of the Trees.* New York: Harper, 1958.

——————— . *The Rose on My Cake.* New York: Harper, 1964.

——————— . *Sand and Snow.* New York: Harper, 1965.

Milne, A. A. *When We Were Very Young.* New York: E. P. Dutton & Co., 1924.

Mitchell, Lucy S., ed. *Another Here and Now Story Book.* New York: E. P. Dutton & Co., 1946.

Richards, Laura E. *Tirra Lirra.* Boston: Little, Brown & Co., 1955.

Sandburg, Carl. *Early Moon.* New York: Harcourt, Brace & Co., 1958.

Stevenson, Robert L. *A Child's Garden of Verses.* London: Collins, 1973.

Tippett, James S. *Crickety, Cricket!* New York: Harper, 1973.

Werner, Jane, ed. *The Golden Book of Poetry.* New York: Simon & Schuster, 1949.

Zolotow, Charlotte. *All that Sunlight.* New York, Harper, 1967.

- *Preparation for an Excursion.* On the day an excursion is to take place, tell the children about it just before the excursion.

  Preparation for the bus excursion discussed on pages 145-146 was made just prior to the story and the actual excursion. Children were prepared by discussion, pictures, and songs.

  For additional information, see section on excursions.
- *Puppets.* Several kinds of puppets are available and add interest to activities. Puppets (sack, finger, hand, sock, tube, clothespin, and stick) can be easily made and used by either children or teachers.

  Make sure the puppets are realistically represented and that correct concepts are taught. This should be a learning experience rather than merely an entertainment.

BIBLIOGRAPHY FOR PUPPETS

Vermeer, Jackie, and Marian Lariviere. *The Little Kid's Craftbook.* New York: Taplinger Publishing Company, 1973, pp. 78-96.

Cole, Ann, Carolyn Haas, Edith Bushnell, and Betty Weinberger. *I Saw a Purple Cow.* Boston: Little, Brown and Company, 1972, pp. 26-28.

- *Rhyming Games.* Read a poem, show objects, or tell the children certain words. Ask them to think of words that rhyme. Some of their responses are interesting.
- *Rhythms.* For specific suggestions, see pages 99-100.
- *Role Playing.* Encourage a child or children to act out a story or activity. Let others guess what it is. Give all a turn who want one.
- *Science.* If you are interested in having all the children together for a science experience, this would be a good time.

  For additional information, see chapter on Science.
- *Songs.* Most children enjoy singing simple songs. Songs which use the names of the children in the group tend to have a magical power to draw children. (See "Mary Wore Her Red Dress," *American Folk Songs for Children* by Ruth Seeger. Moiselle Renstrom also has some delightful songs in her books: *Merrily We Sing, Rhythm Fun,* and *Tune Time.* See Bibliography on Music, pp. 102-103, for complete references and for other sources.)

  Choose songs which deal with familiar experiences of children (about themselves, pets, activities). For information as to how to teach songs to preschoolers, see page 95.
- *Stories with Action.* Have you ever been on an action walk with children? It brings out an element of suspense which delights each child.

  The children and teachers sit on the floor, using their hands to make the sound effects. Clapping can represent walking; rubbing the hands together can represent going through tall grass; gently pounding on the chest can represent going over a bridge; fists pounding on the legs can represent running. Use your own imagination and comments from the children to carry you through an enjoyable experience.

  Here is an example of how this type of activity can be used. (The actual source is unknown.)

Everyone sits down. The teacher begins the story:

Once some people went camping. At night they ate supper and sang songs around the campfire until they were very sleepy (yawn and stretch). Then they crawled into their sleeping bags (wiggle as if getting into the bag) and went to sleep. While they were sleeping, they snored (snore in and blow air out). One child named (use the name of one of the children), snored louder than any of the others (snore, blow). But one man wasn't sleeping, so he went for a walk in the woods.

As he was walking (slap hands rhythmically on legs), he went over some cobble rocks (make click with tongue in mouth); then he went over a bridge (pound fists on legs); then he went over some dry dirt (rub hands together). And do you know what he saw when he got there? He saw a fire in the forest, and the wind was blowing the fire (put arms up in air and wave back and forth, saying "whoo-oo-oo").

When he saw the fire, he ran back over the dry dirt (action), over the bridge (action), and over the cobble rocks (action) to the camp. He woke everyone up and told them of the fire. They all got up and ran to the fire, first over the cobble rocks (action), then over the bridge (action), and last over the dry dirt (action). They saw the fire with the wind blowing it (action) and decided to go back and get some water (go back with actions). They got some buckets and poured some water into them (say "shh-hh-hh-pt"). They went back to the fire (with actions).

When they got to the fire, all the water was gone because there were holes in the buckets. So they went back again for water (actions). They plugged up the holes and put more water into the buckets ("shh-hh-hh-pt") and ran back again (actions). They poured the water on the fire that the wind was blowing ("whoo-oo-oo," slow down) and the fire went out.

They were very tired now, so they decided to go back to the camp and go to sleep. They went across the dry dirt, (and so forth—very slow actions). They crawled into their sleeping bags and all started to snore (action). And guess who snored the loudest of all?

If this activity seems too long for the children, it is possible to delete parts of it without detracting from it.

Another example follows which contains repetition and light suspense:

Down in the box there is a little child who waits and waits as quiet as can be until I open the lid. (Child waits in crouched position.) Pop! (Teacher claps her hands or touches child on his head and he jumps up.)

- *Talking Time for Children.* Language development is very important in the life of a preschool child. Many opportunities should be provided for him to express himself and his ideas as well as to listen to others.

Following are some ideas which have been tried and found to be effective.

Ask the children if they know which children in the group are absent that day. This helps the children to become more aware of each child and of all the children in the group.

Talk about the weather. Has there been a recent change? What kinds of activities can be enjoyed in a particular kind of weather? What kind of wearing apparel is appropriate?

If you know a child has done or is about to do something exciting, give him the opportunity to share it with the group.

If you are trying to promote certain concepts on this day, get feedback from the children so that you will know if more time and information are needed.

Talk with the children about things they have been doing during the

morning. How did the finger paint feel? Was it fun to climb on the jungle gym? The possibilities here are endless.

See other ideas on page 78.

- *"Think" Box.* Provide a good-sized box which is designated as the "think" box. Use it once a week—or more or less often as the value dictates. The teacher brings the box to storytime. She encourages verbal expression from the children. "What do you think is in the box today?" As the children guess, the teacher may add clues. For example, one day the box may include gloves. The teacher says to the children, "What does a glove look like?" "How many kinds (or what kinds) of gloves do you know about?" As the children name some, she takes them out of her box (the children have not seen in the box). The teacher may give added clues, "It's a kind of glove you play a game with," or "You wear it in the winter." (In the box could be a baseball glove, a ski glove, a boxing glove, a lady's dress glove, a child's winter glove).

  Another use of the "think" box is to tell parents and children the day before you use the box to bring things about_____ (something soft, something your favorite color, something about an animal, a picture of something in your house). The enthusiasm of parents and children is usually high. Then the next day have the child place his object in the box (unseen by others). At the appropriate time the child shows and tells about his object. The setting is very informal so that even the shy child participates. Allow enough time for everyone to have a turn.

- *Use of Storybooks.* Select an appropriate book, other than one to be used at actual story time, and show the pictures to the children. Stimulate conversation from children.

  This is a good time to clarify concepts and get an insight into children's thinking about certain things.

  A child may select a book he would like to hear for story time, but another one has been selected by the teacher. Here is a good time to use the child's selection.

  Some children like to hear a certain story every day. It gets boring for some children but not for a few. Use it during the prestory period.

CHAPTER 7

EXCURSIONS

Following are worthwhile purposes for taking young children on excursions:

1. To give them a firsthand experience on their developmental level.
2. To help them learn about their world.
3. To increase and clarify existing concepts.
4. To increase their frame of reference and sense of observation.
5. To help build good relationships with other children and adults through a group experience.
6. To develop initiative and creativeness in dramatic play.
7. To have fun.

Health and safety must always be utmost in the teacher's mind as she plans for an excursion.

READINESS OF CHILDREN

An excursion can either be of benefit to a child, or it can produce an opposite effect. If, for example, a child is taken on an excursion before he feels comfortable in his new setting (the preschool), the experience can produce in him fear and anxiety. A group of four-year-olds was taken for a walk on the university campus of which their nursery school was a part. One child kept repeating, "But my daddy won't know where I am." The teacher tried to assure him that they were close to the school and would return before it was time for his father to pick him up. This was no consolation; the child kept repeating the same concern. He felt uncomfortable the entire time he was away from school. Upon his return, he heaved a sigh of relief and began exploring the play yard.

On the other hand, some children who are not ready for an excursion can be encouraged to participate in the experience. A teacher had planned a bus ride for her group of three-year-olds. The children had been prepared earlier, and the preparation continued as they walked a short distance to the bus stop. As the bus pulled into sight, Melinda began to cry and to withdraw from the group. She said, "I'm not getting on that bus. You can't make me!" The teacher tried to calm her, telling her that if she did not want to go on the bus, the teacher would return to the school with her. As the other children and the other teachers boarded the bus, Melinda stood very close to the teacher. When they were all on the bus except the two of them, the teacher asked Melinda if she would like to look into the bus. She quickly poked her head in and then drew back. The teacher began to explain about the bus until Melinda decided she would like to sit in it for a short minute. She entered the bus, and the bus driver asked the teacher, "Shall I drive off?" The teacher asked him to wait, which he did. Melinda pondered for a moment and then said, "I think I'll ride down to the corner." When she was offered the choice of getting off the bus or continuing her ride as they approached the corner, she decided to continue. Because she had not been forced to take the ride, she became more comfortable, taking several minutes to become less frightened. Throughout the ride she sat close to the teacher, clutching her hand. After the ride she talked freely about it and seemed to have enjoyed it. She had not been ready for the experience when it began, but by the time it was over, she felt comfortable.

PLANNING

In order to avoid unpleasant consequences like the following, teachers should plan well for an excursion. Upon hearing that sheep were to be sheared not too far from the preschool, the teacher arranged to take the children. When they arrived at their destination, they found the man shearing the sheep behind schedule and roughly shearing the sheep as fast as he could, often cutting them so that they bled. The children became upset and wanted to get Band-Aids to cover the wounds. They soon turned to other, more pleasant things. How different this experience could have been.

Excursions should always be planned with the needs, interests, and ages of the children in mind. What would be appropriate for one age may be inappropriate for another. Also, the number of excursions during a given period of time should be based on the characteristics of the children in the group; some children benefit from excursions while others do not. If an experience can be brought to the nursery school, this should be encouraged. See page 137.

The route to be used on an excursion also deserves consideration. Avoiding construction and other dangerous areas and including interesting areas will add to the pleasure of the experience.

On a walk, always take along an empty sack or two for bringing back the many "treasures" which will be found as children explore. Use them in future planning (on a science table or for creative expression).

PREVISIT

One of the prerequisites of a successful excursion is that the teacher make a visit to the location in advance. Too many excursions have ended in failure because the person conducting the excursion directed the information to the teachers rather than to the children. A teacher should ask that person to conduct the tour on a child's level. A successful excursion is one which involves the children and stimulates them to learn more about the particular subject.

TIME

Time is an element deserving much consideration. A student planning an excursion across campus to a botany lab was asked how long it would take to walk there. The student replied, "I can make it in five minutes." The question, "But how long does it take to walk on a four-year-old-level?" was posed. Children like to explore, investigate, and enjoy details as they walk. Make sure, therefore, that plenty of time is allotted. An otherwise successful excursion can be ruined by teachers' hurrying children to a certain place by a certain time. It is better to allow too much than too little time. Avoiding busy times of day is also helpful.

The time during the preschool period for which the excursion is planned is important. It is usually more successful if it occurs near the beginning of the period because children are less likely to be fatigued or involved in another activity.

Excursions near a holiday should be avoided because the children may be either overly stimulated or too fatigued. Also, their interests in an excursion may not be as keen because of their excitement about the holiday.

ADULTS INVOLVED

Before leaving on an excursion, make sure you have enough adult help—at least two, regardless of how few children. If you are going by car, you should have two adults per car so that the driver can concentrate on the driving, and the other adult can supervise the children. If you are walking, an adult for every three to five children, depending upon the ages and activeness of the children, should be sufficient. Always plan for an adult to stay behind at the school or in the car in case a child decides he does not want to participate in the excursion. Planning ahead for this possibility saves confusion and time.

If sufficient staff members are not available, a parent could be asked to participate with the group. Select one whose child is secure in the group setting. An insecure or aggressive child may cause concern to both teachers and parent during the excursion.

PARENTAL PERMISSION

It is wise to check in advance with the parents and obtain written permission from them. Consideration should be given to the parents' wishes; some prefer to take their own children on certain excursions, while others are appreciative if a preschool teacher does it.

One nursery school has found the following form satisfactory:

Dear Parent:

We are conducting an excursion for the children. We will be visiting _____

If you will assume full responsibility and will give permission for your child to go, please sign below.

_____
(Child's Name)

_____
(Date)

_____
(Signature of Parent or Guardian)

This form is used with each excursion on the day the excursion takes place. In this way, parents are informed of the details of the excursion when they bring their children to school. If a form granting permission for events of the entire year is signed by parents ahead of time, they are not aware of the child's current activities and thus lose some of the value of the experience.

TRANSPORTATION

In arranging transportation for excursions, take precautions to see that the drivers have valid licenses, carry adequate insurance, and are capable of the task. Serious concern should be given to this responsibility.

If a parent is asked to help transport the children, she should be an asset to the group. If it is necessary for her to bring along one or two younger children, for example, her value is decreased.

In some instances school buses or public transportation are available. Checking time schedules in advance saves confusion and worry.

SCHOOL POLICIES

Check the policies of your school concerning outings for children before an excursion is planned. Exercise every precaution for the safety of the children.

PREPARATION OF CHILDREN

Children should be prepared for the excursion as near to the time of the excursion as possible. If they are told about it a week or even a day or more in advance, plans might go awry. Perhaps not enough adults are available on the appointed day; perhaps a storm prevents the excursion; perhaps one child happens to be ill and misses the excursion. These are but a few of the unforeseen things that might occur. Charles, for example, had been told of an excursion to take place on Wednesday. He came with his mother, but because he was ill, the nurse asked his mother to take him home. Resisting, he climbed under the nurse's desk and held on with all his might. He did not want to miss that excursion! His mother finally removed him, but he screamed and cried all the way out the door. It would have been better if Charles had been unaware that an excursion was to take place that day.

Give the children a general idea ahead of time what is in store for them on the excursion. If there will be a noise, let them know about it and avoid incidents like the following. A group of children was taken to the local fire station on a wintry day. The building was closed in because of the weather.

When a well-meaning fireman stepped up to the fire truck and turned on the siren, several children became very frightened because they had not known what to expect.

Taking a picnic or snack lunch adds a special air to the occasion. Each child can be given a sack lunch, or a teacher can be responsible for all the food.

As often as possible, plan a walking excursion. Stopping along the way to examine things of interest can enhance the occasion. The children will find many things ordinarily overlooked by fast-paced adults. And a wagon can carry lunches or treasures.

There are several ways to decide which children accompany a certain teacher. One way is to let the children go with the teacher of their choice. Another way is to assign certain children to a particular teacher. Still another way is to have colored name tags—"All children with a blue tag go with Miss _____ , who also has a blue tag"—and so on. In this way each teacher is assured of not getting too many children who are hard to supervise, and each child feels he has someone special to go with.

Limits for the excursion should be clearly defined. Decide on necessary ones and make sure both children and adults understand what they are and why they must be observed.

TEACHING AIDS

There are many ways to increase and stimulate knowledge on an excursion. A bulletin board, for example, with pictures and materials can convey information to children before they go.

Dramatic play is another way in which children can clarify and increase concepts. One teacher was anxious to give children an insight into the needs for and the values of doctors and nurses. So she provided small cots and bandages and placed doctor and nurse kits strategically throughout the preschool. Many of the children wandered about aimlessly, paying no attention to the teaching aids. That morning the class toured a nearby university's campus health center. When the children returned to the preschool, there was much activity. They now had firsthand ideas about nurses, doctors, and a small hospital. It was fascinating and thrilling to see how their ideas had increased.

Dramatic play following an excursion is important. Plan the excursion early enough during the period for the children to try out their new ideas. Provide some props, and let their imaginations do the rest. For example, blocks placed to represent a bus could stimulate dramatic play.

Stories, pictures, songs, and creative materials can add to the learning experience of an excursion. Remember, children need more than one exposure to a thing if they are to develop correct concepts and a sound foundation.

EVALUATION

As soon after the excursion as possible, the experience should be evaluated. What were the strong points? What were the weak points? What concepts were learned by the children? Was the experience of interest to them? How could it have been improved? What teaching aids could be employed to increase the children's knowledge and understanding?

SUGGESTED PLAN FOR AN EXCURSION

Excursion: to nearby construction

Preassessment (several days before excursion)

1. Children are encouraged to look at and identify construction vehicles from replicas or pictures.
2. Pictures of buildings in various stages of construction are placed around the room.

3. Children are asked if they have watched construction, if they know what an architect does, if they know someone who works on construction, and other pertinent questions.
4. Take a walk to see if the children recognize construction materials.

Concepts

1. Heavy equipment helps in construction.
2. Steam shovels dig rapidly.
3. Trucks haul off the dirt.
4. Bulldozers smooth the dirt.
5. Men operate the equipment and do other jobs (pour cement, read plans, hammer, make forms, place steel).
6. Different materials are used for making buildings.

Behavioral Objective: At the end of the experience, the child will be able to:

1. Name three different pieces of equipment.
2. Describe the work done by each piece of equipment.
3. Tell four things the men do in the construction.
4. Name three building materials.

Planning and Preparation

- The bulletin board contains pictures of equipment at work.
- The children have been in the preschool for several months and are now ready for an excursion.
- The teacher makes a previsit to the site to determine the best route and also the best place for the children to observe.
- The following times are allotted: 10 minutes to walk over, 15 minutes to observe, and 10 minutes to walk back. It will take place as soon as all children have arrived at school.
- There will be five children for each of the four adults. (Parents are invited, if needed.) The children help decide which ones will go with which adults.
- Approval is secured from the parents.
- Because the construction is nearby, the children will walk; transportation is not involved.
- The school policies have been checked, and this excursion is acceptable.

Learning Activities

- The children are prepared immediately prior to their departure by the use of pictures and the story "Mike Mulligan and the Steam Shovel" by Virginia Lee Burton. Discussion follows, and the children are told of the excursion.
- The limits are clearly defined as the children help to decide upon them. It will be necessary for the children to stay together as a group. All of the children will wait at the crosswalk to cross together.
- At the site, the teachers point out various jobs of the workmen and the different materials used. Discussion follows.
- Upon returning to the school, trucks, steam shovels, and tractors will be placed in the sand area for dramatic play.
- During evaluation, the teachers discuss the strengths and weaknesses of the excursion.

SUGGESTED EXCURSIONS OF INTEREST TO YOUNG CHILDREN

(Keep in mind that an excursion should be on the *developmental level* of the children involved and should be *fairly close* to the school. Some of these places

would be familiar to some children and unfamiliar to others. For example, John's parents operate a restaurant, and he spends a great deal of time there. He may, or may not, be interested in visiting a restaurant.)

Airport or terminal
Apartment house
Aquarium
Artist's studio
Bakery
Bank
Barber shop
Beauty shop
Boat ride
Body and paint shop
Bus depot
Bus ride
Cannery
Car dealer
Car wash
Circus
Collector (rock, insect, coin)
Construction site
Construction equipment
Dairy
Dance studio
Dentist
Department store
Dock
Doctor's office
Dog kennel
Dormitory
Elevator
Escalator

151

Factory—food, clothing, other
Farm
Fire department
Fish hatchery
Flower garden
Foundry
Gas station
Greenhouse
Grocery store
Harbor
Hobby shop
Hospital or clinic
House—child, teacher
Junk yard
Laundry
Library
Livestock show
Lunch room
Manufacturer—car, household equipment
Marching Band
Music department or rehearsal
Newspaper
Occupations (variety)
Orchard
Office
Park
Pet store
Photo studio
Planetarium
Police station or car
Post office
Pottery factory
Poultry farm
Produce market
Radio station
Railway station
Recreation—bowling alley, gyms, hobby
    display, skating rink, swimming pool
Repair shop—bike, car, shoes, watch
Restaurant
Road repair or equipment building
Rodeo
School
Seed store
Sewage disposal plant
Specialties of community
Stream
Street car ride or station
Subway
TV studio
Truck terminal
Upholstery shop
Walk
Water—dam, lake, river
Woods
Zoo

ESPECIALLY FOR PARENTS

Excursions for parents and children are for two main purposes: (1) to build good relationships with each other, and (2) to increase the child's knowledge as he indicates interest and readiness.

Caution: Too many experiences too fast will defeat the purposes of excursions.

Below are listed some possible trips for parents and child. Some of them may be impossible or inappropriate; look for those which are feasible. These are merely suggestions to help you look around your community and discover places of interest for your child now and in future years.

Consider the following as possibilities:

Airplane ride
Airport
Air show
Amusement park
Animal shelter
Animal show
Aquarium
Assembly line
Athletic event
Aviary
Beehive
Boat races
Boat ride
Bottling plant
Brick plant
Butchers
Camping
Candle maker
Candy factory
Cannery
Canyons
Car manufacturer
Carnival
Carpenter
Carpet weaver
Church
Clock maker
Coal mine
Construction site
Cotton plantation
Dam
Dance rehearsal
Dentist
Doctor
Doll hospital
Drive
Drive-in (food)
Fabric factory
Fair (state, local)
Family reunion
Festival
Fish hatchery
Fishing
Flower show or shop
Frozen food plant

153

Fruit packing shed
Fur breeder
Furniture manufacturer
Glass factory
Gravel pit
Hiking
Holiday celebration
Hospital
Hunting
Indian reservation
Lake
Lock
Lumber yard
Map maker
Meat processing plant
Mountains
Musical instrument factory
Office
Oil drilling
Painter
Paint factory
Paper mill
Parade
Peanut plantation
Piano factory
Piano tuner
Picnic
Power plant
Printer
Radio station
Recording studio
Recycling plant
Repair shop (bike,
    radio, toy, shoe,
    appliance, TV)
Road construction
Rock and mineral show
Rock hunting
Seashore
Seed store
Shoe factory
Shopping
Specialty in community
Swimming
TV station
Toy factory
Train depot
Train ride
Turkey farm
Upholstery shop
Vacation
Veterinarian
Visit relatives
Walk
Warehouse
Zoo

Parents may consider some of the suggestions for excursions more in the category of "necessities" than pleasures. Whenever you can, take your child along with you and explain what is happening—not in complicated, lecture fashion, but in understandable, interesting children's language.

Excursions can support many areas of learning. Previous chapters in this book have dealt with the ways in which they further a child's knowledge of a particular topic (see pages 101-102 and 119-121).

Many excursions can be executed by either parents or teachers, and sometimes by both. Because of time, expense, liability, and availability, however, parents are more likely to take their children to certain places than are teachers.

BIBLIOGRAPHY FOR EXCURSIONS

BOOKS

Hildebrand, Verna. *Introduction to Early Childhood Education.* New York: Macmillan, 1971, pp. 260-75.

Moore, Sallie, and Phyllis Richards. *Teaching in the Nursery School.* New York: Harper & Bros., 1959, pp. 53-69.

Read, Katherine. *The Nursery School.* Philadelphia: W. B. Saunders, 1971, pp. 217-24.

Russell, Helen R. *Ten-Minute Field Trips, a Teacher's Guide.* Chicago: J. G. Ferguson Publishing Co., 1973. (Mainly for grade school children, but some of the ideas can be adapted to younger children.)

ARTICLES

Buschhoff, Lotte K. "Going on a Trip." *Young Children*, March 1971, pp. 224-32.

Cohen, Shirley. "Planning Trips for Vulnerable Children." *Childhood Education* 48 (1972): 192-96.

Hildebrand, Verna. "Trips for Preschoolers." *Childhood Education*, May 1967, pp. 524-28.

PAMPHLETS

Hockman, Vivienne. *Trip Experiences in Early Childhood.* New York: Bank Street Publication, 69 Bank Street.

Mitchell, Lucy Sprague. *Geography with Five-Year-Olds.* New York: Bank Street Publication, 69 Bank Street.

CHAPTER 8

SPECIAL OCCASIONS

Does the celebration of special occasions have value for young children? The following section should answer this question.

GOALS

- To teach a child true concepts about the occasion
- To support or give first-hand experiences on a child's developmental level
- To increase a child's understanding about his world
- To allow a child to interact with others who share ideas in common
- To build social relationships
- To inform a child of other customs and practices (religious, cultural, national, community, family, foreign)

VALUES FOR CHILDREN

Children can benefit from such experiences if they are planned for the individual child as well as for the total group. In planning to celebrate special occasions, consider the following criteria:

- Interest, interest span, and skills of the children
- Possibility of increasing existing knowledge or of clarifying concepts
- Activities: should be child-centered but may be adult-initiated
- Total developmental level of the children
- Possibility of increasing a child's independence
- Use of food: should be child-prepared, simple, nutritional, and in small quantities.

BIRTHDAYS

(For a complete lesson plan, see "It's My Birthday" in *When I Do, I Learn* by Barbara J. Taylor, pp. 40-46, 164-65.)

Concepts to be Taught

1. It is fun to have a birthday.
2. We can share our birthday with others.

The most special of special occasions is a child's own birthday. He deserves, and should get, some recognition on this day. Some preschools have formulated a policy with regard to a child's birthday. Some parents like to send a simple treat. Often it seems more special if the children at school prepare something, such as cookies or cupcakes.

When a luncheon or a snack is served in the preschool group, the child having the birthday can stand while others sing "Happy Birthday" to him; then he can pass out a treat which has been prepared by a parent or the children. In this way he is sharing his birthday with others—a concept which should be cultivated.

Some Suggested Teaching Aids

- Make cookies or cupcakes.
- Decorate cookies or cupcakes.
- Make gelatin.
- Pop corn.
- Freeze ice cream.
- Make pudding.
- Make a birthday card or picture.
- (See other suggestions in Chapters 2 and 10.)

Books for Children

Brown, Myra B. *Birthday Boy.* New York: Franklin Watts, 1963.

Buckley, Helen. *The Little Boy and the Birthdays.* New York: Lothrop, Lee & Shepard, 1965.

Fern, Eugene. *Birthday Presents.* New York: Farrar, Strauss, & Giraux.

Schatz, Letta. *When Will My Birthday Be?* New York: McGraw-Hill, 1962.

HALLOWEEN

Concepts to be Taught

1. Halloween is a time to have fun.
2. Halloween is a make-believe time.
3. Halloween comes in the fall.

This is an occasion which can create fear if witches, goblins, and masks are emphasized. Even costumes can be frightening to some young children and will add to their confusion and discomfort. These things have no part in the life of a preschooler. A four-year-old child watched his older brother put on a grotesque mask. The younger boy, even though he had seen his brother put on the mask, became frightened and began to cry.

Some Suggested Teaching Aids

- Cut a face on a pumpkin and hollow it out. The seeds can be saved for a spring planting experience. The children can talk about the slickness of the inside of the pumpkin, how it feels to cut with a knife, and general conversation. The group, however, should be kept small so that each child can have a chance to participate.
- Make Halloween cookies.
- Serve a pumpkin dessert for snack or lunch. (This may be adult-oriented.)
- Provide a collage so the children can make trick-or-treat bags to take home with them.
- Use appropriate Halloween stories, songs, and pictures.
- Encourage children to draw pictures about Halloween.
- Encourage children to talk about Halloween.

THANKSGIVING

Concepts to be Taught

1. We are thankful for our families, homes, and food.
2. Families get together at Thanksgiving.
3. It is a time for fun.

A young child's understanding of this holiday is rather limited. For this reason it is best to keep things simple. Through conversation with a child you may be surprised at what his ideas about Thanksgiving really are.

Some Suggested Teaching Aids

- Encourage the children to draw pictures about Thanksgiving.
- Obtain ideas from children's suggestions.
- Plan for the individual child. One teacher provided apples and let the children stick colored toothpicks into them for tail feathers. Many of the children had a concept only of putting toothpicks into apples; they could not grasp the concept of putting tail feathers on a turkey.
- Use appropriate stories, songs, and pictures.
- Encourage children to talk about Thanksgiving.

CHRISTMAS

Concepts to be Taught

1. Christmas is a time for fun.
2. We express our love for others through giving.
3. Christmas comes in the winter.
4. We make special things at Christmas time: gifts, cookies, tree decorations.
5. It's Jesus' birthday.

Because of the commercialism at Christmas, children get many confusing ideas. Parents should be free to convey to their children the ideas they want them to have. A safe policy for the preschool staff is to make a "middle of the road" stand, neither encouraging nor discouraging the Santa Claus aspect.

Some nursery schools dismiss for the Christmas holidays a week or more in advance of the special day. For this reason, it is wise to refrain from overstimulating the children. It is difficult for them to wait for a special event.

Some Suggested Teaching Aids

- Expose children to good Christmas music.
- Let children explore with rhythm instruments and Christmas carols.
- Make and decorate Christmas cookies or cupcakes.
- String cranberries or popcorn for tree.
- Make ornaments for tree:
  1. Cut egg cartons into individual sections; paint with easel paint and hang in tree by pipe cleaners.
  2. Cut colored construction paper into strips for making chains.
  3. Decorate small individual pie containers and hang in tree with yarn.
  4. Decorate jar lids with pictures from wrapping paper or old Christmas cards. Punch a hole in one end and hang in tree with yarn or pipe cleaners.
  5. Make aluminum foil decorations.
  6. Use cornstarch dough # 2 (page 44). Roll out. Using Christmas cookie cutters, make ornaments. Make hole near top for string, yarn, or pipe cleaners.

7. Bake flour-salt dough # 3 (page 43) as directed, first making hole for hanger. Paint or decorate as desired. Attach string, yarn, or pipe cleaner. Hang in tree.

8. Paint pine cones and apply glitter.

- Make mobiles (objects to hang from cribs, ceilings, and cupboards), using wire, paper, spools, fabrics, yarn, glitter.
- Stimulate ideas through use of appropriate pictures.
- Encourage children to draw pictures about Christmas.
- Let children paste with cotton (resembling snow).
- Let children make their own Christmas cards to take home. Pictures from old Christmas cards, magazines, or wrapping paper with glitter make interesting cards.
- Use appropriate stories, finger plays, and songs.
- If children are to make gifts to take home, keep them simple. Objects made out of clay or plaster of paris may be easiest for their small hands. However, even this tends to become adult-centered.
- Decorate a 9" nonwaxed paper plate with small macaroni products (noodles, macaroni, shellroni) and spray with gold paint. Place a picture of the child in the center and make a hanger out of yarn. (The picture could be a snapshot or a silhouette cut from construction paper.)

VALENTINE'S DAY

Concepts to be Taught

1. Valentine's Day is a time for fun.
2. We show people we like them by giving them valentines.
3. We enjoy making valentines.

Some Suggested Teaching Aids

- Encourage children to draw pictures about Valentine's Day.
- Provide materials so children can make valentines (lace, paper doilies, colored construction paper, pictures, fabrics, etc.).
- Make heart-shaped cookies.
- Use appropriate stories, songs, and pictures.
- Encourage children to talk about Valentine's Day.

EASTER

Concepts to be Taught

1. Easter comes in the spring.
2. New growth begins in the spring.
3. Easter is a time for fun.

Because of the religious significance of this holiday, this is another time when parents prefer to inform their children. There is much about the occasion that young children do not understand. Their ability to think in abstract or complex terms is just developing.

Some Suggested Teaching Aids

- Acquire an incubator and some chicken or duck eggs.
- Plant a garden.
- Add a new pet to the nursery school family: a bunny or duck.
- Explore the new growth in the play yard.
- Color eggs.
- Make easter baskets from egg cartons (cut so each contains four or six egg sections), cottage cheese cartons, or small boxes. Let the children paint them and fill them with artificial grass. Make handles from ribbons or pipe cleaners.

FOURTH OF JULY

Concepts to be Taught

1. The Fourth of July is the birthday of our country.
2. The name of our country is the United States of America.
3. We celebrate the freedom of our country.
4. The Fourth of July comes in the summer.
5. A flag is the symbol of our country.
6. The colors of our flag are red, white, and blue.
7. The Fourth of July is a time for fun.

Some Suggested Teaching Aids:

- Talk about what freedom means.
- Take the children to see a flag and tell them about it briefly.
- Show the children how to respect the flag.
- Make three-cornered hats out of newspaper or newsprint.
- Have a pasting experience using red, white, and blue.
- Have a parade, using flags, musical instruments, and a march (piano, record, tape).
- Let the children decorate wagons, trikes, and boxes, as though for a parade.
- Use appropriate stories, finger plays, songs, and poems.
- Ask the children what they are going to do to celebrate the "Fourth."
- Show a globe or map and indicate what part is our country.

Exercise for teachers:

Write or plan for some special occasions which would be appropriate for your children and locality. In some sections of our country, a religion, a culture, or a foreign population predominates. Even though all children in your preschool may not be directly involved with such a religion or culture or population, help them to understand and appreciate the ways of others.

ESPECIALLY FOR PARENTS

Celebrating special occasions gives parents an opportunity to take the lead in teaching the values they want their children to have. A teacher might be limited in the information she imparts or the activities she plans because of national or local restrictions.

Parents reminisce about religious and other special occasions and have certain customs or ideas they want to pass on to their children. Because schools are not in session during most holidays, the actual celebration may be with parents or with the family, but preparation for a holiday may or may not begin at school. Sometimes we plan so far in advance of the occasion that by the time it arrives, all the fun is over. Remember, it is difficult for young children to wait for a special time; so decide how far in advance you want to inform him. You have to live with his counting the days and hours.

Because special occasions are such personal matters, only a few suggestions will be given for each occasion. Custom or tradition will likely be a determining factor in each household.

SOME SUGGESTED AIDS

Birthday

- Let your child help make a traditional birthday cake or dessert.
- Give him several possible activities and let him decide how to celebrate.
- If there is a formal party, keep it simple (in number of children, activities, and food).

161

- Encourage him to share the day with others.
- Help the child select several toys or articles of clothing; then let him make the final selection of the *one* he wants.
- Give him special privileges.
- Do something special with your child alone.
- Start a birthday tradition (musical cake plate, activity).
- Help him record events of the day in a book or journal.
- Take pictures.
- Let him help make his favorite foods for dinner.

Halloween

- Make an appropriate costume.
- Make decorations.
- Go to a field and get a pumpkin.
- Carve a pumpkin.
- Start a family tradition.

Thanksgiving

- Observe crops being harvested.
- Make it a family time.
- Make decorations.
- Begin a family tradition.
- Prepare food.
- Visit a turkey farm.
- Prepare for guests (being a guest or having guests).
- Discuss things for which we are thankful.
- Show appreciation for things through attitude and action.
- Share something with others.

Christmas

- Make gifts.
- Show love by doing good deeds for others.
- Go Christmas shopping.
- Make food for holidays.
- Decorate tree and house.
- Wrap presents.
- Make decorative wrapping paper.
- Begin a family tradition.
- Share something with others.
- Teach own values, whether religious, cultural, or commercial.

Valentine's Day

- Make and deliver valentines.
- Make a treat for dinner.
- Express love verbally.
- Do good deeds.
- Make decorations.
- Begin a family tradition.

Easter

- Select and purchase new clothes.
- Go on egg hunt.
- Observe new life in plants and animals.
- Color eggs.
- Make decorations.

- Begin a family tradition.
- Hatch eggs.
- Plant bulbs.
- Get a new pet.
- Teach own values, whether religious, cultural, or commercial.

Fourth of July

- Attend a parade.
- Attend special community activities.
- Display and respect the flag.
- Discuss patriotism.
- Briefly explain why we celebrate the Fourth of July.
- Make decorations.
- Begin a family tradition.

BIBLIOGRAPHY FOR SPECIAL OCCASIONS

BOOKS

Green, Marjorie M., and Elizabeth L. Woods. *A Nursery School Handbook for Teachers and Parents.* Sierra Madre, California: Sierra Madre Community Nursery School Association, 1963.

Hoover, Francis L. *Art Activities for the Very Young.* Worcester, Mass.: Davis Publications, 1967.

Kauffman, Carolyn, and Patricia Farrell. *If You Live with Little Children.* New York: G. P. Putnam's Sons, 1957, pp. 96-126.

Moore, Sallie, and Phyllis Richards. *Teaching in the Nursery School.* New York: Harper & Bros., 1959, pp. 100-124.

Taylor, Barbara J. *When I Do, I Learn.* Provo, Utah: Brigham Young University Press, 1974, pp. 40-46.

Todd, Vivian E., and Helen Heffernan. *The Years before School.* Toronto: Macmillan Co., 1970, pp. 288-305.

ARTICLES

Crystal, Frances H. "The Holiday Dilemma: Celebrating the Holidays in Preschool and Kindergarten." *Young Children*, November 1967, pp. 66-73.

Highberger, Ruth. "Are Celebrations of Special Occasions in the Nursery School for Children or Adults?" *Journal of Nursery Education* 16: no. 2, 1960-61.

PAMPHLETS

Recipes for Holiday Fun. Parents as Resources Project, 1973. Order from DCCDCA, # 42A, $2.00.

CHAPTER 9

OUTDOOR EQUIPMENT

Good planning is necessary in order to get the greatest possible use out of the playground and its equipment. It can be a beautiful yet functional area, with space for freedom of movement a must. Needs of the children can be provided for without involving a great deal of cost, either by having much of the equipment made locally to your specifications or by improvising some of it.

VALUES FOR CHILDREN

Large Muscle Development

It is an observable fact that young children are active. This we know and plan for. The preschool child is exercising his large muscles and needs the proper equipment to help him. One of the best kinds of equipment is a good assortment of sturdy boxes and boards that can be moved easily and arranged in a manner stimulating to the interests and abilities of children. They should be constructed to take the abuse of energetic bodies and colored brightly to attract the attention of children. A board can be used directly on the ground for children who are beginners, then can be raised to various levels as children's imaginations dictate. One minute it may be a road, the next a bridge to crawl under. Boxes should be large enough for children to climb into, onto, or over. An indication of the ingenuity of children, Ted and James, climbing on top of a box, decided to turn the box onto its side and use it for a house. An interesting obstacle course can be made, too, from boards and boxes. If funds are limited, get some large cardboard boxes from the florist or from a furniture or grocery store.

A jungle gym, or climbing apparatus of some kind, should be included in the equipment. One that presents a variety of possibilities for activity is best—an apparatus including a rope ladder, steps, a pole, an inside play area, and a platform on top. Not only will such a piece of equipment stimulate imaginations; it will exercise muscles as well.

An area should be provided for wheel toys, also, such as tricycles and wagons. This area should be paved with cement or asphalt or a similar material to facilitate the use of equipment with wheels. Tricycles and wagons can be

165

used separately or jointly. Most pedal cars, on the other hand, are difficult for preschoolers; the pedals and steering are not coordinated as they are on a tricycle.

Tires or tubes can help children release excess energy. Large truck or airplane tubes are exciting to roll in, climb through, jump on, and bounce on.

Stick horses provide good exercise at a low price. Many different kinds are on the market, but the ones that seem to be most durable are those with molded plastic heads. When not in use, they can be stored conveniently in a tall garbage can.

Either blocks built for outdoor use or large barrels also add interest to the playground.

For information regarding woodworking, see pages 62-64.

Swings have little to offer a preschooler. The child is not coordinated enough to pump the swing; therefore, he gets no muscle exercise and must depend upon a teacher to push him. Accidents happen, also, because children walk into the path of the swing, or the child swinging decides to let go. Moreover, it takes a child away from group or active play. And he has opportunities elsewhere (at home, in a park) for this type of experience.

Moving the equipment around on the playground and putting it in different combinations will stimulate the interest of children. They may even suggest some ideas. In warm weather, materials and activities generally used inside could be taken outside.

Social Interaction or Dramatic Play

Many of the equipment pieces discussed throughout this chapter stimulate socialization and either group or dramatic play. Two or more pieces of the same equipment (tricycles, stick horses, shovels) make this possible.

Often children initiate an unusual use for a piece of equipment. Two children were building with large blocks when one discovered that his arrangement looked "like a horse!"

Role playing can take on a new and vigorous light outdoors. The entire playground is the stage. Most girls (and many boys) enjoy dressing up and taking a doll for a walk. We can learn much from them by listening and observing.

A rowboat is another interesting piece of equipment. It can be brightly painted and strategically placed. Some holes drilled in the bottom facilitate draining if the children use water in it.

Sensory Experiences

Experiences with water can be more fully explored outside, and, when weather permits, water can make an occasion special. Many parents object to their children's playing with water at home; opportunities should be provided them, then, at the preschool. Precautions should be taken, of course, to see that the children are properly dressed for this activity, in bathing suits, boots, or aprons. Washing doll clothes and hanging them outside is one interesting water experience for children. Another is adding water to sand; yet another is "painting" with water; still another is sailing boats; and even watering plants can be fun. (See pages 60-61, 110-111, and 119.) On a hot day it is refreshing to the children to let the hose run on the slide, cooling the slide and adding an extra "zip." A wading pool filled with water at the end of the slide adds zest to the experience. Close supervision is necessary, of course.

Sand is another item which is better used outdoors. It has many possibilities, especially with the addition of props such as strainers, spoons, molds, buckets, shovels, cars, and various toys. (See page 59.)

Learning about Nature

The landscaping around the playground area could be provided in such a way as to stimulate children's interest in nature. Shrubs of differing sizes, colors, and characteristics could be planted either in the ground or in large tubs. A large tree for climbing is desirable if available.

The layout of the playground should provide large areas of space away from the equipment—a garden area, perhaps, providing many opportunities for children, from their using proper tools to their harvesting a crop. Free-flowing paths are inviting to fast-paced youngsters, too. They resemble the curves found on modern highways.

From playing and building outdoors, a child adds to his experiences. Crates and large wooden cartons (pop, beer, milk) are fun to build with as are old tires, wooden and metal frames, and boards. The weight of the object should challenge but not tax the ability of a child. He will also learn about cooperation, interdependence, balance, size, and gravity. And through using his body, he will develop skills and dexterity.

ROLE OF THE TEACHER

The role of the teacher in the outside area is similar to her role in other areas:

- To provide for the individual child and his needs.
- To "pace" the area to be inviting and stimulating.
- To set up and maintain necessary limits.
- To be flexible in her teaching.
- To provide a variety of experiences in the fresh air.
- To stimulate and encourage children to explore.
- To appreciate the interests and the enthusiasm of the children.
- To enjoy being with the children.

167

ADDITIONAL OUTDOOR AIDS

Barrels
Bedspread over box
Blocks, hollow
Boards—for crawling, jumping,
    bouncing
Boxes, large packing
Car (doors removed)
Climbers (wood, metal)—rings,
    ropes, poles, platform
Clocks
Cockpit
Domestic area (see pp. 49-52)
Easels
Fishing net
Gardening equipment
Gas pump
Inner tubes
Ladders—horizontal or perpendicular
    (rope, wood, metal)
Levers
Nylon net over frames
Parachute
Playhouse
Pulley
Pumps—water, tire
Punching bag
Radios

Ramp
Ropes
Sand tools
Saw horses
Signs, road
Slide
Storm drain pipe
Swing, tire
Tent
Terrarium
Tricycles
Wagon, large wooden
Water play
Woodworking equipment

ESPECIALLY FOR PARENTS

Providing outdoor equipment for children is sometimes costly in terms of money and space. However, an effort should be made to see that the child has outdoor experiences that develop large and small muscles, encourage social interaction or dramatic play, provide sensory stimulation, and include learning opportunities. If the equipment is not available at home, take your child often to a park or a playground where he can have these experiences. Outdoor experiences at home are preferable because of the convenience. A child has more opportunities there for spontaneous, sustained play, and the parents may go about their tasks with an eye on the activities.

Home equipment could likely include one or more from each of the following groups (note that some of the items appropriately fit in more than one category):

Muscle Development

Boards
Boxes (wood or cardboard)
Climbing equipment (including ladders)
Digging equipment
Pulleys
Ropes
Sand toys
Stick horses
Trees
Tricycles
Wagons
Wheel toys
Woodworking tools

Social Interaction or Dramatic Play

Creative art materials
Dolls
Dishes
Dress-up (hats, shoes, and other articles)
Open and private areas
Playhouse
Sand toys
Trucks, cars
Trunk or suitcases
Water
Wheel toys

Sensory Stimulation

Aesthetic design (color, arrangement, variety)
Flowers
Garden plot
Sand
Sounds of nature
Water

Learning from Total Outdoor Area

Animals
Different surfaces (dirt, grass, gravel, cement, asphalt)
Open and private areas
Planted areas but also areas for playing and digging
Storage
Sunny and shady spaces
Variety of shrubs, flowers
Water

BIBLIOGRAPHY FOR OUTDOOR EQUIPMENT

BOOKS

Hildebrand, Verna. *Introduction to Early Childhood Education.* New York: Macmillan Co., 1971, pp. 83-101.

Leeper, Sarah H., Ruth J. Dales, Dora S. Skipper, Ralph L. Witherspoon. *Good Schools for Young Children.* New York: Macmillan Co., 1974, pp. 418-38.

Matterson, Elizabeth. *Games for the Very Young.* New York: Heritage Press, 1971.

Read, Katherine H. *The Nursery School.* Philadelphia: W. B. Saunders Co., 1971, pp. 77-80.

Todd, Vivian E., and Helen Heffernan. *The Years before School.* Toronto: Macmillan Co., 1970, pp. 129-44 and 245-52.

ARTICLES

Burns, Sylvia F. "Children Respond to Improvised Equipment." *Young Children*, October 1964, p. 28.

Law, Norma R., and Hui C. Wu. "Equipment: Challenge or Stereotype?" *Young Children*, October 1964, p. 18.

McCord, Ivalee H. "A Creative Playground." *Young Children*, August 1971, pp. 342-47.

Moncure, Jane B. "Something out of Nothing." *Young Children*, October 1964, p. 38.

PAMPHLETS

ACEI. *Space, Arrangement, and Beauty in School.* Washington, D.C.: ACEI, 3615 Wisconsin Avenue, 20016, 1958.

ACEI. *Equipment and Supplies.* Washington, D.C.: ACEI, 3615 Wisconsin Avenue, 20016, 1961.

ACEI. *Playscapes.* Washington, D.C.: ACEI, 3615 Wisconsin Avenue, N.W., 20016.

Baker, Kathryn Read. *Let's Play Outdoors.* # 101. Washington, D.C.: NAEYC, 1834 Connecticut Avenue, N.W.

Found Spaces and Equipment for Children's Centers. New York: Educational Facilities Labs, 477 Madison Avenue, 1972.

Kretchevsky, Sibil, and Elizabeth Prescott. *Planning Environments for Young Children.* # 115. Washington, D.C.: NAEYC, 1834 Connecticut Avenue, N.W., 1969.

Office of Economic Opportunity. *Equipment and Supplies.* Project Head Start Bulletin # 9. Washington, D.C.: OEO Office.

Stone, Jeanette J. *Play and Playgrounds.* # 123. Washington, D.C.: NAEYC, 1834 Connecticut Avenue, N.W., 1970.

CHAPTER 10

FOOD EXPERIENCES AND RECIPES

An area of the curriculum wherein adults hesitate to involve children, yet an area thoroughly enjoyed by children, is that of food. Participation in food preparation is a great source of satisfaction to children. (See pp. 116-117 and 120 for some experiences related to this chapter.)

Because adults are pressed for time, because they do not fully understand the abilities of children and are therefore unwilling to involve them, children do not have enough opportunity to participate in food preparation. Nevertheless, here is an area offering additional experiences for the child to become independent, to learn about his world, to experience accomplishment, and to contribute his services.

Many negative attitudes toward either eating or helping others have been eliminated when children have participated in food experiences. A child who is permitted to help set the table, for example, takes pride in its appearance. A child who has previously shunned certain foods or socialization during snack time or meals bursts forth with a desire to partake of the food and to interact socially because of his contribution to the occasion.

As with any activity, certain precautions should be taken. When children are using sharp knives, the teacher must instruct and supervise. When they are using cords, utensils, and other apparatuses, the teacher should indicate precautions or limits for their own protection—not to create fear but to encourage safety.

After preparing, cooking, and eating applesauce at nursery school one day, Joanie asked her mother if she would buy a bushel of apples on the way home so that Joanie could make more applesauce that afternoon. Following another cooking experience at school, Tammy informed her mother, "I am going to make spaghetti for Dad for supper tonight because I learned how to do it today." Still another child, Val, pleaded with the teacher: "If you'd just let us make doughnuts at school, I'd show you how."

Some children have frequent opportunities at home to help with food preparation and cooking. Of course, different ways exist of doing the same thing. For example, some mothers mix bread with their hands, others with an electric mixer, and others with a hand-turned mixer. Some children aid in the process of bread baking from grinding the wheat through tasting the warm, fragrant product. But even these experiences take on new dimensions when they are done with a group of peers. (Often teachers let children do additional things that parents don't because they realize the importance of the experience to the children.)

In food preparation, new terms and definitions can be added to the vocabulary of the children and opportunities provided for the children to try the words out. Consider some of these terms: measure, ingredients, recipe, beat, stir, fold; or these processes: dipping, scrubbing, shaking, spreading, rolling, peeling, cracking, juicing, cutting, grinding, blending, grating, and scraping. We want different products to have different characteristics. Could you explain why we want to form gluten in bread (so we mix it a lot) and not in muffins (so we just stir until the ingredients are blended)? Why are some products more desirable when they are crisp rather than soft or dry rather than moist?

For an enjoyable experience, help the children prepare a picture recipe, then purchase ingredients, then make and eat the product.

Snack time may be a group experience, or it can be made available whenever a child wants it.

Although food prepared by children may not remain under the most sanitary conditions or may not turn out as a perfect product, participation in its preparation is invaluable to children.

SNACK SUGGESTIONS FROM BASIC FOUR FOOD GROUPS

Milk Group

Butter for crackers or bread
Cheese chunks
Cottage cheese
Creamed cheese on crackers or bread
Kabobs: lunch meat and cheese
Milk: whole, powdered, butter
Puddings

Meat Group

Bacon
Beef jerky
Eggs (boiled, scrambled, other)
Fish sticks
Meat balls
Meat loaf
Meat sandwich fillings
Nuts
Poultry
Vienna sausages
Wieners

Vegetable - Fruit Group

Applesauce
Cooked vegetables: broccoli, beans,
    asparagus, beets, spinach, corn
Dried fruit (or fruit leather)
Fresh fruit: pineapple, grapes, melons,
    bananas, strawberries, dates, pears,
    coconut, cherries, peaches, apricots,
    plums, apples, tangerines
    IMPORTANT: CITRUS: oranges,
    lemons, grapefruit

Fresh vegetables: peas, carrots, radishes,
  cauliflower, cherry tomatoes, celery,
  green peppers, cabbage, lettuce, turnips,
  potatoes, zucchini, cucumbers
Fruit or vegetable salads
Juice: fruit or vegetable
Kabobs: various fruits or vegetables on
  toothpicks
Popcorn
Raisins
Soup
Stew: various vegetables

Bread and Cereal Group

Bread (white, Boston Brown, whole wheat,
  muffins, biscuits, other)
Bread sticks
Chinese noodles
Cooked cereal
Cookies
Crackers
Cupcakes, small
Fruit or nut breads
Macaroni, noodles, other pasta
Melba toast
Pancakes
Prepared cereal
Rice (steamed)
Sandwiches, small
Spaghetti with sauce
Waffles

Miscellaneous

Gelatin
Honeycomb
Marshmallows

Combinations

Apple wedges spread with cream cheese,
    peanut butter, or other spread
Celery stuffed with cottage cheese,
    peanut butter, creamed cheese,
    fruit, raisins
Rice pudding

Support food experiences with community resources, as follows:
- Field trips

  - Bakery
  - Butcher shop
  - Cold storage plant
  - Corn, potato, or peanut field; cabbage or berry patch
  - Dairy farm
  - Dairy processing plant
  - Fish hatchery
  - Fishing at local lake or river (close supervision necessary)
  - Food processing plant
  - Local market
  - Orchard (at appropriate season)
  - Picnic (prepare and/or cook own meal)
  - Poultry or turkey ranch
  - Produce farm
  - Restaurant

- Resource people (with appropriate aids)
  - Baker
  - Butcher
  - Chef from a restaurant
  - Cook at your center (if you have one) or from local school
  - Farmer with some of his produce—how he prepares it for market and how he sells it (crate, truckload, by the pound)
  - Fisherman
  - Grocer
  - Milkman
  - Parent—preparation and/or use of products
  - Poultry rancher

SOME SUGGESTIONS FOR UNCOOKED FOOD

Butter (see recipe on page 182)
Fruit salads
Gelatin
Homemade ice cream (see recipes on page 187)
Icings (see recipes on page 188)
Instant puddings
No-bake cookies (see recipes on pages 184-185)
Peanut butter made with a blender
Sandwich fillings
Vegetable salads

SOME SUGGESTIONS FOR FOOD PREPARED ON A HOT PLATE OR ELECTRIC SAUCE PAN OR FRY PAN (see recipe book accompanying appliance)

Apples, baked
Applesauce
Candy
Cottage Cheese (See recipe, p. 186.)
Dumplings
Doughnuts
Eggs
Fritters
French fried potatoes
French toast
Grilled sandwiches
Jam
Jelly
Meat (bacon, sausage,
    hamburgers, other)
Meatballs
Pancakes
Popcorn
Rice Krispie cookies
    (recipe on box)
Scones
Soup
Spaghetti and sauce
Stew
Stewed fruit
Tacos
Upside-down cake
White sauces

ADDITIONAL TEACHING AIDS FOR FOOD EXPERIENCES

SONGS

Dalton, Arlene, *et al. My Picture Book of Songs.* Chicago: Donahue & Co., 1947.
  "Simple Sal," p. 47
  "Grandpa's Farm," p. 57

Seeger, Ruth. *American Folk Songs for Children.* New York: Doubleday & Co., 1948.
  "Old Aunt Kate," p. 139
  "Do, Do, Pity My Case," p. 136

Wood, Lucille F., and Louise B. Scott. *Singing Fun.* St. Louis: Webster Publishing Co., 1954.
  "Little Seeds," p. 33
  "Gathering Eggs," p. 35
  "I'd Like to Be a Farmer," p. 36
  "If I Were a Farmer," p. 39
  "The Singing Farm," p. 40
  "Ten Yellow Chicks," p. 42
  "Our Milkman," p. 51
  "The Bakery Truck," p. 53

——————— . *More Singing Fun.* St. Louis: Webster Div., McGraw Hill, 1961.
  "A Whistling Farm Boy," p. 61
  "Ice Cream Man," p. 71

BOOKS

Berg, Jean H. *Baby Susan's Chickens.* New York: Wonder Books, 1951.

Collier, Ethel. *Who Goes There In My Garden?* New York: Young Scott, 1963.

Cook, Bernadine. *The Little Fish that Got Away.* New York: Young Scott.

Darby, Gene. *What Is a Plant?* Chicago: Benefic Press, 1958.

——————— . *What Is a Chicken?* Chicago: Benefic Press, 1958.

——————— . *What Is a Cow?* Chicago: Benefic Press, 1963.

——————— . *What Is a Fish?* Chicago: Benefic Press, 1958.

Green, Carla. *I Want to Be a Fisherman.* Chicago: Children's Press.

Green, Mary. *Everybody Eats.* New York: Young Scott, 1950.

Jordan, Helene J. *Seeds by Wind and Water.* New York: Thos. Crowell, 1962.

——————— . *How a Seed Grows.* New York: Thos. Crowell.

Kraus, Ruth. *The Growing Story.* New York: Harper & Row, 1947.

——————— . *The Carrot Seed.* New York: Harper & Bros., 1945.

Martin, Dick. *The Apple Book.* New York: Golden Press, 1964.

——————— . *The Fish Book.* New York: Golden Press, 1964.

McCloskey, Robert. *Blueberries for Sal.* New York: Viking Press, 1966.

Rothschild, Alice. *Fruit Is Ripe for Timothy.* New York: Young Scott, 1963.

Selsam, Millicent E. *Seeds and More Seeds.* New York: Harper & Bros., 1959.

——————— . *All About Eggs.* New York: Wm. R. Scott, 1952.

Smith, Laura & Ernie. *Things That Grow.* Chicago: Melmont, 1958.

Webber, Irma E. *Bits That Grow Big.* New York: Wm. R. Scott, 1959.

——————— . *Up Above and Down Below.* New York: Wm. R. Scott, 1943.

ESPECIALLY FOR PARENTS

Because the child has more meals (and snacks) in the home than in the school, he also has more opportunities for participation. At school other children want and need to share in the activities. At home, start with some simple *possible* activities for your child; as he shows interest and ability, increase the selection in kind and complexity. At first, helping take out the garbage may seem glamorous and important, but if it becomes his lifetime assignment, he will lose interest in a hurry. He needs a variety of things at which he can succeed.

Things other than food preparation make mealtimes pleasant. Making some decorations for the table, setting the table, eating in a different location (outside, for instance), or inviting a guest also adds interest to the occasion. A word of caution here: mealtimes should be happy affairs, with discussions of interesting topics and everyone having a chance to hear and be heard. This is a time family members should look forward to. Unpleasantries can be handled at another time.

To involve your child further in meal planning, let him help you check your supplies at home and make a list of what you will need to purchase. Can you get all of your items at the same store, or do you need to make several stops? Let him help you decide.

If you have a garden, let your child help plant, care for, and harvest the crops. This will give him an understanding about where produce comes from that he would never get by purchasing the produce in the grocery store. If you don't have a garden, let your child go with you to the market. Show him how to select various fruits and vegetables. Sometimes you want produce that is green; at other times you want it bright with color; you may want it firm or soft. Talk with him about how you decide upon the quantity to buy and whether you feel the item is expensive or a good buy. Discuss different ways you could prepare it together and how well it stores. Keep in mind that this is not a formal lecture but a sharing of your thoughts. Upon your return from the market, let your child assist you in putting the groceries in their proper places. When you are ready to use these items, he can get them. He will also learn how to store similar things together and how to make some orderly arrangements. And he learns about different methods of storage (refrigerator, shelf, freezer).

Talk also about the importance of good nutrition with your child. Help him to understand why we need to eat certain foods and either avoid or limit others. The eating habits and attitudes he forms early in life will have a great bearing on his future health. Perhaps posting a chart of the basic four food groups, including a column for your child to record his daily menus, would be an enjoyable and beneficial home activity.

Make food preparation fun rather than dull. Occasional suggestions from your child as to a dish or a menu increase his interest. On more than one occasion my own two sons (at preschool age) said, "Mother, why don't you go to a meeting so we can make something?" or "I can do that for supper." And they said it with such confidence.

Encourage your child to eat a variety of foods. Introduce new foods, one at a time, in small quantities with the suggestion, "Just try it." Forcing a child to eat a certain food often creates a dislike that could have been avoided. Each time you serve it, encourage him to eat a little: "Taste it, and if you want more, you can have it." Compliment him when he does taste it. I have used this technique many times in the classroom. One time a child said, "Well, aren't you going to say you're glad I tasted it?" when I forgot to complete my part.

Serve finger foods to young children—and expect them to use their fingers on other foods as well. It may be difficult for them to manipulate the silverware at first, but they will soon develop the skills and the desire to use them.

Children can also help clear the table—especially their own dishes. Many of them can help wash and dry the dishes. They will want to do these things if

they feel a part of what is going on. Suppose you rotate the jobs—washing dishes, wiping dishes, taking out the garbage, sweeping up crumbs, clearing up the table—so that it doesn't become a monotonous routine but remains an opportunity to help and to learn. (What is your goal here: to get the dishes done and the kitchen cleaned up, or to help the child establish some good work habits? Certainly, it takes longer when the child helps, but look at the long-range goal!)

Here are some possible ways a child *can help* with actual food preparation:

Brush vegetables (potatoes, carrots, turnips)
Peel vegetables or fruit (Hand peelers are easiest for young hands.)
Shell peas or snip beans
Rinse vegetables (lettuce, tomatoes, radishes)
Whip cream or topping
Make gelatin or instant pudding
Knead bread
Make and bake cookies
Frost cupcakes or cookies
Season vegetables
Pour milk, juice, water
Cook meat
Make sandwiches
Make fruit or vegetable salads (or plates)
Process fruit or vegetables (canning, drying, freezing)
Make punch or fruit drinks
Make popsicles
Prepare picnic lunch
Make a special treat
Pop corn
Use suggestions throughout this chapter (see also pages 116-117 and 120).
See *When I Do, I Learn* by Barbara J. Taylor, pp. 93-99.

RECISES

BREAD

White Bread (Method 1)

Scald 1 quart of milk. Add 1½ T salt and 6 T shortening. Cool.

Mix together ½ c. warm water, 6 T sugar, and 2 pkgs. yeast. Let stand about 10 minutes. Add yeast mixture and 2 c. sifted flour to milk mixture. Beat until creamy and smooth. Add 8 c. sifted flour (one cup at a time). Knead 10 minutes. Let rise in covered, greased bowl for 45 minutes. Knead again and shape into loaves. Put in pans. Let rise until double in bulk (about 45 minutes). Bake 350-375° for 30 minutes. Rub top with milk and return to oven for 5 minutes. Remove and cool. Makes 3 loaves.

90-Minute Bread (Method 2)

4 c. warm water	4 T shortening
4-5 tsp. salt	4 pkgs. dry yeast
4 T sugar	8-10 c. flour

Dissolve yeast in warm water in a very large bowl. Add flour (start with 8 c.), salt, sugar, and shortening. Stir together with spoon until it becomes more dough-like; then mix with hand(s). Dough should be medium-soft, not sticky. Add more flour and salt if necessary. Cut dough into four pieces, mold into loaves, and let stand for 15-20 minutes. Beat down each loaf with fist for about 1 minute. Mold into loaves again, place in greased loaf pans, and let rise in a warm place for 30-60 minutes. Bake at 350° for 30-40 minutes. Remove from pans to cool. Makes four loaves.

Streamlined White Bread (Method 3)

1¼ c. warm water (not hot—110 to 115°)
1 pkg. active dry yeast
2 T soft shortening
2 tsp. salt
2 T sugar
3 c. sifted flour

In mixer bowl, dissolve yeast in warm water. Add shortening, salt, sugar, and half the flour. Beat 2 minutes, medium speed on mixer, or 300 vigorous strokes by hand. Scrape sides and bottom of bowl frequently. Add remaining flour and blend with spoon until smooth. Scrape batter from sides of bowl. Cover with cloth and let rise in warm place (85°) until double, about 30 minutes. (If kitchen is cool, place dough on rack over a bowl of hot water and cover with a towel.)

Stir down batter by beating about 25 strokes. Spread batter evenly in greased loaf pan, 8½" x 4½" x 2¾" or 9" x 5" x 3". Batter will be sticky. Smooth out top of loaf by flouring hand and patting into shape.

Again let rise in warm place (85°) until batter reaches ¼" from top of 8½" pan or 1" from top of 9" pan, about 40 minutes.

Heat oven to 375°. Bake 45-50 minutes, or until brown. To test loaf, tap the top crust; it should sound hollow. Immediately remove from pan. Place on cooling rack or across bread pans. Brush top with melted butter or shortening. Do not place in direct draft. Cool before cutting. A sawtooth knife is especially good for cutting. Slice with a sawing motion rather than pressing down, making slices slightly thicker than usual. Makes one loaf.

181

Individual Bun Recipe (Ingredients for each child)

1 tsp. soft margarine	1 tsp. mixed fruit (currants)
1 tsp. sugar	1½ T milk and egg (2 eggs to 1 pint of
1 T flour	milk whipped together)

Blend margarine and sugar in small bowl or plastic carton. Add flour, fruit, and liquid. Stir. Put in baking papers in muffin tin. Bake.

Whole Wheat Bread (Method 1)

4½ c. sifted whole wheat flour
2 c. sifted enriched white flour (approx.)

Keep whole wheat and white flour separate until mixing.
½ cake yeast softened in ¼ c. lukewarm water or ½ T dry granular yeast softened in ¼ c. warm water (110° F.).
Place in mixing bowl:
2½ c. scalded milk
3 T shortening
3 T sugar
1 T salt

When milk mixture is cooled to 90° F., add 3 cups of the whole wheat flour. Beat well. Then add the softened yeast. Add the remaining whole wheat flour. Beat until all the whole wheat flour is thoroughly mixed into the dough. Then add enough of the white flour to make a soft dough. Mix until the dough forms in an elastic, soft ball. Whole wheat dough ferments much faster than white dough. If it gets too light, the finished bread will be coarse and crumbly.

Cover. Keep dough in a warm place away from drafts until it has almost tripled in bulk. Punch it down, turn it over, cover it, and let it rise 30 minutes. Punch it down, turn it over, cover it, and let it rise 20 minutes; divide into balls for loaves. Cover and rest dough 10 minutes. Mold into loaves and put into pans. Cover; let double in bulk. Bake in a moderate oven (375°) about 50 minutes. Makes 2 loaves.

The whole wheat dough will be ready for baking in a shorter time than will white dough.

Whole Wheat Bread (Method 2)

Use recipe for 90-minute bread with following changes: Honey for the sugar; peanut oil for the shortening; and 1 c. white flour with whole wheat flour.

BUTTER

Use ½ pint cream in a pint jar. *Cream should be at room temperature and should be several days old.* Shake it until it thickens (about 10 minutes). Add salt. Drain. Pour cold water over it and keep pouring buttermilk off. Cream with a spoon until all buttermilk is drained off. Add yellow food coloring. (Butter can also be made by putting cream in small baby food jars so more children can participate.)

COOKIES—DROP

Peanut Butter Cookies

1½ c. sifted flour	Dash of salt
1 tsp. soda	½ c. peanut butter
½ c. white sugar	½ c. butter or margarine,
1 c. brown sugar	melted
1 egg	

Sift flour and soda together once.
Mix together dry ingredients.
Add peanut butter, butter, and egg.
Make balls the size of English walnuts, place on oiled cookie sheet 3 inches apart, and press down with fork.
Bake at 375° until light brown. Makes 3 dozen cookies, mild in flavor.

Oatmeal Cookies

1 c. raisins (covered with water and simmered for 5 minutes)

1 c. shortening	2 c. flour
1 c. white sugar	½ tsp. soda
3 eggs	½ tsp. allspice
½ tsp. salt	1 tsp. cinnamon
6 T raisin liquid	½ tsp. cloves
2 c. oatmeal	1 c. nuts

Cream white sugar and shortening; add eggs and beat. Sift dry ingredients and add to creamed mixture. Add raisin liquid alternately with oatmeal. Add raisins and nuts. Bake at 375° for 15 minutes. Makes about 5 dozen.

Light Brownies

2¾ c. sifted flour	2½ c. brown sugar (1 lb.)
2½ tsp. baking powder	3 eggs
½ tsp. salt	1 c. nut pieces
2/3 c. shortening	1 pkg. chocolate chips

Mix shortening and add brown sugar. Mix well and *cool*. Sift flour, baking powder, and salt. Add eggs one at a time to sugar and shortening. Beat well after each addition. Add dry ingredients, nuts, and chocolate chips. Pat into greased pan about 12" x 17". Bake in 350° oven for 25 minutes. Cool for 5 minutes. Cut into squares.

Ginger Creams

¾ c. shortening	1 c. sugar
¼ c. molasses	2¼ c. flour
1 egg	1 tsp. soda
½ tsp. salt	1 T ginger
	1 tsp. cinnamon

Mix together. Chill. Spoon out in walnut-size balls and roll in hands. Dip in sugar. Bake at 375° until done (12-15 minutes).

Chocolate Chip Cookies

1¾ c. flour	14 T shortening
¾ c. brown sugar	¾ c. white sugar
1 tsp. hot water	2 6 oz. pkgs. chocolate chips
1 tsp. soda	1 tsp. salt
2 eggs (unbeaten)	1 c. nut pieces
2 c. oatmeal	1 tsp. vanilla

Cream shortening with brown and white sugar. Add eggs. Mix hot water and soda and add. Sift dry ingredients and add to mixture. Add vanilla, nuts, and oatmeal. Bake at 375° for 8 minutes. Makes about 5 dozen.

Snickerdoodles

1 c. shortening	2 eggs
2½ c. flour	2 tsp. soda
2 tsp. cream of tartar	½ tsp. salt
1½ c. sugar	

Cream shortening and sugar. Add eggs and stir. Sift dry ingredients together and add. Mix well and roll in 1 tsp. cinnamon and 2 tsp. sugar. Bake at 350° for 8-10 minutes.

No-Bake Cookies (Method 1)

½ c. milk	Add: 3 c. oatmeal
½ c. butter	½ tsp. vanilla
2 c. sugar	4 T cocoa
Boil for 1 minute	½ c. nuts
	½ c. coconut (or raisins)

Drop by spoon onto waxed paper. Let stand until firm.

No-Bake Cookies (Method 2)

2 c. sugar
4 T cocoa
½ tsp. salt
½ c. peanut butter

½ c. milk
1 tsp. vanilla
2½ c. quick-cooking oats

In saucepan combine sugar, cocoa, salt, peanut butter, and milk. Bring to a boil and boil 1 minute. Remove from heat and add vanilla and oats. Mix well. Drop by spoon onto waxed paper. Let stand until firm. Makes about 2½ dozen.

COOKIES—ROLLED

Grandma Milne's Sugar Cookies

1 c. shortening
2 eggs
1 c. milk
2 heaping tsp. cream
   of tartar

2 c. sugar
2 tsp. vanilla
2 tsp. soda in a little hot water
5 to 6 c. flour

Cream shortening and sugar; add eggs and soda. Sift flour and cream of tartar. Add dry ingredients alternately with milk. Add vanilla. Bake at 350°-375° for 12 minutes.

Boston Cookies

3 eggs, well beaten
1½ c. brown sugar
1 c. shortening, softened
3¼ c. flour (reserve a little)
1 tsp. baking powder

½ tsp. salt
2 T water
½ tsp. vanilla
½ c. raisins (chopped)
1 c. nuts (chopped)

Combine eggs, sugar, and shortening. Beat well. Add sifted dry ingredients, water, vanilla, floured nuts, and raisins. Mix thoroughly. Chill mixture about 45 minutes. Roll 1/3" thick. Cut. Bake at 350° for about 15 minutes or until delicately browned. Makes about 7 dozen 2" cookies.

Buttermilk Cookies

1 c. shortening
2 c. sugar
3 eggs, beaten
1 c. buttermilk

6 c. flour
1 tsp. soda
¼ tsp. nutmeg or other spice

Cream the shortening; add the sugar gradually and blend thoroughly. Add beaten eggs and buttermilk. Add sifted dry ingredients, mixing well. Chill. Roll to a thickness of about 1/8"; spread with sugar and cut. Place on greased cookie sheet and bake at 375° for 10 – 12 minutes.

Swedish Cookies

½ c. shortening
½ c. confectioners' sugar
1/8 tsp. almond extract
3 egg yolks, hard-cooked

1 c. sifted flour
¼ tsp. salt
red jelly

Cream shortening and sugar. Add flavoring. Blend. Press egg yolks through sieve. Blend with creamed mixture. Work in flour and salt. Chill. Roll 1/8" thick. Cut one half with cookie cutter, the other half with doughnut cutter of same size. Place doughnut-shaped cookie portions atop whole round portions. Bake at 350° for 20 minutes. Cool on rack. Fill center with red jelly just before serving. Makes approximately thirty 2" cookies.

Sugar Cookies (Method 1)

¾ c. granulated sugar	1 tsp. cream of tartar
½ c. melted shortening	½ tsp. baking soda
2 eggs, beaten	½ tsp. salt
2 c. flour	1 tsp. vanilla

Blend sugar well with shortening. Stir in beaten eggs and vanilla. Sift flour, cream of tartar, baking soda, and salt; add to shortening mixture gradually while mixing well. Chill until easy to handle. Then turn out onto lightly floured board. Roll to 1/8" thickness, then cut with floured 3" cutter. Arrange cookies on a greased baking sheet, about 2" apart. Sprinkle with granulated sugar and cinnamon if desired. Bake at 375° for 10 - 12 minutes. Makes about 1½ to 2 dozen cookies. Two tsp. baking powder may replace cream of tartar and soda.

Sugar Cookies (Method 2)

Cream together and beat until light and fluffy: ½ c. shortening and 1 c. sugar. Add and beat well: 2 well-beaten eggs, 2 T cream, and 1 T vanilla or almond extract. Sift together: 3½ cups cake flour and 2 tsp. baking powder. Add sifted dry ingredients to creamed mixture. Shape into mound, wrap in waxed paper, and chill thoroughly. Roll on board lightly powdered with confectioners' sugar, until dough is about ¼" thick. Dip cutters in confectioners' sugar each time before cutting cookie, then place cookie on lightly greased baking sheet. Bake in moderate oven (375°) for about 8 minutes or until delicately browned.

Coloring Sugar Cookies

Beat 1 egg yolk with 1 tsp. water. Divide into containers and add different food coloring to each. Brush onto cookies before baking. If not cooked too long, the color is good.

Carolyn's Cookies

4 c. flour	1 c. shortening
1 c. sugar	4 eggs, well beaten
4 tsp. baking powder	1/3 c. milk
½ tsp. salt	1 tsp. vanilla

Sift together. Cut in 1 c. shortening as in pie dough. Add 4 well-beaten eggs, 1/3 c. milk and 1 tsp. vanilla. Roll out and cut. Bake at 400° until brown.

Gingerbread Men

Simmer 15 minutes 1 c. molasses and 1 c. shortening.
Cream together 1 c. sugar, 1 egg, and 1 tsp. vanilla.
Dissolve 2 tsp. soda in ½ c. hot water. Add hot water and soda mixture to sugar and egg. Sift together 6 c. flour, ¼ tsp. cloves, 1 tsp. cinnamon, 1 tsp. salt, and ½ tsp. ginger. Add to other mixture and stir until flour is well mixed. Roll thin and cut with cookie cutter. Bake 10 minutes in 375° oven. This dough does not stick to the pan. Even a child can handle it.

COTTAGE CHEESE

2 c. whole milk or soured milk
1 T vinegar

Stir and cook milk over medium heat until bubbles begin to form on top. Remove from heat and stir in vinegar. Stir gently and watch for curds, which form quickly. Liquid is whey. Stir occasionally as mixture cools. Gather curds in strainer, gently pressing curds so that whey is removed. Add salt to taste.

ICE CREAM

Homemade Ice Cream (Cooked)
(makes 6 quarts)

4¾ c. sugar
2 qts. milk
5 T flour (mix flour with sugar)
Add 5 beaten eggs
Dash of salt

Cook together, stirring constantly, until mixture eventually thickens and boils. Cool mixture in refrigerator (overnight if desired).
Place custard in freezer.
Add this mixture:

1 pt. whipping cream
2 cans evaporated milk
4 T vanilla (imitation)
1 T lemon

Add enough whole milk to finish filling freezer. Place freezer can in ice, add rock salt, and turn until mixture is frozen.

Homemade Ice Cream (Uncooked)
(24 servings)

8 eggs   2 pts. whipping cream
4 c. sugar   3½ pts. milk
                           4 tsp. vanilla

Beat eggs slightly. Add sugar and beat. Add the cream (as it is, do not whip) and beat just until well mixed. Add the milk and vanilla and mix well. Pour into freezer can and freeze according to freezer directions. Makes one gallon.

ICINGS (FOR COOKIES, CRACKERS, CUPCAKES)

Easy Creamy Icing

Blend 1 c. sifted confectioners' sugar, ¼ tsp. salt, ½ tsp. vanilla or other flavoring (lemon, almond or peppermint), and liquid to make easy to spread (about 1 T water or 1½ T cream). Tint, if desired, with a few drops of food coloring. Spread on cookie with spatula or pastry brush or knife.

Butter Icing

1/3 c. soft butter
3 c. sifted confectioners' sugar
3 T cream (approx.)
1½ tsp. vanilla

Blend butter and sugar together. Stir in cream and vanilla until smooth. Makes frosting for 24 cupcakes.
*To make chocolate icing, stir 3 tsp. unsweetened chocolate (3 oz.), melted, into blended mixture.
*For other variations add different flavorings and a few drops of food coloring.

Quick-as-a-Wink Chocolate Frosting

1 pkg. (6 oz.) semisweet chocolate pieces
2 T butter
3 T milk
1 c. sifted confectioners' sugar

Combine chocolate, butter, and milk in saucepan. Stir over low heat until chocolate is just melted. Remove from heat. Stir in sugar. Beat until smooth, glossy, and easy to spread. (If not glossy, stir in a few drops of hot water.) Makes frosting for 12 cup cakes.

POPCORN

Caramel Corn (Method 1)

Combine and bring to boil: 1 c. dark syrup and 1 pkg. brown sugar.
Add and bring to boil: 1 square butter.
Add 1 c. evaporated milk and 1/3 c. white sugar.
Cook to soft ball stage, stirring constantly.
Pour over popped corn. Makes 2½ to 3 gallons.

Caramel Corn (Method 2)

1 square margarine
1 large can condensed milk
   (Eagle Brand)
1 pkg. brown sugar

Combine ingredients and boil. Stir constantly. Pour over popcorn.

Popcorn Balls (Method 1)

2 c. sugar
¾ c. corn syrup
¾ c. boiling water

Combine ingredients and bring to quick boil. Add 1 tsp. cream of tartar. Cook to soft crack stage. Add 1 tsp. vanilla and 1/8 tsp. soda and stir well. Pour over popcorn.

Popcorn Balls (Method 2)

1 c. white Karo
½ c. white sugar

Bring to a boil. Add one box jello and let cool. Pour over popcorn. Children shape balls. Recipe can be made several hours before use.

Popcorn Cake

1½ c. sugar	2 T butter
1 c. white corn syrupp	½ tsp. salt
1/3 c. boiling water	4 c. popped corn
red coloring	candied fruits

Mix sugar, corn syrup, and boiling water. Color the syrup a light pink. Cook the syrup over low heat to the hard crack stage (290°). At this stage syrup forms a hard thread in cold water. It snaps easily when handled. Remove from the heat. Add butter and salt. Pour syrup over popped corn, mixing well. Butter sides and bottom of large cake pan. Sprinkle brightly colored candied fruits on bottom. Press the popcorn mixture into the cake pan. Allow to harden and cool. Remove from cake pan and slice in wedges. Makes 12 large wedges.

BIBLIOGRAPHY FOR FOOD EXPERIENCES AND RECIPES

BOOKS

Adventures in Cooking. Westfield, New Jersey (07090): Kenyon Chapter of New Jersey Assoc. for Ed. of Young Children, c/o Mrs. Florence P. Foster, 810 Harding Street. (1972) $3.00.

Baking Like Mommy. Minneapolis, Minnesota: Junior Home Service, Pillsbury Co. A storybook on how to cook. Included are recipes and illustrated directions. Part one is for preschool chefs; part two is for primary cooks, ages 5 to 7.

Barlow, Frances, and Captola Murdock. *Food Facts and Fun for Young Children.* (Write to first author at 1235 Cedar Avenue, Provo, Utah, 84601.) 1973.

Croft, Doreen J., and Robert D. Hess. *An Activities Handbook for Teachers of Young Children.* Boston: Houghton Mifflin, 1972.

Croft, Karen B. *The Good for Me Cookbook.* San Francisco: R and E Research Associates, 4843 Mission Street, 1971.

Dishes Children Love. Chicago: Consolidated Book Publishers, 1727 S. Indiana Avenue, 60616. Dozens of simple, step-by-step recipes that children enjoy are in this cookbook. $1.00.

Ferreira, Nancy J. *The Mother-Child Cookbook.* Menlo Park, Calif.: Pacific Coast Publishers, 1969.

Hildebrand, Verna. *Introduction to Early Childhood Education.* New York: Macmillan, 1971, pp. 276-92.

ARTICLE

Ferreira, Nancy. "Teacher's Guide to Educational Cooking in the Nursery School—an Everyday Affair." *Young Children*, November 1973, pp. 23-32.

CHAPTER 11

MATHEMATICS

With mathematics, as with all other curriculum areas, the experiences should be casual rather than forced; they should be within the developmental abilities of the individual child and should be of interest and value.

GOALS IN TEACHING MATHEMATICS

1. To stimulate an interest in numbers and their uses
2. To show how number concepts can aid in problem solving
3. To increase knowledge about the everyday world by using mathematics
4. To introduce number symbols and terms as the child indicates readiness

By the time a child goes to preschool (whether he is three, four, or five), he has already had some contact with numbers. He has generally been taught to hold up the appropriate number of fingers to indicate his age and perhaps say the number. He may be able to count a few numbers in the proper sequence. He has heard and seen others use numbers. He is developing an interest in numbers, but his comprehension of symbols or meanings is very limited; even if he is able to count to ten or higher, he has learned by rote and does not have an understanding of mathematics.

Mathematics is a shortcut and an aid in many daily activities. Adults know how to use addition, subtraction, multiplication, division, fractions, and geometry so that their use becomes somewhat automatic. Children, too, need to have concrete experiences in order to understand mathematics. For instance, at snack time, how many chairs or napkins will we need? An adult can rapidly count the children (or subtract the number absent from the total enrolled). A child would more likely say, "A chair for John, a chair for Helen, a chair for. . . ." Eventually he may be able to count the children, then the chairs.

Addition is the first form of mathematics learned by a child. "We need two more blocks to make this stack as high as that one"; "Peter needs a cowboy hat, so we'll have to find one more"; and "We don't have enough cookies for everybody to have two" are common examples.

A further step in mathematics is subtraction. "If I give you two of my colors, we'll each have four"; "You have more brushes than I do"; and "If you give me some of your cars, I can play with you" indicate a reduction on one

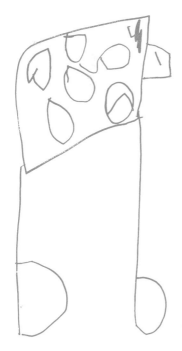

part and an increase on the other. Often this is more than a transfer of material things: it is social technique, sharing, and cooperative involvement.

The formal teaching of addition and subtraction comes later, followed even later by more advanced forms of mathematics, such as multiplication, division, and use of fractions.

Referring to goal number one (to stimulate an interest in numbers and their uses), we find that we have many daily opportunities to interest children in number manipulation. The first step would be similar to counting the chairs (one for John and one for. . . .). The next step would be to help a child count a small number of people or objects followed by a representation for that number (a written symbol). All of these steps should take place in a category of special interest to the children in your group. Pushing all the children simply because one is ready, or holding them all back because one is not ready, is inappropriate. Ideas and materials should be made available for those who indicate interest. Ways of stimulating interest in others should also be provided.

As opportunities arise, capitalize upon them to show the children how numbers help us (goal number two). "We have five children at our table today. How many napkins will we need? Cups? Do we have enough cupcakes for each person? Let's count and see." "There are twelve blocks on the floor. If each of us takes four to the shelf, they will all be put away." "How many children are wearing the color red today? They can go with this teacher. How many children are wearing blue? They can go with this teacher." "Does each teacher have the same number of children? How could we do that?"

Suppose some of the children are playing in water or sand. You provide some measuring spoons, cups, or other utensils and they begin to measure and pour. How long do you think it would take them to find out how many teaspoons make a tablespoon, how many tablespoons in a cup, or how many cups in a quart? Do *you* know? Now try this one. Using a recipe, make something for a snack or for lunch. Talk to the children about what you are including, how much of each ingredient, and why you use different amounts. What would happen if you used the same amount of salt and sugar in cookies? What would happen if we didn't measure anything? What is the purpose of including each of the ingredients? Another example: "We have one apple and four children. How shall we cut it so all can have the same size piece?" These are just a few simple examples of ways in which you can increase the child's knowledge about his world through using mathematics (goal number three). See how simple and enjoyable mathematics can be? We may not use the term "math" with the children, but, more important, we are helping them to form attitudes and skills.

Some preschool children can read the written symbols for some numbers. When trying to preassess my group of children, I made ten cards (5" x 8") on which I wrote one number per card, using the numbers one to ten. I showed the cards to each child and told him I wanted to see if he knew what was on each card. Naturally, I mixed up the numbers. Most of the children recognized that these were number symbols, but some thought they were letters in the alphabet. Regardless of the sequence of the numbers on the cards, most of the children counted by rote from one to ten. A couple of the children knew some of the numbers, but no child knew all of them. That gave me a starting point. That week we did some casual number experiences. No child was forced or pushed beyond his interest or ability. Later, when I showed the cards to the children individually, most of them could recognize at least some of the numbers. It was challenging to the teachers to provide stimulating number experiences (dominoes, games, puzzles, pegs, and numbers) so that each child participated in one or more of the activities daily. They thoroughly enjoyed it. Some of the children spent time writing the numbers because *they* wanted to. It was a way of expressing something they were interested in (goal number four).

There may be children in your group who know a great deal about numbers. One boy, four, had some coins in his pocket. The teacher asked him if he could identify the coins—which he correctly did. Then as a challenge, the teacher asked if he knew which coin could buy more than the others. He did. Moreover, he went on to tell her how many pennies were in a nickel, a dime, and a quarter. Most children would rather have a penny than a dime because it is larger, but this child knew the relative value of coins.

You can introduce mathematical terms to children as long as these terms are defined and the child has an opportunity to understand the meaning through a firsthand experience (also goal number four). "When you want (or need) more of something, you add (get more). When you want less (or not as many), you subtract (or take away). If we don't have enough cups for a snack, what do we need to do? If we have too many, what do we need to do?" Some children can understand what an equal sign means. ("You have the same number of things on one side of the sign as you have on the other." Try it.) "We have three boys on this side of the line and three boys on that side. That means we have an equal number of boys on each side of the line. How can we make an equal number of girls on each side of the line? Hats? Shoes?"

"If we have one carrot, and we want to give an equal part (or half) to the white rabbit and an equal part to the black rabbit, how shall we do it?" You can explain that two halves make one whole. Demonstrate it, and let the children use other objects to make sure they have the idea. This may be the limit that most children can understand at this time; however, another child may be building with unit blocks and arrive at the marvelous discovery that if he wants to make a circle, he has to use four rounding blocks.

Maria Montessori felt that the concept of "zero" (or nothing) was worth special teaching. She devised some games, activities, and materials for teaching it. Perhaps this particular concept is given less importance today, but it still has meaning. Montessori also teaches numbers in a series of nine rather than ten (as is more common) just to give special emphasis to zero.

Can you imagine how we would get along in this complex world without some methods of simplification (mathematics, for example)? Number symbols are used so much in our daily lives that we take them for granted. How could we tell houses (or cars or other objects) apart without our present numbering system? How could we follow a recipe? Of what value would the telephone, a

cash register, or a computer be without symbols and meanings? Try to think of all the happenings in your life today that involve numbers.

Here are some suggestions you might like to share with your children at school:

- Provide various methods of measurement (length, weight, time, size, amount).
- Talk with the children about the difference between cardinal (1, 2, 3) and ordinal (first, second, third) numbers.
- Show them how grouping things helps in counting them.
- Provide opportunities for linear measurement (use a string, a stick, a measuring tape, a yard stick).
- Go on a picnic. What will we need to take? How much of it?
- Play games with a spinner (number symbols).
- Use a die (dots to represent numbers; written symbols could be included).
- Make a die out of a large block or cover a cube with contact paper.
- Tell a story and have the children supply number parts (number of legs on an animal, a distance).
- Count the number of children with certain color clothing, type of shoes, physical characteristics.
- Set table for lunch or snack. How many chairs and napkins do we need?
- Make and follow a recipe.
- Make a store. Provide cans, boxes, money, a cash register. Write number (cost) on articles and amount on money. Make it simple.
- Pour liquid or dry ingredients into measuring containers (large and smaller).
- Bake or make something special. Sell it for snack.
- Use a token system.
- Have tickets for snack or lunch.
- Have objects and articles of different sizes and shapes. Have the children make different combinations (little and round and others).
- Look around the room and yard for objects of the same shape.
- Provide a large clock with numbers.
- Weigh each child, measure his height, and post information about him on visible chart or on wall.
- Have a display of coins. Discuss characteristics and amounts of each.
- Provide a scale for weighing objects (could also be used in a store).
- Count and name the parts of plants or objects.
- Introduce a thermometer and have ways for them to use it (hot and cold).
- Use math vocabulary (add [more], subtract [less], wide-narrow, large-larger-largest, middle, various shapes).
- Have duplicate cards showing certain number of objects or dots on one and a corresponding written symbol on the other.
- Use egg cartons for separating articles from symbols (beans, rocks).
- Count the number of times a ball is bounced, hands are clapped, feet are stamped.
- Take a shoe box and make openings of different shapes. Pass same shaped object through openings.
- Make sandpaper shapes and written symbols.
- Use stories ("One Bright Monday Morning" by Baum, see page 89), poems ("One, two, buckle my shoe"), fingerplays ("Ten Little Indians"), songs that contain numbers ("Over in the Meadow").
- Have a discussion in block area (shapes, sizes, number, relationship to each other).
- Talk about objects which have numbers: speedometer, ruler, yard stick, phone, timer, clock, watch, license plates, scales, money, measuring spoons and cups, sport players, tickets, cards, cash register, bottles, boxes, calendar, road signs, flash cards.

- Discuss balance and how it is achieved.
- Introduce the concepts of "zero," "equal," "half" as the child is ready.

ESPECIALLY FOR PARENTS

Parents need to be aware of their role in helping their children build correct and positive attitudes towards mathematics. Saying, "I always hated math in school," or "I just never learned how to balance a budget or figure something" is in opposition to our goals. True, everyone does not enjoy mathematics, but influencing a child before he has had a chance is really unfair to him. So is it unfair to push him when he is neither ready nor interested.

From a very young age your child can have enjoyable counting experiences with you. You might count "One, two, three buttons on your sweater" as you help him fasten them. "One shoe, two shoes." "Daddy, mommy, baby: one, two, three." "One for you, one for brother, and one for me." As he grows older, he can have more complex experiences: "Everybody needs a knife, a fork, and a spoon—three things." "Let's bake some potatoes for supper. How many will we need? One for Daddy, one for Mommy, and one for you: one, two, three."

Provide experiences which help rather than hinder concept development. One family had a very modernistic clock in their living room which had a gold ball where each of the twelve numbers should appear. Then they wondered why their children were having difficulty learning to tell time. The same principle would apply to having Roman numerals, which many people have difficulty reading when the numbers get beyond ten.

What do you think will happen when we change our current measurement system to the metric system? How easy do you think it is going to be to teach us a new system? Will there be a mathematics gap? How easy or difficult has it been for the people in England to adjust to their new monetary system? These situations are similar to what children face. They will need to learn and use methods which are common in the society in which they live. We can assist

them or we can confuse them by the early experiences we offer and the attitudes we display. Mathematics is too important to our everyday living for us to have a fear of or a dislike for it.

Perhaps parents will want to try some of the following ideas:

- Provide games which have dice (or one die) or a number spinner.
- When possible, point out written number symbols and tell the meaning. (A road sign reads "50." Show the child how that number should correspond with your speedometer.)
- Using a calendar, show how many days until a certain event (for your sake limit too much advance warning).
- For a birthday, show how the candles represent the years of a person's life.
- When looking at books or pictures, count the number of similar objects.
- Let him help set the table with the proper number of utensils.
- Show him where to look on bottles, cans, and boxes to find out how much is in that container.
- Tell him how you compare prices, quantity, and quality at the store.
- Show him how much material (fabric, yarn) you would need to make him a certain article of clothing.
- Ask the shoe salesman to show the child the instrument he uses to measure feet.
- Give him his own tape measure or metal tape and encourage him to measure and compare different things.
- Hand him an object. Ask him if it is large or small. Then compare it to another object. Ask if it is larger or smaller. Show him how it can be larger than some objects and smaller than others.
- Teach him the concept of "middle" ("There is one object on this side of it and another on the other side, so it is now in the middle").

- Ask a cashier to show the child how he knows what numbers to "ring up" and how much money to ask the people for.
- Tell your child you want five pounds of potatoes, and let him put them into the scale.
- Assist him in learning to count (meaningful experiences, not just rote).
- Teach him the proper way to dial the telephone, and teach him your number.
- Assist him in making something for a meal (from a recipe).
- If you are going to build something (bird house, dog house, fence), show him how you figure the amount of materials needed.
- Let him help you prepare a shopping list (how much you already have, what you will need to buy).
- Buy some shoe laces (how many eyelets are there, how long should the strings be?)
- Show him your house number and help him learn his address.
- Take him to an athletic event and point out the numbers on each player and tell him how scoring occurs ("When the ball goes over that line [or through that hoop], the players get points").
- Let him experiment with measuring spoons and cups.
- Make candy, using a thermometer.
- Make a coin card (five pennies equal one nickel; two nickels equal one dime).
- Take the child to the bank and explain some of the simple procedures.
- Go to the post office and see the stamps with different numbers on them.
- Let him help you fill your car with gas; point out the quantity and how much you must pay.
- Let him observe or participate in bowling (numbered pins and scoring).
- Make a chart showing what amount of money he can earn by doing certain jobs.
- Show him how numbers help us in our everyday life (the numbers on a pencil tell us about the softness of the lead, patterns tell us how large or small to make things, recipes tell us how much of each ingredient to include).

- Make up an enjoyable activity, using numbers. (Take one button, two spools, three ribbons, and four marshmallows. What can you make with them?)
- Help him to understand ordinal numbers (first, we have to get dressed; second, we wash our hands; third, we. . . .).
- Get him a bank that he can see into.
- Show him how to locate a radio station or a TV channel.
- Provide opportunities to make comparisons (more–less, little–littler–littlest, shapes [number and length of sides], temperature changes).
- Talk about things you do that involve numbers.
- Ask him to put a certain number of objects in certain piles.
- Help him relate a written symbol to a group of objects of that same number.
- Help him make a picture recipe of something he can make.
- Ask stimulating questions. ("What shall we do—we have only three oranges and there are five children?" "Two children want to paint and we have only one brush?" "How can we find out how tall each child is?" "How many blocks does it take to make the scale balance?")

BIBLIOGRAPHY FOR MATHEMATICS

BOOKS

Ashlock, Robert B. "Planning Mathematics Instruction for Four- and Five-Year-Olds." In Mills, Belen (ed.). *Understanding the Young Child and His Curriculum.* New York: Macmillan & Co., 1972, pp. 341-45.

Carmichael, Viola S. *Curriculum Ideas for Young Children.* Pasadena, Calif.: 1886 Kinneola Canyon Road, 91107.

Croft, Doreen J., and Robert D. Hess. *An Activities Handbook for Teachers of Young Children.* Boston: Houghton Mifflin Co., 1972, pp. 148-70.

Hildebrand, Verna. *Introduction to Early Childhood Education.* New York: Macmillan Co., 1971, pp. 163-65.

Leeper, Sarah H., Ruth J. Dales, Dora S. Skipper, and Ralph L. Witherspoon. *Good Schools for Young Children.* New York: Macmillan Co., 1974 (3rd edition), pp. 234-58.

Mills, Belen (ed.) *Understanding the Young Child and His Curriculum.* New York: Macmillan Co., 1972, pp. 344-46 (bibliography and selected readings).

Montessori, Maria. *The Montessori Method.* New York: Schocken Books, 1964.

Read, Katherine. *The Nursery School.* Philadelphia: W. B. Saunders Co., 1971, pp. 214-15.

Sharp, Evelyn. *Thinking Is Child's Play.* New York: Dutton, 1969.

Spodek, Bernard. *Teaching in the Early Years.* Englewood Cliffs, New Jersey: Prentice-Hall, 1972, pp. 137-53. (Also see selected readings on page 153.)

Vance, Barbara. *Teaching the Prekindergarten Child.* Monterey, Calif.: Brooks/Cole Pub. Co., 1973, pp. 269-82.

Withers, Carl. *Counting Out Rhymes.* New York: Dover, 1970.

ARTICLES

Ashlock, Robert. "What Math for Fours and Fives?" *Childhood Education,* April 1967, p. 469.

Heard, Ida Mae. "Number Games with Young Children." *Young Children,* January 1969, pp. 147-50.

_____ . "Mathematical Concepts and Abilities Possessed by Kindergarten Entrants." *Arithmetic Teacher* 17:4 (1970), pp. 340-41.

Maertens, N. W. "Who's Afraid of Modern Math?" *Parent's Magazine*, August 1971.

Rea, R. E., and R. E. Reys. "Mathematics Competence of Entering Kindergarteners," *Arithmetic Teacher* 17:1 (1970), pp. 701-5.

PAMPHLETS

Adkins, Dorothy C. *et al. Preschool Mathematics Curriculum Project. Final Report.* ERIC Document 038 168, November 1969, 28 pp.

Cahoon, Owen W. *A Teachers' Guide to Cognitive Tasks for Preschool.* Provo, Utah: Brigham Young University Press, 1974.

Hucklesby, Sylvia. *Opening Up the Classroom: A Walk Around the School.* University of Illinois. Urbana, Illinois: ERIC Clearinghouse on Early Childhood Education, 1971. (Ideas to teach math and science using stones and sticks.)

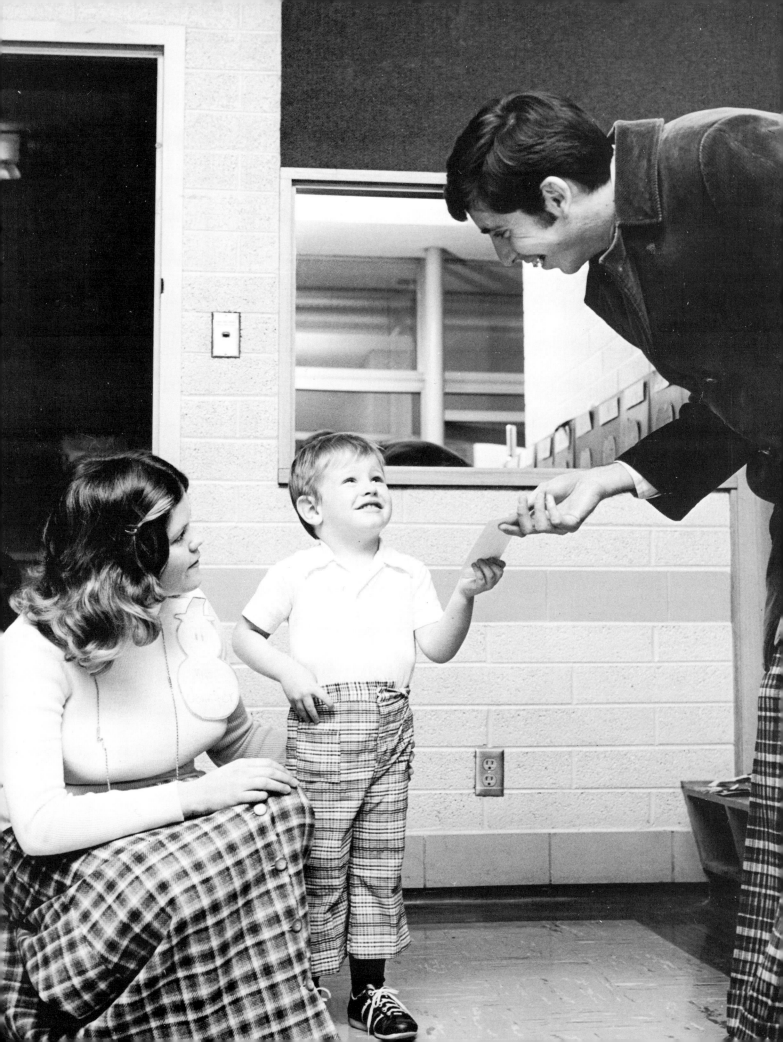

CHAPTER 12

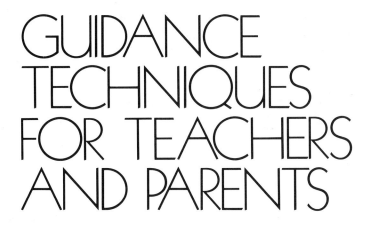

GUIDANCE TECHNIQUES FOR TEACHERS AND PARENTS

Having given consideration to the curriculum, we turn now to some workable techniques for child-adult interaction. It is true that adults respond in various ways to children. Teachers, for example, are less emotionally involved and therefore often act in a more objective way than parents do. It is easier to work with someone else's child. Moreover, parents have more at stake than a teacher because a child is a reflection of and upon his parents.

For the person who is research oriented or who is a depth seeker, there is an extensive bibliography at the end of this chapter. To the person who is looking for some simple techniques that are easy to initiate and that show results, read on. These techniques are not in any particular order. They just work. As you read through them, pick out one or two that you would like to try. Be persistent. Give each one a fair trial. After you have mastered a few, select others. Undoubtedly it will mean a change in behavior for both you and the children you teach.

LISTEN *TO* THE CHILD AND TALK *WITH* HIM

Have you ever heard a child who was questioned about a certain act reply, "But you (or someone else) said I could!" His response is a result of someone's not listening! We often give our undivided attention to another adult, but fail to hear the words of children. Sometimes it is necessary for them to tug and pull at us before we give them even divided attention. Children do have important things to say and ask. We should listen, because listening is the beginning of understanding.

One way to give the child your undivided attention is to stoop or kneel so that you have eye-to-eye contact. Then concentrate on his words. His vocabulary is somewhat limited, and it may be difficult for him to convey the message he desires. Showing him you are interested helps him communicate.

Besides being poor child-listeners, we may talk differently to him than to others—talking down to him in tone of voice or ideas. Listen attentively and speak normally. He wants and needs information from you but dislikes long, unnecessary lectures. Talk with him about things he is interested in and stimulate his thinking with new ideas. Appreciate and enjoy your conversations with young children. They are refreshing and enlightening.

A child often comes up with a very good suggestion. Let him know it is good. "That's a very good idea; let's try it" will encourage him to make suggestions at other times.

KNOW THE ABILITIES OF THE CHILD AND PLAN "SUCCESS" EXPERIENCES FOR HIM

A young child needs to have successful experiences at least 80 percent of the time. We all like to have successes, but it is especially important for a young child. He is just beginning to unravel his world; his knowledge and skills are limited. He needs to be encouraged to try new activities and repeat old ones. Nothing breeds success like success.

Observe a child carefully, then give him responsibilities and privileges accordingly. Express your honest appreciation frequently.

If a child has only experiences that he can easily manage, he will tend to repeat them and ignore challenging situations. If his experiences are always too difficult for him to succeed, he will turn away from them because failure is an unpleasant feeling. Watch him. See what his interests are and how he attacks various problems. See that he has some experiences that will encourage him to develop his problem-solving abilities. Toys and materials that have endless experiential possibilities are a must for preschool children. This is an excellent time to stimulate the curiosity of a child; he has the time and the interest to find out about his world. Plan to introduce him to some new experiences to widen his horizons, but make sure these experiences are based on his needs, his level of development, and his interests. Don't push him into experiences he isn't ready for, but keep his curiosity alive by giving him some new and different experiences he *is* ready for.

SEND AND RECEIVE CLEAR MESSAGES

When you make a request of a child, be sure he understands it. Often, he may not respond because he is unsure of what is expected of him. It may be necessary for you to define the situation or give him valid reasons—not in a bribing way, but in a way of clarification.

At preschool, Charles began a habit of standing near the playground gate until no one was looking, then running out into the parking lot. Because it was a busy lot and because he was unsupervised when he left the playground, the teacher told him that if he ran out of the gate again, she would have to call his mother to come and get him. She showed him how many cars there were in the lot, how fast they went past the gate, and how difficult it was to see him because of his height. Her words went unheeded; the next chance he had to slip out of the gate, he was gone again. Because of her warning and the presence of real danger, the teacher felt responsible for calling his mother—which she did. His mother came and took Charles home. The next day when Charles arrived at school, he went to each child and said, "Do you know what happens if you run out of the gate?" and then went on to explain, "Your mother comes and takes you home." He had omitted the part about the reasons, but he was clear on the result.

Requests made of children should be reasonable, clear and simple. Too many commands, something that seems unreasonable or complicated, causes a child to hesitate rather than respond. He may even ignore the request because he doesn't know where to begin.

As well as sending good messages to children, we must be alert to receiving the messages they are sending to us. Are their words saying what they mean? Are there nonverbal messages? Gestural language often conveys more clues than verbal language. It may be necessary for you to let a child know you understand his feelings by defining them for him. "I know that you are mad because you can't swing. It's Lisa's turn, but when she is through, it will be your turn.

We'll find something else to do while we are waiting." "It really hurts when you fall on the cement. Let's put a cool cloth on the bump."

Be honest in your praise of a child or his accomplishments. He will appreciate your sincerity.

REINFORCE ACTIONS YOU WANT REPEATED

Often we forget to comment on behavior that is acceptable, but we spare no time in complaining about adverse behavior. Perhaps the only times we communicate with a child are to describe his "bad" behavior; so in order to get any recognition at all, he repeats the action we would like to help him eliminate. Is it better to have negative attention than none at all?

Suppose a child picks up his toys. If you say something like, "I like the way you put your toys in the box. It makes your room look so nice," you are increasing the possibility of toy-picking-up behavior. But if you say nothing, he may think, "Why should I pick up my toys? Mother (or teacher) doesn't care. She'll just pick them up later." This affirmative kind of communication is not always possible, of course. How do you show approval for something that hasn't ever happened (the child has never picked up his toys)? Sometimes you have to "catch" the child doing something good. Even if he picked up one toy, say, "That truck looks good on the shelf. Now it won't get stepped on." The next time he may pick up two toys. Again give honest praise. He will probably continue until all the toys are picked up if he gets more recognition for toy-picking-up than toy-lying-around behavior.

If you look for good behavior and reinforce it by comment or by some other reward, you are likely to find good behavior. If you look for the bad, you will probably also find it. The more closely a reinforcement (a reward, an approval, a privilege) follows an action, the more likely that action is to be repeated. In fact, if you reinforce a child's action every time he exhibits good behavior, then begin to taper off to occasionally, reinforcing less frequently, he will continue to repeat that pattern.

If the child shows bad behavior (a tantrum, for example), and we pay attention to it, he is more apt to repeat it. Since we want to get rid of tantrum behavior, we must follow the above guide. If we ignore the behavior, it is likely to first increase, then decrease. If we give the child attention during tantrums (even if we punish him), he is likely to continue them in more intensity. A four-year-old was very angry at his mother. He began yelling, screaming, and acting out all sorts of undesirable behavior. The mother said calmly, "If you want to scream and carry on like that, you can do it in your room." The child did. He yelled and screamed louder and louder to make sure the mother heard him. But she went right on about her tasks trying to "keep her cool." After an extended length of time, the child ended his own tantrum. He found that he was getting no attention. It was a matter of waiting it out on the part of the mother.

USE A POSITIVE RATHER THAN A NEGATIVE APPROACH

When I make the above statement to my college students, some of them rebel. A familiar comment is "We had nothing but negative comments from our parents. Now you give us an opposing technique and expect us to adopt it just like that!" It is difficult for these students to see value in and to use this technique at first. But through diligent effort they try it, and they see that it makes the children respond more favorably than to negative statements.

When you are always told what you can't do, it creates in you a defiant attitude. Turn that around: when you are told what you can do, it opens up all sorts of possibilities; it gives you a different attitude and encourages rather than discourages your participation.

Think how you would respond to the following statements:

"Hammer your nail in some of that wood," or "Don't hammer the table."

"Hang your jacket in your locker," or "Don't throw your jacket on the floor."

"Pour just the amount you want to drink," or "Don't waste that juice."

If it appears that the three statements on the left are too commanding, read them again; you will realize that the child is being redirected—given a possible response—an appropriate action. On the other hand, the statements on the right leave him hanging: "Well, what do you expect me to do?" He may continue with that behavior because he has no alternative.

Positive statements work well with anyone. If a person knows how he is expected to act, the chance of his acting that way is very good. Most people respond better when addressed in a positive way. They feel respected and appreciated. The world of a preschooler is so full of "don'ts," "quits," and "stops" that it leaves him with the feeling, "Whatever I do, it is wrong." Using the positive approach opens new avenues for him and his behavior.

As a little "homework" or "school work," keep track of your interaction with a child (or adult) for a few days. Mark down every time you respond to that person and see if your positive responses outweigh your negative ones.

PROVIDE GUIDELINES (LIMITS) FOR BEHAVIOR

Where limits are necessary, define them for a child. You want to protect his health and safety while giving him as much freedom as possible. As he grows and develops, alter the guidelines. His developing reasoning power, skills, and experiences will cause him to act increasingly independent. Be consistent in the enforcement of guidelines, but not inflexible. Certain conditions may call for altering guidelines—not breaking them or removing them.

If at all possible, let the child help establish rules. "What do you think we ought to do about. . . ." "Can you think of something that would make that situation safer?" "If you had a trike, where could you ride it?"

When you think danger might be involved, set up guidelines before an incident arises ("When we cross the street on our walk today, we will wait at the corner and all cross together"). With prior admonition, a child will know what is to occur and as a consequence will behave acceptably.

SHOW RESPECT FOR THE CHILD

When a child is engaged in an activity, he often totally immerses himself in it. If the activity needs to be terminated before the child is finished, give him a little warning ("It's about time to pick up the blocks," or "Lunch will be ready in a few minutes"). This gives him an opportunity to finish his activity without feeling cut off. Lee was used to a few minutes' warning before lunch, but he finished his activity early one day. He called, "Mother, aren't you going to tell me it's a few minutes before lunch?" She replied, "Not quite yet." Lee stood silently by the kitchen door for several minutes until Mother did remind him that lunch was about ready. Happily, he went to the bathroom to wash and then to the table. Children involved in school activities, too, need and appreciate a similar warning.

Another way to show respect for a child is by respecting his belongings. His things belong to him, and sharing *follows* possessing. (How would you like it if someone passed your valuables around?) Encourage him with good social techniques, but never force him. ("Molly doesn't have anything to play with. Could you let her use some of your things?" "If each of you would give some of your clay to someone else, there would be enough for everyone.") If a child has a particular possession that he doesn't want to share, say to the other child (or children), "This is very special to him. He wants to keep it now, so let's look for something for you." The child is not made to feel guilty because he doesn't share; rather, he feels that his rights are respected. At school this problem may not arise so frequently because all the toys belong to everyone.

Still another positive method is to respect a child for the individual he is, for what he can do, and for just being himself. Help him build a good self-image by pointing out his assets ("You are able to do that so well." "You have the prettiest blue eyes." "My, but you are strong"). Show him in words and actions that you value him as a person. Avoid comparing his abilities, characteristics, activities, and behavior with those of other children. Such comparison breeds dislike and unhappiness.

GUIDE THROUGH LOVE RATHER THAN THROUGH FEAR OR GUILT

Sometimes it is necessary to rebuke a child for his behavior. In such a circumstance, make sure he is aware of the seriousness of the offense, then let him know you reprimand him because of your love for him; you really do care about him.

Define the situation for the child—or ask him to define it: "Do you know why you can't_____?" Then explain: "Because it is very dangerous, and you might get hurt. I love you, and I would feel very sad if something happened to you." Or "I care enough about you to stop you when you are doing something that could hurt you or someone else."

Trying to rule a child through fear or guilt is a growth-stunting procedure. He will never learn to make valid decisions because he will be unable to see the true issues involved. Instead, build a loving relationship with him so that you will be able to survive the inevitable rough times.

BE A GOOD MODEL

The mere fact that we are moving, speaking beings means that we are providing a model for someone. When someone imitates your good qualities, you are flattered. But when they imitate your bad qualities, it can be embarrassing. As parents or teachers we often see our behavior reflected in the words and actions of children (a comment, a gesture). Sometimes we recognize these behaviors as ours; sometimes, oblivious, we wonder where they could have seen or heard such a thing!

If we have a happy attitude, the children around us are likely to have the same attitude. If we are harsh and critical, so will the children be. "Actions speak louder than words." Be sure your words and actions say the same thing. If you tell your child to get ready for supper, you get ready, too. If you continue to sit and read the paper while you are telling him to hurry, he becomes confused. If he sits (as you are doing), don't get angry with him for imitating you. He usually follows your example in action more readily than he does your words. When your actions and words do not support each other, you are sending a double message to your child.

Did you ever stop to think that one of the best ways to change someone else's behavior is to change your own? If you are always defensive, so will be the person you encounter. Try being more understanding and patient. Look at a point from another's view, especially if that person seems defensive. Pleasant understanding reduces tension.

BE ON GUARD FOR WARNING SIGNALS

There are times when immediate action is called for: when the child is hurting himself or someone else, or when he is destroying property. You need to step in immediately and stop the behavior; otherwise, damage to person or property will result. If verbal means deter the action, fine ("Put that shovel down," or "Don't hit him with the shovel"). If that doesn't stop the action, physical means may be necessary ("I'll have to hold onto your arm so you won't hit him with the shovel"). Then discuss the situation with those involved. "When he stepped on your road, it made you want to hit him; but when you hit him, he doesn't know what you want. Tell him with words." Let the child know that you understand his behavior but that there are other, more positive ways of expressing it. Children will not learn the value of property if they are allowed to destroy it. Being inquisitive is one thing, but deliberate destruction must not be tolerated.

AVOID POWER STRUGGLES OR BATTLES OF WILLS

We may make a demand or a request of a child. When he doesn't comply, we become angry. We tell or ask him again. Still no compliance. We become

defensive—especially if the child asks "why" or ignores us. Does he have the right to question us? When we tell him to do something, he should obey. Or should he? Is the request reasonable? Does he understand the nature of the request? What do your actions mean to the child? Is he being deliberately disobedient? If you and he can analyze the situation together, if you can tell him why you made the request, if he can tell you why he didn't comply, you may be able to resolve the problem. If, on the other hand, each of you decides stubbornly that you will win, you will have a power struggle. What a difficult situation for both of you. No matter who "wins" (if there is such a thing), both of you come out of the struggle with uncomfortable feelings.

The best plan is not to let a situation develop into a power struggle, or battle of wills. But if it does, resolve it mutually ("What do you think we ought to do about it?" or "What would seem fair to you?" or "Let's see how we can resolve this").

OFFER LEGITIMATE CHOICES AND BE ABLE TO ACCEPT THE CHILD'S DECISION

Choice making should be a practice developed from early childhood. Choices should be ones which help build a child's character; they should be within his ability and should be legitimate.

Some interesting research from the Gesell Institute of Child Development regarding the ease or the difficulty of choice making suggests that it is related to the child's age. It indicates that the average child of three, five, seven, or ten has an easier time making decisions between two alternatives than children at other ages because the child is under less "inner stress and strain" at these ages and is therefore able to accept choices without too much emotional conflict. Some other times when children do not make good decisions are when they are ill, fatigued, bombarded, or pressured. Are adults any different?

If a child has a legitimate choice, it is good to let him practice decision making. Bearing in mind that you must be prepared to accept his decision, be careful to form appropriate choices ("You can wear your blue shirt or your green one," "You can play inside or outside," or "You can either hear one

more story or play a short game before bedtime"). If he has no choice, you make a simple outright statement about what is to occur ("Put on your blue shirt," "You will have to stay inside," or "It is time for bed now"). To offer a child a choice ("Do you want to drink your milk?") and then refuse to accept his answer ("Well, that's too bad; you have to, anyway") increases the negative aspect of his world. Also, remember that when a question is worded in such a way that either "yes" or "no" can be answered, the child at this age is most likely to answer in the negative, even if he really wants to be positive.

Sometimes we think we are being democratic in offering choices to children, when in reality we are weighting the questions in our favor ("Do you want to watch TV, or do you want to help me so we can go and get a treat?" or "Do you want to pick up your toys or go to your room?").

If children are going to be able to make good decisions, they need to develop a sound basis upon which to make choices. They need some legitimate choices for practice.

ENCOURAGE INDEPENDENCE IN THE CHILD

A preschool child likes to do things himself. Often, in the interest of time or energy, the parent or teacher will assist the child or will actually do the task rather than let the child try his skill or problem-solving ability. Admittedly, there are some tasks too difficult for the preschool child to attempt. Here, the adult can offer assistance and encouragement in those aspects of the task that the child can handle. If it is a task the child can handle by himself with suggestions, let him do it. It takes longer, but the result is worth the patience required to let him achieve.

Encouragement is essential in building independence. "You try, and if you need help, I'll help you" is often enough incentive to get the child started. Then remain near. If he needs you, help him—through either verbal or physical means (tell him something he might try, or demonstrate for him). At the completion of the task, give him some honest praise ("You did a good job," or "I'm glad you tried. I think you will be able to do it by yourself next time").

We seek the long-range goals—the development of good work habits in a child and his initiative and ability to tackle a job—rather than those dictated by expediency.

PROVIDE ACCEPTABLE AVENUES FOR RELEASE OF FEELINGS

Frustration and anger come easily to a preschooler. He needs to express these feelings in such a way that he feels better—not worse. If he is hitting, tell him he can hit the clay, the stuffed animal, the punching bag, the pillow, or another suitable object but that he can't hit the baby, the TV set, or even you. Large muscle activities, such as painting with big strokes, moving to music, riding a stick horse, throwing a ball, or fingerpainting, are often suitable outlets. At any rate, you need to look for an activity that helps each child to release his feelings.

The younger the child, the more likely he is to use physical rather than verbal release. He knows he gets action when he attacks someone or something physically (see the shovel example on page 206). With encouragement, experience, and practice, he will learn acceptable verbal ways of releasing his feelings.

HELP THE CHILD LEARN THROUGH PARTICIPATION

It is possible for a child to learn through observation or lecture, but the true test is in the doing. Instead of always telling the child, provide opportunities for him to have the experience. Allow plenty of time and materials for his exploration and investigation.

When you ask him to perform a task, let him do it his way. You may offer some suggestions, but give him the freedom to try his ideas. He may find a better way than yours.

ONE FINAL NOTE—

As you will recall from chapter one, various teaching methods and their effects upon children have been investigated. Repeatedly, research has shown that the single most important factor in children's learning is the effectiveness of the teacher. Similarly, in counseling, regardless of the method employed, it is the counselor who makes the difference in the therapy. As adults involved with young children, we are both teachers and counselors. We have the responsibility of seeing that our attitudes and personal attributes are such that they will be more instrumental in helping children reach their potential than if our lives had not crossed theirs.

BIBLIOGRAPHY

Books

Becker, Wesley C. *Parents Are Teachers*. Champaign, Ill.: Research Press Co., 1971.

Bushell, Don. *Classroom Behavior*. Englewood Cliffs, N.J.: Prentice-Hall, 1973.

Hildebrand, Verna. *Introduction to Early Childhood Education*. New York: Macmillan Co., 1971, pp. 66-79.

Hymes, James L. *Behavior and Misbehavior*. Englewood Cliffs, N.J.: Prentice-Hall, 1955.

Krumboltz, John D. and Helen B. *Changing Children's Behavior*. Englewood Cliffs, N.J.: Prentice-Hall, 1972.

Madsen, C. K., and C. H. Madsen, Jr. *Parents/Children/Discipline: A Positive Approach*. Boston: Allyn and Bacon, 1972.

Moore, Dewey J. *Preventing Misbehavior in Children*. Springfield, Ill.: Charles C. Thomas, 1972.

Moore, Shirley G., and Sally Kilmer. *Contemporary Preschool Education*. New York: John Wiley & Sons, 1973, pp. 27-34.

Leeper, Sarah H., Ruth J. Dales, Dora S. Skipper, and Ralph L. Witherspoon. *Good Schools for Young Children*. New York: Macmillan, 1974 (3rd ed.), pp. 58-82.

Read, Katherine H. *The Nursery School*. Philadelphia: W. B. Saunders, 1971, pp. 119-42, 266-366.

Skinner, B. F. *About Behaviorism*. New York: Alfred A. Knopf, 1974.

Smith, J. M., and D. E. P. Smith. *Child Management: A Program for Parents and Teachers*. Ann Arbor, Mich.: Ann Arbor Pub., 1966.

Spodek, Bernard. *Early Childhood Education*. Englewood Cliffs, N.J.: Prentice-Hall, 1973, pp. 18-26, 62-77.

Todd, Vivian E., and Helen Heffernan. *The Years before School.* New York: Macmillan, 1970, pp. 504-44.

Vance, Barbara. *Teaching the Prekindergarten Child.* Monterey, Calif.: Brooks/Cole, 1973, pp. 148-89.

Articles

Elkind, David. "What Preschoolers Need Most." *Parents' Magazine,* May 1971, pp. 37-39, 92-94.

Katz, Lilian G. "Early Childhood Education as a Discipline." *Young Children,* December 1970, pp. 82-89.

———— . "Condition with Caution." *Young Children* 27 (1972): 277-80.

Osborn, D. Keith. "Permissiveness Re-Examined." *Childhood Education,* January 1957, pp. 214-17.

Taylor, Barbara J. "Help Me Be Me." *Family Perspective,* Fall 1972, 7: 51-55.

Veatch, Jeanette. "Learning, Training and Education." *Young Children,* January 1974, pp. 83-88.

Pamphlets

Erikson, Erik. *A Healthy Personality for your Child.* Washington, D.C.: U. S. Gov't Printing Office. Midcentury White House Conference on Children and Youth, 1950.

Feelings and Learning. Washington, D.C.: ACEI, 3615 Wisconsin Ave., N.W.

Galambos, Jeanette. *A Guide to Discipline,* # 302. Washington, D.C.: NAEYC, 1834 Connecticut Ave., NW, 20009, 1969.

INDEX

NOTES